The Philosophy of Fear

The Philosophy of Fear

Historical and Interdisciplinary Approaches

Edited by Ami Harbin

BLOOMSBURY ACADEMIC
NEW YORK • LONDON • OXFORD • NEW DELHI • SYDNEY

BLOOMSBURY ACADEMIC
Bloomsbury Publishing Inc, 1359 Broadway, New York, NY 10018, USA
Bloomsbury Publishing Plc, 50 Bedford Square, London, WC1B 3DP, UK
Bloomsbury Publishing Ireland, 29 Earlsfort Terrace, Dublin 2, D02 AY28, Ireland

First published in the United States of America 2025

Library of Congress Cataloging-in-Publication Data
Names: Harbin, Ami editor
Title: The philosophy of fear : historical and interdisciplinary approaches / edited by Ami Harbin.
Description: New York : Bloomsbury Academic, 2025. | Includes bibliographical references and index.
Identifiers: LCCN 2025016221 (print) | LCCN 2025016222 (ebook) | ISBN 9781666945683 hardback | ISBN 9781978749344 epub | ISBN 9798765165102 pdf
Subjects: LCSH: Fear–History
Classification: LCC B105.F43 P45 2025 (print) | LCC B105.F43 (ebook) | DDC 152.4/6–dc23/eng/20250410
LC record available at https://lccn.loc.gov/2025016221
LC ebook record available at https://lccn.loc.gov/2025016222

ISBN: HB: 978-1-6669-4568-3
ePDF: 979-8-7651-6510-2
eBook: 978-1-9787-4934-4

Typeset by Deanta Global Publishing Services, Chennai, India

Contents

Acknowledgments

I thank Jana Hodges-Kluck and Lauran Jones for their support to this volume and all the authors for their excellent contributions.

Introduction

Fear in the Philosophical Archives and Beyond

Ami Harbin

Philosophers since 500 BCE have considered fear from a number of different methodological approaches. Early on, Confucius, Plato, Aristotle, and the Stoics to some extent shared an approach which situated fear within broader conversations about virtue, living well, and justice. For many of them, fear was a subject of practical advice within their accounts of virtuous action: in many cases, the advice centered on how to avoid or limit it. In the writings of some medieval philosophers, human experiences of fear were situated in the context of faith in God and responses to death. Again, fear was often approached with practical questions in mind: How should Christians respond to fear in ways that are consistent with their faith? In early modern philosophers, and in the work of Descartes especially, we see growing attention to epistemic dimensions of fear—fear as prompted by what we cannot know, and as being most relevant for its relation to other aspects of human agency: beliefs, expectations, and desires. Near the same time, Hobbes' approach to fear was positioned thoroughly within a political view: fear was treated as part of the human condition that could help support arguments in favor of or against certain forms of state power. In the 1800s and early 1900s, some approaches in European philosophy focused on the human experience of fear given a lack of supernatural or otherworldly sources of meaning. Existentialists contended with fears as part of a refocus on human freedom and individual responsibility in the absence of religion. Around the same time, some pragmatists in the U.S. context were articulating views on the philosophy of emotion focused on what emotions themselves are, and fear was one of their foci.

As we can see, philosophy has been ecumenical in its approaches to the subject of fear. And these are only some highlights. But, despite it being a key part of our moral and psychological lives, philosophers have not yet fully attended to fear and all the interesting philosophical questions it raises.

The Philosophy of Fear: Historical and Interdisciplinary Approaches is a collection of fourteen chapters from contemporary philosophers who reflect on the significance of fear as an emotion in the history of Eastern and Western philosophy and at the intersections of contemporary philosophy and other disciplines (cognitive science, neuroscience, psychiatry, developmental psychology, and U.S. history).

Even in the small sample from the history of philosophy above, we can begin to see tensions between the ways different philosophers understand fear. Some position fear as more of an individual experience or mental state, while others focus more on fearfulness in a community or population. Some see it as fundamentally an issue of epistemic function or dysfunction, having its origins in what individuals know or fail to know. Others advise individuals in ways suggesting fear is largely up to individuals to cultivate or diminish, and within thiis group of views, we see disagreement about whether fear is better addressed by mental, physical, or spiritual activity. Others still do not provide advice at all: they are interested in what fear is, more than in how humans respond to it. Some philosophers assume fear is morally damaging, while others are not so pessimistic. Some see it as a natural part of human life, while others see it as such only under non-ideal social or political conditions.

Many empirically informed accounts of fear in philosophy, particularly in the last century, have drawn on research in psychology, cognitive science, or neuroscience. In these engagements, methodological tensions become even more pronounced. When philosophers engage with empirical accounts of fear, they may or may not take on a number of background assumptions that are built into those empirical approaches. For instance, we can see certain frameworks for understanding fear at work in behaviorist approaches to psychology, where fear was regularly believed to be acquired through learning (e.g., individuals would feel fear toward an object and maintain fear of that object by classical conditioning). By contrast, in evolutionary psychology, discussions of fear are often positioned as inevitable components of in-group/out-group relations. Threat detection is understood to be a key aspect of evolutionary development. A variety of psychological schools of thought are represented in empirically informed philosophy of emotions and moral psychology. We see evolutionary psychological approaches informing, for instance, research on racist bias and fear responses. Underlying the experiment design and data collection on, for instance, which groups of people are most likely to respond with fear to which other groups, are conceptions of what fear is, what kind of neurological process it involves, how fears are acquired, the extent to which fears are fundamentally experiences of *individuals*, the role of expression in fearing, and the extent to which fears can be unlearned.

At this point in an already long history of academic research on fear, philosophers have many perspectives within many disciplines to draw on to help us understand what fear is, how cognitive and knowledge processes are involved in and affected by fear, how fear is and should be responded to in moral lives, and how fear is part of our communities and societies. In other words, fear is a topic that can be approached by metaphysicians, epistemologists, philosophers of mind, ethicists, and political philosophers, and all of these philosophers can draw on various historical, scientific, and social scientific archives in their empirically engaged philosophy of fear.

I raise these issues of methodological diversity to make a point which will be important in orienting toward this book: one of the strengths of the philosophy of fear is the ability to *critically reflect* on tensions and conflicts between the background assumptions at play in different approaches to fear. Philosophers are trained to identify and question assumptions which might shape how we approach understanding fear. We do not need to reach full agreement on what fears are or how to understand all their features, but we should strive for clarity about where we do not, or perhaps will not ever, agree.

I encourage readers to hold in mind these questions as they move through the chapters to come: How does this author, or the philosopher or approach they describe, understand *what fear is*? What key cognitive and knowledge processes are involved in fearing in this view? Are there implications suggested for how we should respond to fear in our moral lives? Are they articulating how fear is part of communities and societies, either now or in the past?

In my own work on fear, I have found significant differences among the methodological commitments of philosophers, which have major implications for the accounts of fearing they produce. One question which reliably highlights these differences is *how they determine what an individual is really fearing*. Asking about how a philosopher identifies fearers' objects of fear and, in particular, how they determine the *reliability of fearers in identifying the objects of their fears* can reveal differences among the methodological approaches of philosophers.

For instance, I elsewhere present a case where a person says that they drew a weapon because they feared for their life (Harbin 2023, 33–34). I suggest that of course such a claim must be understood in the legal context where it occurred—in the United States where "fear for one's life" can be taken as exculpatory, and in some cases as a justification for violent action that would not otherwise be easily justified. My account raises the question of how we know what another person is really fearing or whether what they are feeling is really fear. Is the fearer always authoritative? Can a fearer's own claim about what they are feeling or about the object of their fear be disputed? Can others be more reliable judges of the object of that person's fear?

The arguments I present about fearers as fallible judges of their own objects of their fears, and of all of us as having a role in the interpretations of others' fears, are expressive of my methodological commitments: I approach fears as being partly contingent on the interpretive work of those outside the fearer. Fears are not the exclusive property or accomplishment of individual fearers. This means, in part, that it is possible for other people to challenge or dispute a fearer's own beliefs about the object or cause of their fears. When we interpret the feelings of others in any case, and especially when we are in no type of relationship with them but interpreting from afar, we are working from only some information, and we might be wrong. The person with the feeling might themselves also be wrong. The more limited the expressive and interpretive resources, the more challenging it is to appropriately interpret.

In my own work on fear, I have come to think that identifying fear in others is, perhaps most significantly, *an action of relating to* others that can have significant effects on both relationships and future actions. More than such an interpretation is an epistemological claim (i.e., a claim about a belief about what the person felt), or an ontological claim (i.e., a claim about the feeling that existed), it is a moral interaction: it creates certain relationships, modes of relating, or possibilities for interaction. And, to make matters more complicated, the principal effect of the interpretation of another's feeling is not only a moral interaction between interpreter and interpreted but also with other agents who are witnesses to the interpretive interaction. In some (perhaps most) cases, when I interpret another's feeling, I am creating a certain relationship, mode of relating, or possibility for interaction with the person whose feelings I am interpreting.

All of this reflects a particular approach to emotions and their position in moral life. My own approach departs from the approaches of many in the history of philosophy and from some other philosophers writing about fear now. As I noted above, we do not need to reach full agreement on what fears are or how to understand all their features, but we should strive for clarity about where we do not, or perhaps will not ever, agree. My hope is that this book will contribute to such clarity.

As we have seen, fear has played a significant role in philosophical accounts of *other things*—of emotions, virtue, politics, knowledge, freedom, religion, and death. Not many philosophical accounts have had as their central goal *understanding or analyzing fear itself*. The pieces in this volume are exceptions. Here, authors have the goal of providing insights on what fear is, how fear has been addressed by philosophers across the last twenty-five centuries, how fear relates to other emotions and attitudes, how fear intersects with mental health and illness, the epistemic dimensions of fear, and the intersection of fear and trauma.

The volume is divided into two parts: (I) Fear in the History of Philosophy (chapters 1–7) and (II) Interdisciplinary Insights on Fear (chapters 8–14).

Part I begins with two chapters considering the centrality of fear in Confucian ethical-political thought. In "Fear in Early Confucian Thought," Lok Chui Choo outlines fear as central to Confucian ethics and, in particular, to the Confucian conception of the virtuous agent and the cultivation of virtues, showing that it is an important component in the development of virtue for Confucians.

In "Fear and Courage in Early Confucianism," Songyao Ren highlights the specific position of fear in the Confucian account of unity of the self. On this account, the integrated self acts courageously *through* fear, rather than by controlling fear.

These are followed by three chapters reflecting on fear in the ancient Greek philosophy of Aristotle, whose account of fear and virtue was one of the most foundational in the history of philosophy. Two chapters offer distinct perspectives on the question of the extent to which, in Aristotle's view, courageous agents *feel*, *master*, or *avoid* their fears, and a third reflects on Aristotle's virtue ethics in light of recent research on the effects of trauma and post-traumatic recovery.

In "Aristotle on Fear's Contributions to the Virtue of Courage," Andrew Culbreth identifies two puzzles in Aristotle's treatment of courage and fear: first, the question of whether the brave person experiences fear while exhibiting courage, and second, the question of whether the courageous person who experiences fear is exhibiting self-control or virtue. Culbreth shows how Aristotle has the resources to meet both challenges, thanks to his distinction between courageous and non-courageous fear.

In "Do the Brave Master Their Fears—or Avoid Them?" Lawrence Lengbeyer contests a view of courage attributed to Aristotle as involving properly experiencing fears and argues in favor of a view of courage as fearlessness which involves courageous people preventing the arousal or continuation of fear.

And in "Moderating Fear After Trauma? An Aristotelian Analysis," Lily M. Abadal considers how the moral psychology of fear is impacted by trauma, which may affect the development of virtue on Aristotelian frameworks.

We then reflect on the medieval period, and in "Anselm on Fear, Duty, and Moral Motivation," Parker Haratine examines Anselm of Canterbury's account of moral motivation and the specific question of how Anselm explains moral motivation in cases where an agent is afraid for their well-being.

In the final chapter of the section, "Fear as a Reactive Attitude," Robert Pál-Wallin builds on mid-twentieth-century philosopher P. F. Strawson's account of reactive attitudes, with an argument that the account should be expanded to include fear.

Part II considers the work contemporary philosophers are doing to expand the variety of approaches to fear, building connections with work in neuroscience, psychiatry, developmental psychology, and history. We begin the section with two chapters addressing the question of *what fear is*.

In "Reasons for Fear: Against the Reactive Theory of Emotion," Rodrigo Díaz and Christine Tappolet present an account of what kind of thing fear is, engaging in debates about whether fear is a *response* or a *perception*. They argue against the reactive theory of fear and suggest that there are non-evaluative reasons for fear. This is a welcome result for rival theories, such as perceptual theories, according to which fear allows individuals to gain knowledge about danger.

In "Fear as Preventer," Timothy R. Kearl and Robert H. Wallace consider the kind of thing fear is from a different perspective, arguing that we ought to pay close attention to the *function* of fear as a preventer or obstacle, which renders agents unable to act in certain ways.

We then turn to four chapters reflecting in diverse ways on the question of *what fear can do* in a variety of complex social settings.

In "Art-Horror, Social Anxiety, and the Moral Imagination," Saraliza Anzaldúa draws our attention to the role of fear in the context of art-horror. Considering horror films and other sources, Anzaldúa asks what attracts us to art-horror, what makes us willing to tolerate the unpleasant experience of fear while observing such sources over time, and how might these fears play an important role in the processing of social anxiety?

In "Fear and Motivated Reasoning: Lessons from the Satanic Panic," Guy Crain considers the experiences the social phenomenon of the Satanic Panic (circa 1980–1992), where there were a number of ultimately discredited allegations that Satanists were harming children. Crain outlines how fear functioned to alter individuals' reasoning processes during this time, in support of their drawing frightening but ultimately incredible conclusions.

In "Biased Fear: Implicit Bias, Responsibility, and Emotion," Kris Goffin discusses what fear can do in contexts of racist bias, where even when an individual explicitly condemns racism, they can nonetheless experience biased fears that associate racialized groups with threats. Goffin draws on the work of Robert Solomon to explore the question of moral responsibility for actions borne out of biased fears.

In "Fear, Pathology, and Feelings of Agency: Lessons from Ecological Fear," Charlie Kurth and Panu Pihkala take up the question of how fear functions in contexts of climate crisis and environmental degradation. They argue that we can and should be helping mold eco-fears into eco-courage.

And in the final chapter of the volume, we consider the significance of fear in situations where one is reflecting on how their life has gone. In "The Fear of Having Wasted One's Life," Christopher Cowley draws on E. M. Forster's novel *A Passage to India*, specifically referencing a character who reflects on his life and wonders whether he has been successful as a human being or whether he ought to have been working at something else the whole time. Cowley distinguishes this experience from alternative descriptions of the phenomenon and presents a reflection on it as one insufficiently addressed in philosophy thus far—the fear of having wasted one's life.

Though always present in the history of philosophy, and one of the key points of contact between philosophy and other empirically informed disciplines, fear as an emotion has received surprisingly little concerted attention within philosophy. There exists no collection from contemporary philosophers with the express goal of reflecting on fear in the history of philosophy nor does there yet exist any volume collecting perspectives on fear from philosophers working at the intersection of the disciplines reflected above. We present these contributions in the hopes that the field of philosophy of fear will continue to grow in the years to come.

Bibliography

Harbin, Ami. 2023. *Fearing Together: Ethics for Insecurity*. New York: Oxford.

Part I

Fear in the History of Philosophy

1

Fear in Early Confucian Thought

Lok Chui Choo

Fear is an emotional response to perceiving certain stimuli as dangerous or threatening. Like most emotions, fear represents its intentional object in characteristic ways. Fear is generally fear of something in particular, apprehended as dangerous or threatening to the subject. Martha Nussbaum observes that when feeling fear, we perceive an object or situation as a threat, but one that leaves room for potential escape (Nussbaum 2004, 183). Perceiving or judging an object as threatening often gives rise to what is known as the fight-or-flight response. According to Jacek Debiec and Joseph LeDoux, fear emerges when the brain's defense system is active in a self-aware organism (Debiec and LeDoux 2004, 807–818). This recognition ties fear to the primal instinct of self-preservation and survival. In this primal respect, fear is important because it arises in response to a specific object or situation, prompting immediate action.

Consider, for example, encountering a large mountain lion while on a hike, leading to an intense feeling of fear. Several things will characterize this emotional episode of fear. First, it involves certain broadly cognitive characteristics: evaluating or judging the situation as a threat and heightened focus and attention on the perceived threat. In addition, there will be certain bodily or physiological characteristics, such as increased heart rate and blood pressure. Correspondingly, certain unpleasant sensations will be a feature of your experience of these changes and certain expressive and behavioral responses, such as raised upper eyelids, dropped open jaw, horizontally stretched lips, and the inclination to flee.

In Western philosophy, the emotion of fear has featured centrally in debates in the philosophy of emotions between those that emphasize the cognitive dimensions of emotions (specifically, thoughts, judgments, and appraisals) and those that emphasize the bodily dimensions of emotions (that is, physiological and motivational changes). The early Confucians did not separate the cognitive dimensions of emotions from the bodily dimensions of emotions. They ascribed both cognitive and bodily dimensions of emotion to the heart or heart-mind (*xin* 心), the faculty considered central to moral development and ethical conduct.[1] The early Confucians were interested in the role of the heart-mind in connection with the cultivation of moral virtues—which for them included benevolence (*ren* 仁), righteousness (*yi* 義), propriety (*li* 禮), and wisdom (*zhi* 智)—to attain personal and social harmony (*he* 和). Moral cultivation was taken to involve intellectual development while nurturing physical well-being and emotional balance.

It is often said that there is a practical orientation to Chinese Philosophy. The Classical or Early Chinese philosophers were interested in developing and articulating a conception of *dao* 道. This term can mean a path or road (as in the modern Chinese compound *daolu* 道路, meaning roadway). In both Chinese and English, there is a natural metaphorical extension from "way" in the sense of a literal path to "way" in the sense of how to go about doing something. In the case of the Classical Chinese thinkers, "way" came to refer to the right way to live one's life and organize society. Early Chinese philosophers thus sought to relate their conceptions to views about the way human beings are constituted and shared background understandings about the larger cosmos.

It is thus not surprising that Confucian treatments of fear emphasize its significance in relation to moral cultivation and social harmony. Confucianism places significant emphasis on social relationships and ethical behavior within society. The practice of ritual propriety (*li* 禮) and the observance of proper conduct in social interactions were crucial for maintaining harmony in interpersonal relationships and social harmony. These concerns with moral cultivation, ritual propriety, and social harmony are reflected in their reflections on the nature and significance of fear in ethical life. In what follows, I explore how fear is central to Confucian ethics, specifically in the way the Confucians conceived of the virtuous agent, the different moral virtues, and moral self-cultivation. My discussion is organized as follows: the first section considers the variety of terms in early China akin to the notion of fear. The second section examines how notions of fear figure in Confucian understandings of the *virtuous person*, or the *junzi* 君子. The third section explores how several specific Confucian virtues—such as courage, righteousness, benevolence, and ritual propriety—relate to fear. The fourth section examines how fear bears on moral self-cultivation.

Dimensions of Fear in Early China

In this section, I discuss the variety of terms in early China akin to the notion of fear. Early Confucian texts have a term, *kongju* 恐懼, that refers to sentiments akin to what I call fear. There are other terms connoting a spectrum of related sentiments, including concern (*pa* 怕), anxiety (*you* 憂), distress (*huan* 患), awe (*wei* 畏), doubt (*yi* 疑), and panic or alarm (*huang* 慌). When experiencing *kongju*, individuals often grapple with feelings of apprehension and unease. The character *kong* 恐 typically refers to the bodily or physiological manifestations of fear. According to *The Yellow Emperor's Classic of Medicine*, there exists a correlation between the five fundamental emotions and the five internal organs (Ni 1995, 29). In this paradigm, each organ is intimately linked with a specific emotional state: joy is associated with the heart, anger with the liver, concentration with the spleen, anxiety with the lung, and fear with the kidney. It shows that the feeling of fear is connected to a part of our body.

When individuals are in a state of *kong*, they may find themselves gripped by panic, leading to a departure from their usual demeanor and behaviors. For example, individuals experiencing *kong* can be frightened out of their wits. Moreover, the term *kong* can also connote a sense of apprehension or doubt, particularly when paired with the character *wei* 惟. This nuanced usage suggests a connection between *kong* and a cautious, questioning attitude. For instance, in *Mengzi* 2B:3: "the populace expresses concern over their king's failure to assert his authority through displays of anger, as they expect their ruler to exude confidence and assurance." Similarly, in *Mengzi* 4A:19: "a ruler fears that his subjects may not remain obedient due to their expectation of respectful and temperate leadership."

The character *ju* 懼—which typically follows kong—represents certain cognitive aspects, including thoughts, judgments, and appraisals. When one experiences *ju*, one assesses something as inherently threatening or malevolent. According to the *Kangxi Dictionary*, "*ju* is the essence of what we are in awe of (*wei*畏), and *kong* often precedes *ju*." *Ju* is intimately linked with awe (*wei*). In the *Shuowen Jiezi*, an example of "*wei*" describes a terrifying creature with a spectral visage and tiger-like claws (Xu 2018, book 10). Additionally, the object of our *wei* can extend to Heaven (*tian* 天) or anything perceived as vastly superior to us. In *Analects* 16.8: "The Master said, 'The gentleman stands in awe of three things: the Mandate of Heaven, great men, and the teachings of the sages. The petty person does not understand the Mandate of Heaven, and thus does not regard it with awe; he shows disrespect to great men, and ridicules the teachings of the sages'" (Slingerland 2003, 195). Here, these objects of awe—the Mandate of Heaven, virtuous persons, and the teachings of sages—represent a superior level of metaphysical identity and self-cultivation over the petty (that is, vicious) person.

As the *Kangxi Dictionary* notes, awe, which is typically accompanied by a sense of sacredness and respect, is predominantly directed toward our interaction with Heaven. For example, it elucidates that prolonged feelings of awe and reverence are often precipitated by the Mandate of Heaven. It underscores the notion that Heaven manifests its authority through its people, utilizing them as conduits to display its eminent stature. Indeed, Heaven exercises its power by rewarding benevolent rulers or punishing tyrants, thus orchestrating the ebb and flow of nations and their ascendancy to power. Understanding *kongju* in this light allows us to draw connections to the traditional concept of "anxiety or concerned consciousness" (*youhuan yishi* 憂患意識). As noted earlier, the characters *you* 憂 (anxiety) and *huan* 患 (distress) were associated with a sense of fear in Chinese. The term *you* typically denotes deep-seated anxiety or concern, while *huan* refers to a state of distress, suffering, or hardship. Both notions carry an underlying implication of fear, indicating that fear played a significant role in the conceptualization of these emotional states during that time period. This notion of "anxiety or concerned consciousness" has been extensively explored by the contemporary Confucian philosopher Xu Fuguan 徐復觀. He examined its relevance to the tumultuous context of the Zhou Dynasty, characterized by warfare, uncertainty, and societal upheaval (Xu 1975, 20–24). Kwong loi Shun explains this concept as the understanding of anxiety or concerned consciousness as "a sense of mission that involves a dedicated concern to work toward the public good, a moral transformation of the social and political order, and the transmission of what is of value in one's cultural heritage to future generations" (Shun 2016, 4).

During the Zhou Dynasty, rulers sought to legitimize their authority through the Mandate of Heaven, which posited divine sanction for their governance. Within this framework, the people believed that Heaven ordained virtuous rulers to lead. While this belief stemmed partly from the context of the preceding Shang Dynasty's considerable power, the Zhou rulers attributed their ascendancy not solely to military prowess but also to their possession of moral virtues. Consequently, they grappled with a profound sense of anxiety or concerned consciousness in their dedicated efforts to work toward the public good and moral transformation. The Zhou rulers feared their virtue might not suffice to earn Heaven's approval or meet its expectations, worrying that their rule could be destabilized if they failed to align with the divine mandate and transmit valuable cultural heritage to future generations.

Fear and the *Junzi*

In this section, I consider how Confucian reflections on the *virtuous person* make essential reference to fear. More specifically, a key characteristic of the *junzi* 君子 (a virtuous or exemplary person) is the fear of not conforming to *dao* 道 (*the way)*, that is, the way to conduct personal life and order the state.

I begin with the Confucian conception of the virtuous person, or *junzi*. The term "*junzi*" is commonly translated as "gentleman" or "noble person." In Confucianism, a *junzi* is an individual who embodies moral integrity, cultivates virtue, and adheres to ethical principles in both personal conduct and interactions with others. Traditionally, the *junzi* is characterized by qualities such as benevolence (*ren* 仁), righteousness (*yi* 義), propriety (*li* 禮), and wisdom (*zhi* 智). Kongzi emphasized the importance of aspiring to become a *junzi* and believed that individuals could contribute positively to society and bring about social harmony and order through self-cultivation and ethical behavior. As we find in *Analects* 2.4: "The Master said, 'At fifteen, I set my mind upon learning; at thirty, I took my place in society; at forty, I became free of doubts; at fifty, I understood Heaven's Mandate; at sixty, my ear was attuned; and at seventy, I could follow my heart's desires without overstepping the bounds of propriety'" (Slingerland 2003, 9).

The motivational or developmental path to becoming *junzi* is partly driven by a kind of fear that is connected to one's moral focus or conscientiousness. In *Analects* 14:30: "The Master said, 'Do not worry [*huan* 患] that you are not recognized by others; worry rather that you yourself lack ability'" (Slingerland 2003, 166). In this passage, Kongzi emphasizes the humility of the virtuous person (*junzi*), who is more concerned with his or her own potential shortcomings than with receiving recognition or praise from others. A certain kind of fear—anxiety or distress—caused by a sense of personal inadequacy can be seen as an emotional response that influences our attitudes and behaviors in a fitting and helpful manner with respect to virtue. Put differently, the possession and display of certain virtues involve the agent's susceptibility to certain moments of fear; at the same time, the susceptibility to fear also aids the agent in further developing or maintaining a virtue characteristic.

Scholars have proposed various interpretations of Confucians' perspectives on fear. Lee H. Yearley and Donald Munro argue that, according to Mengzi, a morally cultivated person with an unmoved heart[2] precludes the feeling of fear. Van Norden distinguishes between "being afraid" and "feeling afraid," suggesting that the virtuous person, in Mengzi's view, understands what is fearful and the potential consequences of fear-inducing situations but does not actually feel fear or disturbance when facing danger. Jiang Xinyan also makes a similar differentiation between "the emotion or attitude of fear" and the "feeling of fear." I agree with Ivanhoe's reservation about the distinction and share the view that being afraid of something entails feeling afraid of it. According to the Confucian conception, the virtuous person does experience fear (See Yearley 1990, 144–159; Jiang 1997, 274 and 288, note 14; Munro 1969, 153; Van Norden 1997, 248–249; Ivanhoe 2006, 227–229).

An important theme in Confucian ethics is that the virtuous person (*junzi*) is fearful of certain things and not fearful of certain other things. This view is not unlike the Aristotelian notion of virtue as involving the proper sort of response, in the proper degree and extent, in the proper manner, and in the proper circumstance. For example, we find in *Xunzi* 2.12: "In seeking profit, the gentleman acts with restraint. In averting harms, he acts early. In avoiding disgrace, he acts fearfully [*ju*]. In carrying out the Way, he acts courageously. Even if living in poverty, the gentleman's intentions are still grand. Even if wealthy and honored, his demeanor is reverent" (Hutton 2016, 15). Here, we see that fear of disgrace is an important moral motive for the virtuous person. In the next passage, we find the claim that the virtuous person is not without the susceptibility to feeling fear when confronted with troubling situations. Yet, the virtuous person will strive to manage these fears if the fears are bound up with pursuing what is morally right, as can be seen in *Xunzi* 3.2: "The gentleman is easy to get to know, but difficult to become intimate with. He is easily made apprehensive, but difficult to intimidate. He fears [*ju*] troubles, but will not avoid dying when it is for the sake of what is *yi* [righteous]" (Hutton 2016, 17).

In Xunzi's description, the virtuous person displays a kind of due care in which fear plays a role. Even when things go well, the virtuous person remains humble, ever prepared that things might go wrong. This unwillingness to be morally overconfident, or to take things morally for granted, involves a kind of fear or anxiety. According to *Xunzi* 7.6:

> Thus, the way that the wise person conducts affairs is that when he is most successful, then he takes thought for humility. When there is calm, then he takes thought for hazards. When there is safety, then he takes thought for danger. He makes comprehensive and abundant preparation, as though fearful of encountering disaster, and for this reason in a hundred acts he never meets with a downfall. (Hutton 2016, 51)

The phrase "takes thought for" connotes practical deliberation. The idea that we get in this passage is that, even when the wise person achieves success, the wise person engages in a kind of mental preparation for the possibility of encountering failure. Similarly, in the realization of calm or safety, the wise person takes heed of and prepares for potential hazards. The *junzi*'s disinclination to overconfidence exists at the level of both judgment and action. The *junzi* manifests a kind of epistemic humility about the possibility of error in grappling with questions about ethical matters, and this humility implies a lack of certain fearlessness. There is also, relatedly, a kind of practical humility—a refusal to be overconfident in one's agency and an awareness of the role of fortune, good or bad. That is, the *junzi* recognizes that one's ability to carry out or implement successfully in action one's judgment about ethical (or more broadly, practical) matters is never guaranteed. This is because our actions are bound up in the world in which they take place, and so cannot be understood as separate from the messiness and contingencies of the world. In short, the *junzi* is not someone in whom fear is wholly absent. Being "fearful of encountering disaster" enables the virtuous agent to take due care and avoid the defect of negligence.

While claiming that the *junzi* is not someone in whom fear is wholly absent, Xunzi also claims that there are differences between the virtuous and the vicious person that can be registered in terms of fear:

> Zilu asked Confucius, "Does a gentleman have worries [*you*]?" Confucius said, "When the gentleman has not yet succeeded, then he takes joy in his ideals, and when he has succeeded, then he takes joy in bringing good order to affairs. Thus, he has joy to the end of his life, without a single day of worry. As for the petty man, when he has not yet succeeded, then he worries that he will never succeed, and when he has succeeded, then he fears that he will lose it. Thus, he has worry to the end of his life, without a single day of joy." (Hutton 2016, 328)

Interestingly, in *Xunzi* 29.7, we find that the virtuous person has a kind of confidence, or freedom from fear, that the vicious person lacks. The vicious person is described as fearing, worrying, or feeling anxiety about the possibility of failure when striving to achieve a goal, and even in success, the vicious person is afraid that the success will be temporary. The virtuous person, on the other hand, is oriented toward the ideals that govern his goals and feels joy or satisfaction in success, rather than anxiety that the success may simply be ephemeral.

The Confucian classic *Doctrine of the Mean* or *Zhongyong* emphasizes the importance of maintaining balance and moderation in emotions and behavior, which is related to managing fear: "What *tian* 天[heaven] commands (*ming* 命) is called natural tendencies (*xing* 性); drawing out these natural tendencies is called the proper way (*dao* 道); improving upon this way is called education (*jiao* 教). As for this proper way, we cannot quit it even for an instant. Were it even possible to quit it, it would not be the proper way. It is for this reason that exemplary persons (*junzi* 君子) are so concerned about what is not seen, and so fearful [*kongju* 恐懼] about what is not heard" (Ames and Hall 2001, 89, modified). This passage highlights the importance of constant vigilance and ethical mindfulness in the conduct of the virtuous person (*junzi*). It suggests a proactive approach to ethical behavior that may involve fearfulness and awareness of potential consequences. These passages reflect Confucian teachings on the cultivation of moral character and ethical behavior, which implicitly touch upon the role of emotions such as fear in guiding human conduct.

In addition, the passage also emphasizes that what heaven has bestowed upon individuals is their inherent Nature, and adhering to this nature constitutes the Way. It is important to adhere to the Way and moral integrity without deviation. The notion of not straying from the path suggests a strong sense of commitment and responsibility, possibly influenced by the desire to avoid negative consequences or moral transgressions. The virtuous person (*junzi*) is therefore mindful and cautious in their actions, fearing that what they see and hear may not align with the Way. Consequently, they maintain a constant vigilance to ensure their actions remain in harmony with the Way. This aspect underscores the notion of *youhuan yishi* 憂患意識, or "anxiety or concerned consciousness," previously discussed. The virtuous person is dedicated to working toward the public good, moral transformation, and value transmission because they experience a fear rooted in the awareness that their actions may deviate from the Way prescribed by Heaven. This fear is not reactionary but proactive, propelling them to uphold moral integrity and fulfill their responsibilities without faltering.

Consider another passage from *The Great Learning* or *Daxue*: "The virtuous person [*junzi*] is watchful over himself when he is alone. There is no evil to which the mean man, dwelling retired, will not proceed, but when he sees a virtuous person, he instantly tries to disguise himself, concealing his evil, and displaying what is good. The other beholds his true character, and scrutinizes him" (Legge 1971, 366–367, modified). While fear is not explicitly mentioned in this passage, it emphasizes the *junzi*'s self-awareness and self-discipline in adhering to ethical principles even when alone. The *junzi*'s vigilance over his behavior suggests a concern for conformity to the Way and a desire to avoid moral failure.

Fear and the Virtues

Confucianism, with its emphasis on ethics and social harmony, often discusses virtues in relation to fear and its management. For the Confucians, these virtues include not just courage, but also righteousness, benevolence, and ritual propriety. In what follows, I consider how fear is related to these Confucian virtues. In general terms, the idea is that possessing certain virtues involves being afraid of certain things and not being afraid of certain other things. The emphasis here is on virtue's relation to the proper objects of fear—that is, fearing the correct objects and not fearing the incorrect objects. This does not mean that the Confucians deny the relevance of considerations such as fearing to the right degree or right manner, but the emphasis is on what is feared, and the ability to manage or overcome one's fear of those objects that one should not fear.

Courage is not simply the absence of fear but the mastery of one's susceptibility to experience it in certain circumstances or toward certain objects. For the Confucians, true courage lies in facing one's fears and managing them in the sense of maintaining self-control in the face of their presence. In the *Analects*, Kongzi emphasizes that courage is the willingness to confront challenges and dangers without being deterred by fear. In *Analects* 7.37: "The Master said, 'The gentleman is self-possessed and relaxed, while the petty man is perpetually full of worry'" (Slingerland 2003, 77). This suggests that courage is characterized by inner composure and fearlessness in the face of adversity. The idea is that courage involves being free of fear of being insulted, disputed, and dominated by others. In general terms, the idea is that possessing certain virtues involves being afraid of certain things and not being afraid of certain other things.

Arguably, the most important treatment of courage in the early Confucian tradition is found in the *Mengzi*. Mengzi distinguishes between different forms that courage can take. In particular, he distinguishes "petty courage" (*xiaoyong* 小勇) from "great courage" (*dayong* 大勇). Someone with petty courage is concerned primarily with personal "honor." Such concerns can involve maintaining an outward facade of respectability and composure in the face of physical or social threats by others. But they can also involve retaliating and resorting to violence when it is required as a response to affronts to one's honor. Both cases of "petty courage" require some degree of internal management of fear. Great courage, by contrast, is more explicitly connected with one's pursuit of the ethical good (*Mengzi* 2A:2; see Van Norden 2008, 36–37). For Mengzi, an important mark of great courage is steadfastness in the pursuit of the good and the right, which provides the person in possession of great courage with the strength to face challenges. The same can be said of Kongzi. Consider *Analects* 12.4:

> Sima Niu asked about the gentleman. The Master replied, "The gentleman is free of anxiety and fear." "'Free of anxiety and fear'—is that all there is to being a gentleman?" "If you can look inside yourself and find no faults, what cause is there for anxiety or fear?" (Slingerland 2003, 126)

The idea is that one's commitment to goodness provides the necessary internal strength to manage one's fear and confront potentially dangerous situations to pursue worthwhile ends.

It is instructive at this point in the discussion to highlight some differences between this Confucian picture and the picture of fear and courage that we find in Aristotle. For Aristotle, as well as thinkers in the Homeric Greek tradition, the battlefield was taken as the paradigmatic context in which the ethical ideals of courage and fear figured centrally. Indeed, in the Homeric context, fear and courage were taken as important in their relation to one's ability to achieve personal honor and social esteem, which often required success on the battlefield. Courage and the overcoming of fear were thus tied to emotions like pride and a sense of honor. Aristotle had a more ethicized conception of courage and the regulation of fear than the traditional Homeric conception. For Aristotle, courage is bound up with the noble (or fine) and with furthering the good of the community (polis). But even Aristotle's picture contrasts with the view of courage and fear that we find in the Confucian tradition, which focuses on courage and fear in the different contexts of moral self-cultivation and familial relationships.

Another point of contrast is that whereas, in the Aristotelian view, virtue in the context of fear (and more precisely, courage) required having certain feelings to the proper degree, this focus on having the right degree of feelings was not emphasized by the Confucians. For the Confucians, the focus was on the proper objects of one's fear and not so much on the dimension of the proper degree of one's feelings toward certain options. Another point of contrast concerned the relation of courage (including the proper regulation or management of fear) to the other virtues. Aristotle, who was committed to the unity of virtues, thought that there were important relations between courage and other virtues such as justice, wisdom, and generosity. By contrast, Kongzi and Mengzi do not see courage (that is, the ideal regulation of fear) as necessarily unified with what they take as other virtues. For example, Kongzi mentions in *Analects* 14.4 that "those who display courage are not necessarily Good [*ren*]" (Slingerland 2003, 155). Mengzi allows that there are "petty" forms of courage that, though directed at improper *objects* of fear, may still count as courage insofar as they involve the control and management of one's inner feelings of fear. Great or higher courage, which for Mengzi is properly oriented toward the good and is a feature of the *junzi* (the well-cultivated person), does seem to bear greater relations of unity with other virtues, such as benevolence, righteousness, and wisdom.

Righteousness (*yi* 義) in Confucianism involves acting in accordance with moral principles, even in the face of fear or opposition. Kongzi teaches that righteousness is the courage to stand up for what is morally right, regardless of the consequences. In the *Analects* 14.30, Kongzi emphasizes the importance of upholding righteousness despite distress: "The Master said, 'Do not distress [*huan*] that you are not recognized by others; distress (*huan*) rather that you yourself lack ability'" (Slingerland 2003, 166, modified). There is another passage in *Analects* 1.16: "The Master said, 'Do not be distressed [*huan*] about whether or not others know you; be distressed about whether or not you know others'" (Slingerland 2003, 7, modified). Consider another passage in *Analects* 4.14: "The Master said, 'Do not be distressed (*huan*) that you lack an official position, but rather distress yourself with the means by which you might become established. Do not be distressed that no one has heard of you, but rather strive to become a person worthy of being known'" (Slingerland 2003, 34, modified). These passages imply that true righteousness is not swayed by fear of insignificance but rather by the fear of moral inadequacy or failure. Such fear is a necessary or fitting aspect of moral virtue.

Benevolence (*ren* 仁), another important Confucian virtue, is characterized by a lack of fear and a genuine concern for the well-being of others. Kongzi teaches that benevolence arises from a compassionate heart free from selfish desires and fears. In the *Analects*, Kongzi emphasizes the importance of cultivating benevolence and overcoming the fear of others. For instance, in *Analects* 14.28: "The Master said, 'The Way of the gentleman is threefold, and yet I have not been able to achieve any aspect of it: The benevolent are not anxious [*you*], the wise are not confused, and the courageous do not fear [*ju*]'" (Slingerland 2003, 165, modified). Also, in *Analects* 9.29: "The Master said, 'The wise are not confused, the benevolent person is not anxious [*you*], and the courageous do not fear [*ju*]'" (Slingerland 2003, 96, modified).

Xunzi provides an interesting observation about the perspective of the benevolent person. "The person of *ren* [benevolence] is sure to show respect for others. There is a proper way to show respect for others. If they are worthy, then one values them and shows them respect. If they are unworthy, then one fears them and shows them respect" (Hutton 2016, 139, *Xunzi* 13.7). While respect is granted to both those who are morally good and those who are morally bad, only the former are valued, whereas the latter are feared.

Ritual propriety (*li* 禮) concerns the proper conduct and etiquette in social interactions. Rituals include ceremonies marking life-passages such as birth, coming of age, marriage, and death, as well as rituals of everyday interaction, such as greeting people on the street, having meals with others, gathering to listen to a musical performance, and giving and receiving gifts. Kongzi teaches that ritual propriety involves overcoming the fear of social disapproval and adhering to traditional customs and norms. In the *Analects*, Kongzi emphasizes the importance of observing ritual propriety as a way to cultivate virtue and harmony in society. For example, in *Analects* 15.32, "The gentleman devotes his thoughts to attaining the Way, not obtaining food. In the pursuit of agriculture, there is the possibility of starvation; in the pursuit of learning, there is the possibility of salary. The gentleman is anxious [*you*] about the Way and anxious not about poverty" (Slingerland 2003, 187, modified). This suggests that ritual propriety involves a fear of failing to uphold one's own moral integrity rather than a fear of external judgment.

Xunzi believed in the innate selfishness of human nature and the importance of education and ritual propriety in cultivating virtues. In the following passage, Xunzi discusses the role of ritual propriety (*li*) in managing fear:

> In the ritual for "personal welcoming," the father stands, facing south. The son kneels, facing north. The father performs a libation and commands him: "Go and welcome your helpmate, to accomplish our ancestral tasks. Reverently guide her to serve respectfully as the successor to your mother. Thus may we have constancy." The son says, "Yes. I only fear [*kong*] that I may not be capable of this. How would I dare forget your command?" (Hutton 2016, 291, *Xunzi* 27.15)

While ritual practices can enable one to manage fear, for Xunzi, the virtue of ritual propriety also involves a sense of fear—or more precisely, alertness and cautiousness.

> To be reverent and respectful makes for ritual propriety. To be accommodating and harmonious makes for musicality. To be careful and cautious makes for benefit. To go brawling and raging makes for harm. And so, the gentleman rests in ritual propriety and musicality, employs alertness and cautiousness, and avoids brawling and raging. For this reason, in a hundred actions he commits no errors. The petty man is the opposite of this. (Hutton 2016, 139, *Xunzi* 13.8)

It is often noted that the Confucian rituals enable people to strengthen the attitudes and emotions they are committed to, such as care, respect, and gratitude. The idea is that by acting in accordance with ceremonies conventionally established to signify and convey these attitudes, one can strengthen them in oneself. However, the passage in the *Xunzi* suggests that reverence and ritual propriety may presuppose certain varieties of fear, such as alertness or cautiousness.

In Confucianism, a recurring theme is that political power and authority based on the ruler's virtue are both preferred to and more effective than governance by regulation and coercion. Wise rulers possess the characteristics of sages: they are benevolent, courageous, and righteous. According to *Mengzi* 7A:14,

> Mengzi said, "Benevolent teachings do not enter people as deeply as the report of benevolent actions. Good regulations do not win over the people as well as good instruction. People are in awe of [*wei*] good regulations, but they love good instruction. Good regulations will get material resources from the people, but good instruction will win over the hearts of the people." (Van Norden 2008, 174)

The notion of fear thus bears on the distinction between ruling by instruction and ruling by regulation. Good instruction is said to be met with love, whereas regulation is met with awe or fear. Relatedly, consider *Xunzi* 11.8:

> When the ruler himself is not capable, but knows to fear [*kongju*], about this and seek someone who is capable, then one such as this will be strong. When the ruler himself is not capable, but does not know to fear about this and seek someone who is capable, and instead accordingly employs only those whom he favors, those close to him, and those who ingratiate themselves to him, then such a one will be endangered and have his state diminished, and taken to the extreme, he will perish. (Hutton 2016, 103, modified)

This passage expresses an important theme in Confucian political philosophy: the political virtue of being a wise ruler involves fearing well.

Fear and Moral Self-Cultivation

Confucians emphasize moral self-cultivation, and fear is taken to play a crucial role in this process. In this section, I discuss two main ideas. The first is that moral self-cultivation is very difficult, if not impossible, under conditions in which one is gripped by terror (in, say, a condition of political instability or upheaval). The second is the attainment of different stages of moral self-cultivation, manifesting in the agent's susceptibility (or not) to various sorts of fear.

Kongzi often takes up the importance of moral self-cultivation and the role of fear in shaping one's character. In the *Analects*, Kongzi emphasizes the need for self-reflection and self-improvement to cultivate virtue. He often addresses the fear of not living up to moral standards as a motivation for moral self-cultivation. For example, in *Analects* 2.4 (quoted in Section 2), Kongzi reflects on his seventy-year journey of moral self-cultivation, suggesting that the fear of ignorance and moral failings motivated him to strive for self-improvement throughout his life.

Confucians often emphasize the importance of stable social and political conditions for moral self-cultivation. Many Confucians argued that moral self-cultivation is difficult, if not impossible, under terror or political instability conditions. For example, Mengzi frequently discusses the influence of external factors, such as social and political conditions, on moral self-cultivation. Consider the discussion of how adverse conditions can hinder moral development in *Mengzi* 6A:7:

> Mengzi said, "In years of plenty, most young men are gentle; in years of poverty, most young men are violent. It is not that the potential that Heaven confers on them varies like this. They are like this because of what sinks and drowns their hearts. Consider barley. Sow the seeds and cover them. The soil is the same and the time of planting is also the same. They grow rapidly, and by the time of the summer solstice they have all ripened. Although there are some differences, these are due to the richness of the soil and to unevenness in the rain and in human effort. Hence, in general, things of the same kind are all similar. Why would one have any doubt about this when it comes to humans alone? We and the sage are of the same kind." (Van Norden 2008, 150)

This passage suggests that without the proper conditions for moral self-cultivation, such as stability and security, individuals may struggle to develop virtue and may be hindered or stunted in their moral development.

These ideas are not unlike those we find in Thomas Hobbes's work, arguably the preeminent philosopher of fear in the Western philosophical tradition. Hobbes famously claimed that fear is one of the most important as well as one of the worst consequences of being in "the state of nature." Hobbes characterized the state of nature as a war of "every man against every man," and in this state, everyone has reason to fear everyone else; it is a state of "continual fear, and danger of violent death . . . the life of man solitary, poor, nasty, brutish, and short" (Hobbes 1998, 84). Like Hobbes, who observed that "a life of continual fear is scarcely a life at all," the early Confucians also acknowledged the badness of fear and that a life dominated by fear is terrible. In a Hobbesian vein, Xunzi points out how being in a state of fear can lead one to be manipulable. He points out how one can make use of a lord's fear in *Xunzi* 13.4:

> Being able to exert transformative influence, and at the appropriate times to win him over—these are what is *yi* [righteous] in the service of a violent lord. Treat him like riding an unbroken horse, like caring for a newborn, like feeding a starving person. And so, take advantage of his fearful [*ju*] moods to correct his mistakes. Take advantage of his anxious [*you*] moods to scrutinize his habits. Take advantage of his joyful moods to rein in his ways. (Hutton 2016, 137, modified)

In Mengzi, we also find the Hobbesian idea that fear is incompatible with social life. Fear undermines social relations and destroys the conditions that make stability and "commodious living" possible. For Hobbes, we can mitigate or reduce the awful human condition of unremitting fear only through the realization of a stable political society. Indeed, for Hobbes, the fear of death is the first of "the passions that incline men to peace" (Hobbes 1998, 86). Again, Mengzi would agree and add that successful moral self-cultivation would be unlikely without the conditions of a reasonably stable society in which we can be free from a life dominated by fear. Hobbes holds that fearful people could not truly sustain rewarding forms of interpersonal exchange, while Mengzi holds that a life gripped by terror was not conducive to moral cultivation. Mengzi asserts that when people are so impoverished that they do not have enough resources to care for their parents and children and can barely save themselves, they do not have the spare time to pay attention to propriety and righteousness (*Mengzi* 1A:7; see Van Norden 2008, 7–15). This is also reflected in Mengzi's view that, "in times of poverty, people are much more prone to violence, and this is due to the external circumstances of poverty, which sinks and drowns their hearts" (*Mengzi* 6A:7, quoted above).

Confucians understood the different stages of moral self-cultivation partly in terms of the individual's susceptibility to various types of fear. For example, Kongzi discusses the relationship between moral self-cultivation and fear in several passages, such as *Analects* 12:4 (quoted in Section 3), where he claims that those who find no faults within themselves have nothing to fear. In this passage, Kongzi suggests that the virtuous person, who has cultivated moral integrity, is not swayed by fear of poverty or lack of recognition. Instead, they remain steadfast in their ethical commitments and do not succumb to fear.

In Xunzi's philosophy, we find these same Confucian themes about fear. For instance, in *Xunzi* 23.23, we find the following statement about the person who possesses the highest kind of courage:

> The former kings had a certain way, and he dares to carry out his understanding of it. Above, he does not follow along with the lords of a chaotic age. Below, he does not conform to the people of a chaotic age. He considers no impoverishment or hard times to follow from affairs involving *ren* [benevolence]. He considers no wealth or honor to follow from affairs lacking ren. If the world recognizes him, then he wishes to share the world's pain and joy over things. If the world does not recognize him, then independently he stands alone between Heaven and Earth and does not fear or be in awe [*wei*]. Such is the highest kind of courage. (Hutton 2016, 256, modified)

And in *Xunzi* 8.15, we find the following statement about the sage:

> How properly he holds to culture and good form! How magnanimously he takes joy in people's goodness! How apprehensively he fears [*kong*] people's wrongdoing! (Hutton 2016, 59–60)

These Confucian texts highlight the connection between moral self-cultivation and the individual's susceptibility to various types of fear. They suggest that as individuals progress in their moral development and cultivate virtues such as courage, kindness, and integrity, they become less susceptible to fear and more capable of facing challenges with equanimity. However, the broad Confucian picture is not that one should aim to achieve a condition of total fearlessness, nor is it that the development of virtue correlates with a greater degree of fearlessness. To be sure, fear remains a regular component in the development of virtue for the Confucians.

Acknowledgment

I would like to thank George Tsai for helpful discussions and extensive comments on multiple drafts.

Notes

1 In speaking of the *Classical or Early Confucian tradition*, we refer to the foundations of Confucian thought and practice: that is, the philosophy of Kongzi (551–479 BCE) and his followers down to the third century BCE, an era that is sometimes called the Warring States period. "Confucius" is the Latinized name that Jesuit missionaries assigned to Kongzi. He is the central figure in the tradition of thought and practice called Ruism (*Rujia* 儒家, lit. "school of the learned"), which we refer to in English as "Confucianism." Kongzi saw himself as a teacher and scholar trying to transmit and reframe values that he believed were held by earlier kings and cultural heroes ("Sages") of Chinese civilization. The era of Classical Confucianism begins with Kongzi and the *Analects* or *Lunyu*, a text composed by generations of students presenting their understanding of the Master's ideas. Kongzi's teachings came to be seen as touchstones for many who sought to improve their society and their own lives. They influenced later Confucian thinkers such as Mengzi (Mencius), Xunzi, and the Neo-Confucian thinkers Zhu Xi and Wang Yangming.

2 As noted by Chengzi, the heart can be unmoved if it is dominated by something, such as caring about victory and the Way (See Van Norden 2008, 36–38).

Bibliography

Chen Tingjing 陳廷敬and Zhang Yushu 張玉書, eds. 2015. *Kangxi zidian* 康熙字典 [Kangxi Dictionary]. Beijing: Shehui kexue wenxian chubanshe 社會科學文獻出版社 [Social Science Academic Press].

CTP Dictionary. 2022. *Chinese Text Project*. https://ctext.org/instructions/dictionary. Accessed January 8, 2023.

Debiec, Jacek, and Joseph LeDoux. 2004. "Fear and the Brain." *Social Research* 71, no. 4: 807–818.

Hobbes, Thomas. 1998. *Leviathan*. Edited by J. C. A. Gaskin. Oxford: Oxford University Press.

Hutton, Eric L., trans. 2016. *Xunzi: The Complete Text*. Princeton: Princeton University Press.

Jiang, Xinyan. 1997. "Mencins on Human Nature and Courage." *Joumal of Chinese Philosophy* 24: 265–289.

Kwong loi, Shun, 2016. "Studying Confucian Thought from the Inside Out." In *Dao: A Journal of Comparative Philosophy* 15, no. 4: 511–532.

Legge, James. 1971. *Confucian Analects, The Great Learning & The Doctrine of the Mean*. New York: Dover.

Munro, Donald J. 1969. *The Concept of Man in Early China*. Stanford: Stanford University Press.

Ni, Maoshing. 1995. *The Yellow Emperor's Classic of Medicine: A New Translation of the Neijing Suwen with Commentary*. Boston: Shambhala.

Nussbaum, Martha. 2004. "Emotions as Judgments of Value and Importance." In *Thinking about Feeling: Contemporary Philosophers on Emotions*, edited by Robert C. Solomon, 183–199. New York: Oxford University Press.

Revised Mandarin Chinese Dictionary. 2022. National Academy for Educational Research. https://dict.revised.moe.edu.tw/index.jsp. Accessed January 8, 2023.

Slingerland, Edward, trans. 2003. *Analects: With Selections from Traditional Commentaries*. Indianapolis: Hackett Publishing Company.

Van Norden, Bryan. 1997. "Mencius on Courage." In *Midwest Studies in Philosophy Volume XXI. Philosophy of Religion*, edited by Peter A. French, Theodore E. Uehling, Jr., and Howard K. Wettstein. Notre Dame: University of Notre Dame Press.

Van Norden Bryan W., trans. 2008. *Mengzi: With Selections from Traditional Commentaries*. Indianapolis: Hackett Publishing Company.

Xu Shen 許慎. 2018. *Shuowen jiezi* 說文解字. Guilin: Lijiang Chubanshe 漓江出版社 [Lijiang Publishing Limited].

Xu Fuguan 徐復觀. 1975. *Zhongguo renxing lunshi: xian Qin Pian* 中國人性論史: 先秦篇, 2nd ed [A History of Chinese Views of Human Nature: The Pre-Qin Period]. Taipei: Shangwu yingshuguan 商務印書館 [Commercial Press].

Yearley, Lee H. 1990. *Mencius and Aquinas: Theories of Virtue and Conceptions of Courage*. Albany: SUNY Press.

2

Fear and Courage in Early Confucianism

Songyao Ren

A distinctive feature of the early Confucian ideal consists in the attunement of the self as a whole to the *Dao*. Not only does the noble person make the correct choice and act on it, but she also has the appropriate emotion that supplies her with the desire to do it. This is best articulated by Confucius' mini autobiography, which suggests that by the age of seventy, he was able to follow the desires of his *xin* 心 (heart-mind) without overstepping the boundaries (*Analects*, 2.4). Thus, Confucian ethical development culminates in complete congruence between what one wants to do and what one ought to do such that one can meet ethical demands spontaneously and effortlessly by acting on one's desires (Virág 2017; Ivanhoe 2017).

This ideal of the integrated self, where one's judgment, desire, and action all align harmoniously with the *Dao*, fits nicely with many Confucian virtues. However, it is unclear how it applies to the virtue of *yong* 勇 (courage). Confucius lists courage as one of the three cardinal virtues, along with *ren* 仁 (benevolence, humaneness) and *zhi* 智 (wisdom) (*Analects*, 9.29, 14.28). It refers to the ability to persevere in the face of danger and is exemplified by the soldier who marches into battle to defend her country even though this puts her own life in jeopardy.[1] However, some people might be inclined to think that fear is an appropriate response to danger and involves an impulse to avoid the danger. If so, courage appears to be a form of self-control, as the courageous soldier cannot follow her fearful desire, but rather has to overcome it in order to fulfill her patriotic duty. This raises a puzzle: How can the virtue of courage, which seems to require the suppression of fear, fit into the Confucian ideal of perfect integrity?

This chapter attempts a solution to this puzzle. Drawing from the *Analects*, *Mencius*, and *Xunzi*, I argue that although the Confucians acknowledge the presence of appropriate fear in courage, this is not disruptive to the unity of the Confucian self.[2] The integrated self does not act courageously by controlling its fear; it acts courageously through the fear, which makes a valuable contribution to the courageous action (Pears 1980, 180). My solution is inspired by Pears' (1980) Aristotelian analysis of courage. Pears focuses primarily on developing an account of courage that allows for a perfect match between one's medial feelings and medial actions in virtue. In this chapter,

I show that Pears' insights are not only present in Confucian thinking but also further developed by it.

The rest of this chapter is structured as follows. I first present the Confucian ideal of perfect integrity in order to explain the puzzle in more detail. I then discuss and reject a popular reading of Confucian courage as a form of fearlessness. Next, I survey the treatment of fear in the primary texts to show that the noble person has appropriate fears, which are scaled to the magnitudes of the dangers. Finally, I explain how the Confucian account of courage, in which fear is a crucial component, reconciles with the ideal of perfect integrity.

The Confucian Ideal of Perfect Integrity and a Puzzle about Courage

In 4B19, Mencius says,

> That wherein human beings differ from the birds and beasts is but slight. The majority of people relinquish this, while the noble person retains it. Shun was clear about the multitude of things and observant of human relationships.[3] Humaneness and righteousness were the source of his actions; he did not just perform acts of humaneness and righteousness.[4]

According to Mencius, human nature is that which differentiates humans from birds and beasts. This consists of a feature of the cognitive-affective faculty *xin* 心 (heart-mind), namely, its desiring and taking delight in *liyi* 理義 (principle and righteousness) (*Mencius*, 6A7, 6A14).[5] If one makes sustained and painstaking efforts in cultivating one's *xin* 心 (heart-mind), one can acquire the virtues, such as *ren* 仁 (benevolence, humaneness) and *yi* 義 (righteousness). In order for one to count as virtuous, however, it does not suffice that one correctly judges what one ought to do and does it. One's action also needs to flow spontaneously from and express one's virtuous attitudes and dispositions.[6]

That virtue involves a kind of harmony between feeling and action is a distinctive feature of the early Confucian tradition. This is further reflected in the discussion of *li* 禮 (ritual). For the Confucians, rituals encompass more than formal ceremonies, such as coming-of-age ceremonies, ancestral worship, and the burial of parents. They cover a broad range of customs and practices that spell out appropriate behaviors in many aspects of everyday life: how to greet others, compete with them, share meals with them, and so on. Observing rituals is an important virtue because it allows people to assume roles that define their appropriate relationships with each other. It is through observing rituals, for example, that the ruler becomes the ruler, the minister becomes the minister, the father becomes the father, and the son becomes the son (*Analects*, 12.11).

Throughout the *Analects,* Confucius condemns those who wreak havoc by not practicing rituals or by misappropriating rituals meant for social stations other than their own.[7] Confucius also deplores the inauthenticity in ritual performances, as exhibited by those who simply go through the motions but lack the corresponding affective attitudes. He says, "one who dwells in the ruler's seat and is not tolerant, one who performs a ritual and is not reverent, one who joins a funeral and does not grieve—how can I bear to see them" (*Analects*, 3.26)?[8]

This shows that ritual performances should be authentic expressions of appropriate emotions. *Zhi* 質 (substance), representing the inner attitudes, and *wen* 文 (patterned refinement), representing the outward expressions, should be in balance, with neither prevailing over the other (*Analects*, 6.18).[9] With respect to mourning rituals, for example, Confucius remarks that they should give form to appropriate grief and stop at that (*Analects*, 19.14). In a conversation with his student Zaiwo, Confucius even says that if one does not possess sufficient filial sentiments, there is no point in strictly observing the three-year mourning ritual (*Analects*, 17.21). This is because rituals ungrounded in appropriate emotional sensibilities become ritualistic—"meaningless gestures without genuine feelings to authenticate them" (Virág 2017, 33).

Thus, for the Confucian sage, different aspects of the self, that is, judgment, emotion, and action, are fully integrated with each other and work in tandem in following the *Dao.* As Confucius suggests, "knowing it is not so good as loving it; loving it is not so good as taking joy in it" (*Analects,* 6.20).[10] Correspondingly, Confucian virtues are inclinational: the virtuous person simply acts on her desires and inclinations, which consistently track the good (Yearley 1990). The benevolent person, for example, feels alarm and distress upon seeing a child about to fall into a well, and this compassion motivates her to save the child (*Mencius,* 2B6). The filial son has respect and affection for his parents, and this motivates him to take over difficult chores and serve them wine and food first at meals (*Analects,* 2.7, 2.8).

Although this ideal of perfect integrity fits nicely with many Confucian virtues, it seems to give rise to a puzzle about *yong* 勇 (courage). Confucius sees courage as one of the three cardinal virtues possessed by the noble person, alongside *ren* 仁 (benevolence, humaneness) and *zhi* 智 (wisdom) (*Analects,* 9.29). According to Lai (1985), *ren* 仁 (benevolence, humaneness) tells us what to do, *zhi* 智 (wisdom) tells us how to do it, and *yong* 勇 (courage) gives us the ability to do it (201). Although Mencius does not include courage in his list of the four basic virtues, he likewise believes that it is an important component in living a good life. This is implied by Mencius' admiration for the great courage 大勇 of the ancient sage kings, which he deems crucial to their bringing peace to the world (*Mencius,* 1B3).

The ancient Chinese dictionary *Shuo Wen Jie Zi* 說文解字 (Explaining and Analyzing Characters) defines courage as not yielding despite obstacles.[11] More specifically, courage refers to the ability to persevere toward an external goal amid danger, such as the prospect of injury or death (Pears 1980; Sreenivasan 2020).[12] It is sometimes thought, however, that the perception of danger, that is, the possibility of suffering harm, elicits fear, which involves, among other things, a desire to flee.[13] As LeDoux (2020) suggests, the defensive survival circuit, which often partly underlies fear, is activated in the presence of danger and produces defensive behaviors that maximize the probability of survival.[14] If so, courage appears to be a form of self-control: the courageous agent cannot follow her fearful desire to avoid the danger, which conflicts with her external goal, but rather has to overcome it in order to perform the courageous action. This leaves us wondering, how does courage fit the Confucian ideal of perfect integrity? Confucius suggests that the noble person's actions are authentic, flowing from her appropriate emotions. But doesn't courage require the suppression of a wayward inclination, thus displaying the exact kind of inauthenticity that Confucius deems objectionable?

The Fearlessness Interpretation of Confucian Courage

To solve the above puzzle, some interpreters propose that the Confucian courageous person is free from the feeling of fear. This view seems to receive support from several important discussions of courage in the texts. For example, Confucius says, "the wise have no perplexities, the benevolent have no worries, and the courageous have no fears 勇者不懼" (*Analects,* 9.29, 14.28). Mencius also associates courage with having an unmoved mind 不動心 (*Mencius,* 2A2). This is achieved through nourishing the *qi* 氣, the basic stuff in the *xin* 心 (heart-mind), with *yi* 義 (righteousness), so that it becomes vast and strong, filling the space between Heaven and earth (2A2).[15] Based on this, Brooks and Brooks (1998) claim that the noble person is free from vacillations of the mind, including fear, since they negate the virtues (56). Munro (1969) says that the goal of Confucian self-cultivation is a state of tranquility in which one is no longer disturbed by external objects (153).

The most elaborate version of the fearlessness interpretation is developed by Yearley (1990). In his view, the unmoved mind is one where the vast, flowing *qi* 氣 fully empowers the righteous action without any distraction. In the case of courage, all one's *qi* 氣 is gathered toward the pursuit of the external goal, leaving one with "no fear of the objectionable results" or "the loss of real goods" (156). More specifically, Yearley identifies three components in fear: the cognitive judgment about the danger, the desire to avoid the danger, and various physiological changes. He claims that the courageous person who pursues the external goal under dangerous conditions knows that this pursuit is dangerous, but "neither inclines to flee from it nor manifests normal physiological reactions" (156). In other words, the appropriate cognitive judgment occurs, but the conative and physiological components in fear do not.

Proponents of this interpretation believe it can reconcile the virtue of courage with the Confucian ideal of perfect integrity (Yearley 1990; Jiang 1997; Van Norden 1997). Consider a courageous person who sees a deranged person about to attack a child (Yearley 1990, 156). The courageous person judges that it is dangerous for her to interfere, but "lacks the desire to flee and numerous physiological reactions" (156). In fact, "those noncognitive reactions that do appear arise from another judgment and lead to virtuous actions" (156). That is, she judges that "the child is in danger and should be helped," and this judgment is accompanied by the desire to save the child and various physiological changes (156). Thus, the courageous person has no fearful desire that conflicts with the advancement of her external goal. She has nothing to overcome and her courageous action simply springs from her benevolent concern for the child.[16]

The fearlessness interpretation is influential in Confucian scholarship, but its separation of the feeling of fear from the judgment about the danger raises some worries. In particular, there is a wide consensus among philosophers and affective scientists across the theoretical spectrum that emotions play an important epistemic role. In part, they make salient aspects of the world that are relevant to our cares and concerns and inform us about the ways in which they matter to us. As Brady writes,

> Emotions can improve the speed at which we notice the relevant objects and events in our environment, and in a way that is relatively "cost-free." As a result, emotions can have value in so far as they facilitate a "fast and frugal" detection of important objects and events. Another aspect of this is that emotion is very often the way in which the value of significant things registers with us, such that without emotion the importance of many such objects and events would pass us by. (2013, 13)[17]

Thus, emotions provide us with access to the evaluative world. In the absence of emotions, it is difficult, if not impossible, for us to notice important objects and events and become aware of their value or disvalue.

The claim about the epistemic value of emotion poses a problem for the ideal of fearlessness. If the Confucian sage lacks the urge to flee and the concomitant physiological responses, how can she reliably detect dangers and make correct evaluations about them? Even supposing that she can, the mechanism that allows her to do so can hardly be as good as the fear system. This is because the fear system is a product of evolution designed to detect and respond to dangers quickly, automatically, and with minimal cognitive cost (Ekman 1992; LeDoux 2020). An alternative mechanism, if there is one, likely involves deliberate efforts, which consume significantly more cognitive resources, making it much slower and less efficient than the time-tested gift from nature (Brady 2013; Sreenivasan 2020).

One might respond that while the Confucian sage initially feels fear about the danger, once she realizes that the external goal is worth the danger, her fear disappears. In Yearley (1990)'s example, the sage is afraid of being attacked by the deranged person, but upon judging that saving the child is the right thing to do, her fear goes out of existence. On this view, the sage can quickly be alerted to the danger by virtue of her initial fear. But since such fear soon vanishes, there remains no adverse inclination that needs to be controlled when she performs the courageous action.

While this partial fearlessness interpretation may bypass the epistemic objection targeting complete fearlessness, it is nevertheless subject to a general worry that arises from the appropriateness of fear. That is, the emotion of fear, including its conative and physiological components, is not only elicited by danger but also justified by it (Sreenivasan 2020, 234). The fact that an agent is in a dangerous situation gives her a reason to preserve herself, thus rendering her fearful desire appropriate. This undermines both the ideal of complete fearlessness, where the agent has no fear at all, and the ideal of partial fearlessness, where the agent stops fearing upon realizing that the external goal takes precedence over avoiding the danger. In the latter case, the fact that the danger is outweighed does not mean that it has vanished. As long as the danger persists, fear continues to be called for as the appropriate response and "part of the agent's equipment for navigating it well" (234).

The Treatment of Fear in the Early Confucian Texts

We have seen that the fearlessness interpretation is philosophically implausible. In this section, I further show that it is, in fact, not the view that the early Confucians endorse. Through an examination of the treatment of fear in the primary texts, I argue that while the noble person lacks many kinds of fears that affect ordinary people, she has appropriate fears directed at genuine dangers. Along the way, I also show that the apparent textual evidence for the fearlessness interpretation can be explained away.

Consider first the kinds of fears that are objectionable. Confucius claims that the noble person should not fear that she has no position or that no one recognizes her (*Analects,* 4.14, 14.30). Rather, she should be concerned with whether she has what it takes to merit a position or recognition. Nor should the noble person have a fear of poverty (*Analects,* 1.14, 4.5, 15.32). This is implied by Confucius' praise of his student Yan Hui, who, despite "living on a shabby lane" with only "a simple bowl of food and a dipperful of drink," was "unchanging in his joy" (*Analects,* 6.11).[18] The reason that these fears are inappropriate is because wealth and fame are not genuine goods and the prospect of being deprived of them does not pose much danger to the noble person.[19] In fact, it is a recurring theme in the texts that while the noble person may pursue fame and wealth when circumstances permit, she should never be excessively focused on them (*Analects,* 7.12, 7.16, 8.12, 8.13; *Mencius,* 3B7, 6A10).

As has been noted, some interpreters are led to the fearlessness interpretation in part by Confucius' remark that the courageous have no fear (*Analects,* 9.29, 14.28). A closer look, however, reveals that this remark is made in a particular context and that a qualification needs to be added to it. In *Analects* 12.4, Confucius' student Sima Niu asked him what it takes to be a noble person. Confucius responded that the noble person is not beset with worry or fear. When asked to explain what he means, Confucius said, "surveying himself within and finding no fault, what worry or fear could there be?"[20] This shows that the claim about the noble person's fearlessness should be understood in the context of self-reflection, where he has no fear because he has a clear conscience and finds little wrongdoing within himself.[21] This, however, gives us no ground to infer that the noble person is free from fear in the absolute sense.

In fact, many passages indicate that the noble person does experience fears, but, unlike ordinary fears, they are fitting or appropriate. As D'Arms and Jacobson (2000) suggest, the fittingness of an emotion has two dimensions—shape and size (73). An emotion is unfitting in shape if it represents its object as having an evaluative feature that it in fact lacks. An emotion is unfitting in size when it is out of proportion with the evaluative feature of the object. On this view, an episode of fear is fitting or appropriate when the object that it represents as dangerous is indeed dangerous and its strength is proportionate to the magnitude of the danger.

One object that the noble person fears is the moral decline of the world. Confucius was afraid that "deviant speech and oppressive actions again became prevalent" and that "there were cases of ministers murdering their rulers and of sons murdering their parents" (*Mencius,* 3B9).[22] This prompted him to write the *Chunqiu* 春秋 (Spring and Autumn Annals), the first Chinese chronicle, as a way to propagate the Confucian *dao.* In a similar vein, Mencius feared that licentious thoughts would block the path of humaneness and righteousness. This motivated his engagement in arguments with rival philosophers so as to "correct people's minds," "stop deviant speech," "resist perverse actions," and "carry on the work of the three Sages" (3B9).

The objects of the noble person's fears extend further to the dangers in the personal realm. In particular, the Confucian tradition ascribes significant value to personal relationships. This not only gives rise to various duties to promote those relationships, but also calls for different kinds of fears depending on the ways in which they are threatened. Take, for example, the parent–child relationship, the most important relationship in Confucian thought.[23] Confucius says, "one cannot fail to know the ages of one's parents: on one hand, these are a source of happiness, on the other hand of fear" (*Analects,* 4.21).[24] Insofar as one cares about one's parents, one has mixed feelings toward their advancing years. On the one hand, their advancing years indicate that they have lived long and rich lives and thus warrant joy. On the other hand, they signal their increased frailty and approaching death and thus warrant fear.

Another source of fear is physical harm to oneself. According to the Confucian classic *Xiao Jing* 孝經 (Classic of Filiality), "one receives one's body, hair, and skin from one's parents, and one dares not injure them. This is the beginning of filial piety."[25] This suggests that one's body is not merely one's own possession, but a gift from one's parents, reflective of their care and nurture (*Mencius*, 4B30). Because of this, one should fear the loss of physical integrity and be motivated to avoid it out of respect and gratitude toward one's parents.

That one should fear the loss of physical integrity is also because it prevents one from serving one's parents to the fullest. The *Analects* 11.23 recounts a story in which Confucius was in danger in the state of Kuang. He and his entourage were surrounded by the Kuang people, who refused to let them go for several days. Amid the chaos, Yan Hui fell behind the main group. When he finally caught up, Confucius said to him, "I thought you had died."[26] Yan Hui replied, "while you are alive, Master, how would I dare to die?" Yan Hui's response can be made intelligible in light of the father-son-like relationship that he had with Confucius. As Mather (1995) suggests, filial piety demands "not only cheerful obedience to parents during childhood but also reverential support of them through their old age, and faithful worship of their spirits after their death" (113). Because of this, Yan Hui carefully preserved himself out of fear of death so that he could continue to serve Confucius.

The Confucian noble person has general fears of genuine dangers. This allows her to correctly gauge the magnitude of the danger in a particular circumstance and motivates her to avoid it accordingly. Further, even in circumstances that call for courage—where the right thing to do is to confront the danger in order to achieve an external goal—the noble person remains fearful of the particular instance of the danger. Contrary to what the fearlessness interpretation suggests, a complete absence of fear is not a constituent of courage, but an impediment to it.

To see this, consider the example of Zilu. The eldest among Confucius' disciples, Zilu was a former warrior known for his love of courage. But in the eyes of Confucius, Zilu possessed only a semblance of courage, not real courage. Once Confucius praised Yan Hui for his ability to adapt to different situations (*Analects,* 7.11). Zilu became jealous and tried to steer the conversation toward what he perceived to be his strength, that is, courage. He asked Confucius, "Master, if you were put in charge of the three army divisions, then whom would you wish to have with you?"[27] Rather than hearing the praise he expected, Zilu was scorned by Confucius, who said, "Those who fight tigers with their bare hands, wade across rivers, and are willing to die without regret—I would not want their company. I would certainly want those who approach affairs with a proper sense of fear and who like to lay careful plans for success." In fact, Confucius foretold that Zilu would not be able to live out his natural years due to his reckless disposition (*Analects,* 11.13). This is validated by the historical account of Zilu's death recorded in the *Shi Ji* 史記 (Records of the Grand Historian).[28] During a coup d'état in the state of Wei, Zilu charged into battle out of loyalty to a ruler whom he knew had already been killed. He heedlessly exposed himself to great danger, which resulted in his violent death.

Zilu took pride in his fearlessness on the battlefield. He experienced no motivational conflict and was wholeheartedly devoted to victory. Confucius, however, deemed this a display of recklessness rather than courage. That is, Zilu's lack of fear led him to march into battle, oblivious of the danger it involved. This exposed him to unnecessary risks and led him to die in vain. By contrast, true courage requires a proper sense of fear, which instills heightened vigilance, enabling the individual to carefully navigate the dangerous situation while pursuing the external goal. Thus, for the early Confucians, true courage involves having appropriate fears, not having no fears.

Fear, Courage, and the Ideal of Perfect Integrity

Let's take stock. Courage refers to the ability to persevere toward an external goal amid danger, such as the prospect of death or injury. Also, the Confucian courageous agent is not fearless; she has appropriate fear, the size of which matches the extent of the danger in her situation. If so, doesn't the fearful desire need to be controlled in order for the courageous agent to persevere? This section resists such a view. The Confucian courageous agent does not act by controlling her fear; rather, she acts through her fear, which makes a valuable contribution to the courageous action (Pears 1980, 180). As has been mentioned, my argument draws on the insights offered by Pears (1980) in his reconstruction of an Aristotelian account of courage. I show that these insights are not only present in Confucian thinking but also further substantiated by it.

Let me start by adding a qualification to the account of courage developed so far. Confucian courage has a normative aspect. It is not simply a matter of persevering toward the external goal in the face of danger, but doing so in accordance with *yi* 義 (righteousness). As Confucius says, "to see the right thing and not do it is to lack courage" (*Analects*, 2.24).[29] Mencius also says,

> I desire fish, and I also desire bear's paws. If I cannot have both of them, I will give up fish and take bear's paws. I desire life, and I also desire righteousness. If I cannot have both of them, I will give up life and take righteousness. It is true that I desire life, but there is something I desire more than life, and therefore I will not do something dishonorable in order to hold on to it. I detest death, but there is something I detest more than death, and therefore there are some dangers I may not avoid. (*Mencius,* 6A10)[30]

In the Confucian tradition, *yi* 義 (righteousness) does not always enable one to identify the right action by itself. Rather, one has to weigh competing values in order to satisfy its requirement.[31] The Chinese term for weighing is *quan* 權, which is that by which we know which things are light and which are heavy (*Mencius*, 1A7, 4A7). In the case of courage, one needs to correctly weigh the external goal—"the hoped-for state of affairs that animate the action," against the countergoal—the unfortunate state of affairs that may result from the action (Yearley 1990, 114). One's perseverance aligns with *yi* 義 (righteousness) if, on the objective side, the value of the external goal exceeds the value of avoiding the danger; and on the subjective side, the courageous agent makes the corresponding judgment that pursuing the external goal is worth the danger (Sreenivasan 2020, 204). When both the objective and the subjective requirements are satisfied, the courageous agent will be persevering in accordance with *yi* 義 (righteousness), that is, "*when* (objective) and *because* (subjective) the perseverance is worthwhile" (204).[32]

According to *Mencius* 6A10, Mencius detests death. Suppose, however, that in a particular circumstance the value of avoiding death is outweighed by that of a competing goal, such as saving a child from the attack of a deranged person. Then Mencius will not shy away from the danger, since doing so is in conflict with *yi* 義 (righteousness). Suppose further that Mencius' fear of death is appropriate and scaled to the disvalue of the potential death. Does it hinder his courageous action and need to be controlled? No, because other than the fearful desire to avoid death, Mencius also has a stronger desire for the external goal. Both desires are appropriate and in proportion to the values of their objects. It follows that when Mencius perseveres toward the external goal, there is no need for him to interfere with his fearful desire to avoid danger. Insofar as the fearful desire is the weaker one between the two, it will simply be outweighed by the stronger desire for the external goal (Pears 1980).

This further allows us to see *Mencius* 2A2, a passage Yearley (1990) describes as "elliptical, even cryptic," in a new light (151). Mencius says that the courageous person possesses an unmoved mind 不動心. Through harmonizing with *yi* 義 (righteousness) and the Way, her *qi* 氣 becomes "consummately great and consummately strong."[33] Proponents of the fearlessness interpretation take this to imply that the courageous person is unmoved by danger, with all her *qi* 氣 pointing to and empowering the pursuit of the more important external goal (Yearley 1990). On my view, however, adhering to *yi* 義 (righteousness) does not entail being unmoved by danger. In fact, being moved by danger is not a distraction from *yi* 義 (righteousness) but is as integral to it as being moved by the external goal is. This suggests that an unmoved mind is achieved through a correct balancing of *qi* 氣 for the danger and *qi* 氣 for the external goal such that the resultant *qi* 氣 always travels in the same direction as *yi* 義 (righteousness). This is what it means to possess the vast, flowing *qi* 氣 that is moved by nothing other than *yi* 義 (righteousness).[34]

Pears (1980) claims that an appropriate fearful desire, even when outweighed, makes a correct contribution to the courageous action. Specifically, it may "rightly modify the way in which the agent tries to attain the external goal" (181). This view is further developed by Xunzi in his discussion of semblances of courage and real courage (*Xunzi*, 4.5).[35] Xunzi says there is the courage of dogs and pigs, which is "to struggle over food and drink, ravenously seeing only the benefit of food and drink" (4.5). There is the courage of merchants and robbers, which is "to strive for benefit in all affairs, to struggle over goods and wealth" (4.5). There is the courage of petty men, which is "to treat death lightly and act impetuously" (4.5). As for the courage of noble men, Xunzi says, "wherever *yi* 義 (righteousness) lies, not to be swayed by power, nor to focus on benefit, not even changing his glance when offered the whole state in bribery, to uphold *yi* unswervingly while yet taking death seriously—such is the courage of well-bred men and gentlemen" (4.5).

The petty person proceeds toward the external goal with little regard for the danger doing so poses to her life. Even supposing that the external goal is indeed worth the danger and her desire for it is appropriate, lacking the appropriate fear of death, she acts recklessly, failing to steer clear of unnecessary risks.[36] By contrast, the noble person takes death seriously. Even when she rightly decides that the value of the external goal outweighs the value of avoiding the danger and acts on that decision, her fear of death informs and shapes the manner in which her action is undertaken. For example, she will be mindful of the danger in her situation and try to minimize it when doing so does not compromise the attainment of the external goal. That is, she will opt for the safest course of action among all that are equally effective in terms of satisfying the external goal. Thus, although the noble person and the petty person both try to attain the external goal, the manners in which they do so differ, making one an exemplar of courage and the other a cautionary tale of recklessness.

Appropriate fear of death contributes to courageous action further because it animates the courageous action when the value of avoiding the danger exceeds that of the external goal (Pears 1980; Sreenivasan 2020). As Xunzi suggests, dogs and pigs risk their lives to pursue food and drink just as merchants and robbers risk their lives to pursue profit and wealth (*Xunzi,* 4.5). They all represent semblances of courage because the external goals that they pursue have significantly less value than life and are not worth the danger. Were a noble person placed in this situation, her fear of death would be much stronger than her desire for food, drink, profit, and wealth. Her fearful desire would lead her to abandon these external goals, in accordance with what courage requires.[37]

This point is vividly illustrated by the story of Bian Zhuangzi. We know very little about Bian other than that Confucius regards him as an exemplar of courage (*Analects,* 14.12). Fortunately, an account of his words and deeds can be found in the *Han Shi Wai Zhuan* 韓詩外傳, which consists of historical accounts and anecdotes collected by the Han dynasty Confucian scholar Han Ying.[38] It is said that when Bian's mother was alive, he fought three battles and fled three times (10.13). His friends disapproved of him and his ruler humiliated him, but Bian accepted it without any change in his expression. When his mother had died and he had mourned for her for three years, Bian requested to join the army. Upon being received by the general, he said, "Previously, my mother was still with me, and that is why I fled the battle and brought shame upon myself. Now that my mother has passed away, please allow me to make amends" (10.13).

Bian's fleeing from the battles does not undermine his courage, but rather is a reflection of it. When Bian's mother was still alive, his filial duty to support her through her old age outweighed his duty to protect his state. Since his being alive and well was a necessary condition for fulfilling this filial duty, it was courageous of Bian to flee whenever he was sent to the battlefield to avoid being injured or killed. This further shows that the fearful desire can animate courageous action when the evaluative balance favors avoiding danger. That is, Bian fled out of fear of death, which, grounded in the more important filial duty, outweighed his desire to gain victory for his state.

To sum up, the presence of fear in courage does not undermine the Confucian ideal of perfect integrity. When the correctly perceived value of the external goal exceeds that of avoiding the danger, the courageous agent's fearful desire does not need to be controlled since it will simply be outweighed by her stronger desire for the external goal. Also, even when outweighed, the fearful desire contributes to the courageous action by rightly modifying the way the agent pursues the external goal. When the value of avoiding the danger exceeds that of the external goal, fear rightly leads the agent to give up the external goal, in accordance with the demand of courage. Thus, fear does not need to be overcome because it is not an impediment to courageous action, but rather a contributing element to it.

Conclusion

This chapter has identified a tension between the virtue of courage and the Confucian ideal of perfect integrity. On the one hand, for the Confucian noble person, different aspects of the self, that is, feeling, judgment, and action, are fully integrated with each other and travel together in following the *Dao*. The noble person simply acts on her desires and inclinations, which consistently track the good. On the other hand, courage consists in persevering toward the external goal in the face of danger. Fear, which involves a desire to avoid the danger, is not only elicited but also justified by the presence of the danger. This appears to render courage a form of self-control: the courageous agent cannot act on her fear, but has to overcome it in order to perform the courageous action.

Through an examination of the treatment of fear and courage in early Confucian texts, I have argued that the tension is apparent, not real. In particular, Confucian courage has a normative aspect. It consists in persevering in accordance with *yi* 義 (righteousness), that is, when and because the external goal is worth the danger. It is true that the courageous agent has an appropriate fearful desire, which is scaled to the value of avoiding the danger. But she also has a stronger desire for the external goal, which reflects its greater value. Because of this, the courageous agent does not need to control her fear, since it will simply be outweighed by her stronger desire for the more important external goal (Pears 1980). Moreover, fear, even when outweighed, rightly modifies the way in which the agent pursues the external goal. Thus, fear does not hinder courageous action but contributes to it. Courage is not about acting despite fear, but about acting through appropriate fear.

Acknowledgment

Thanks to Ami Harbin and Christopher Cowley for their helpful comments on a previous version of this chapter.

Notes

1. I borrow the useful expression "persevere in the face of danger" from Sreenivasan (2020).
2. Occasionally, I draw from other Confucian classics and historical accounts to supplement the above texts.
3. Shun was a legendary emperor of the golden age of antiquity.
4. Bloom (2009)'s translation with my modifications (89).
5. This is a point of agreement between Mencius and Xunzi despite their otherwise different views on human nature. See, for example, *Xunzi,* 9.19.
6. Ivanhoe (2010) refers to this as cultivated spontaneity, which is achieved through "engaging in concerted and sustained efforts at learning, reflection, and practice" (187).
7. For Confucius' critique of ritual misappropriation, see the *Analects,* 3.1, 3.2, 3.22, and 17.21.
8. Eno (2015)'s translation with my modifications (13). Elsewhere, Confucius says that Zigong is a precious ritual vessel (*Analects,* 5.4). Zigong strictly observes the codes of

conduct that *li* 禮 (ritual) prescribes but lacks the emotional substance characteristic of virtue.

9 *Wen* 文 literally means patterns. According to Eno (2015), they are "forms of cultural refinement basic to the ritualized conduct of *li*" (28).

10 Trans. Eno 2015, 27.

11 *Bu nao er zhe* 不撓而折. Retrieved from https://ctext.org/shuo-wen-jie-zi.

12 That is, the obstacles that need to be surmounted in courage are of a specific kind, constituted by danger.

13 In presenting the puzzle, I remain neutral about the exact nature of fear and rely only on the widely accepted claim that fear often involves the desire to avoid danger.

14 LeDoux (2020) thinks that the defensive survival circuit is often involved in fear, but is not the same as fear. This is because fear requires the further cognitive representation that one is in danger at the present moment.

15 More generally, *qi* 氣 is the basic stuff-energy that makes up the whole world.

16 Van Norden (1997) likewise suggests that the Mencian sage manifests "motivational harmony" (249). He writes, "a sage who has a feeling of alarm because a child is about to fall into a well is not of two minds and is not pulled in two directions about what to do. The only thing the sage wants to do is to save the child" (249).

17 See also Frijda (1986), Damasio (2005), and Tappolet (2016), among others.

18 Trans. Eno 2015, 26.

19 Although material wealth has little intrinsic value, it can facilitate the acquisition of virtue. Mencius says, "It is only a gentleman who will be able to have a constant mind despite being without a constant means of livelihood. The people, lacking a constant means of livelihood, will lack constant minds" (*Mencius*, 1A7, trans. Bloom 2009, 11).

20 Eno (2015)'s translation with my modifications (60).

21 In this case, moral wrongdoing is bad, but the noble person has no fear of it because he is confident in his virtue.

22 Trans. Bloom 2009, 70.

23 The parent–child relationship is primary and serves as the model for all other relationships. As Master You says, *xiao* 孝 (filiality), the virtue of serving and respecting one's parents, is the root of *ren* 仁 (benevolence, humaneness) (*Analects*, 1.2). This suggests that one's care for people outside the family should resemble one's care for one's parents. This does not imply that care is impartial, though. One's care should reflect the intimacy of the relationship such that other things being equal, one should give priority to one's own parents over the parents of others (*Analects*, 13.18, 17.21).

24 Trans. Eno 2015, 16.

25 Retrieved from https://ctext.org/xiao-jing.

26 Trans. Eno 2015, 55.

27 Trans. Eno 2015, 31.

28 Retrieved from https://ctext.org/shiji. See also Eno (2015)'s comments on *Analects* 11.13, 54.

29 Trans. Eno 2015, 8. See also the *Analects* 15.9 and *Mencius* 2A2.

30 Bloom (2009)'s translation with my modifications (127).

31 Pears (1980) likewise says that reflections on nobility do not allow one to know what courage requires because nobility is a resultant property, not a constitutive property (185).
32 Although the Confucians admit instances of "courage" that are separate from the other virtues, it does not follow that they deny the unity of virtues (*Analects,* 8.2, 14.4, 17.8, 17.23). This is because true courage is in accordance with righteousness and always accompanied by the other virtues (Jiang 1997, 275).
33 Trans. Bloom 2009, 30.
34 Although *Mencius* 2A2 is ambiguous and can be interpreted in different ways, my interpretation has the advantage of making it better align with passages that underscore the importance of fear.
35 Hutton's (2014) translation with my modifications (24–5).
36 Here we are reminded of Zilu. Even if displaying loyalty to his ruler was the more worthy goal, it was still wrong for Zilu to be oblivious to the danger and risk his life heedlessly.
37 Mencius, quoting Zengzi, says, "If, on looking inward, I find that I am not in the right, I must be in fear of even a poor fellow in coarse clothing. If, on looking inward, I find that I am in the right, I may proceed against thousands and tens and thousands" (*Mencius,* 2A2, trans. Bloom 2009, 29, with my modifications). Thus, even when the magnitude of the danger is small, as long as the value of avoiding it outweighs that of the external goal, the courageous action will travel in the same direction as the fearful desire.
38 Retrieved from https://ctext.org/han-shi-wai-zhuan.

Bibliography

Bloom, Irene (trans.). 2009. *Mencius*. Columbia University Press.

Brady, Michael. 2013. *Emotional Insight: The Epistemic Role of Emotional Experience*. Oxford University Press.

Brooks, E. Bruce, and A. Taeko Brooks. 1998. *The Original Analects: Sayings of Confucius and His Successors*. Columbia University Press.

Damasio, Antonio. 2005. *Descartes' Error: Emotion, Reason, and the Human Brain*. Penguin.

D'Arms, Justin, and Daniel Jacobson. 2000. "The Moralistic Fallacy: On the 'Appropriateness' of Emotion." *Philosophy and Phenomenological Research* 61 (1): 65–90.

Ekman, Paul. 1992. "An Argument for Basic Emotions." *Cognition and Emotion* 6 (3–4): 169–200.

Eno, Robert (trans.). 2015. *The Analects of Confucius*. Retrieved January 15, 2024 from https://scholarworks.iu.edu/dspace/handle/2022/23420.

Frijda, Nico H. 1986. *The Emotions*. Cambridge University Press.

Hutton, Eric L. (trans.). 2014. *Xunzi: The Complete Text*. Princeton University Press.

Ivanhoe, Philip J. 2010. "The Values of Spontaneity." In *Taking Confucian Ethics Seriously: Contemporary Theories and Applications,* edited by Kam-por Yu, Julia Tao, and Philip J. Ivanhoe, 183–207. SUNY Press.

Ivanhoe, Philip J. 2017. *Oneness: East Asian Conceptions of Virtue, Happiness, and How We Are All Connected*. Oxford University Press.
Jiang, Xinyan. 1997. "Mencius on Human Nature and Courage." *Journal of Chinese Philosophy* 24 (3): 265–289.
Lai, Whalen. 1985. "Yung and the Tradition of the Shih: The Confucian Restructuring of Heroic Courage." *Religious Studies* 21 (2): 181–203.
LeDoux, Joseph E. 2020. "Thoughtful Feelings." *Current Biology* 30 (11): R619–R623. https://doi.org/10.1016/j.cub.2020.04.012.
Mather, Richard. 1995. "Filial Paragons and Spoiled Brats: A Glimpse of Medieval Chinese Children in the *Shishuo Xinyu*." In *Chinese Views of Childhood*, edited by Anne Kenney, 111–126. University of Hawaii Press.
Munro, Donald J. 1969. *The Concept of Man in Early China*. Stanford University Press.
Öhman, Arne, Anders Flykt, and Francisco Esteves. 2001. "Emotion Drives Attention: Detecting the Snake in the Grass." *Journal of Experimental Psychology: General* 130 (3): 466–478.
Pears, David. 1980. "Courage as a Mean." In *Essays on Aristotle's Ethics*, edited by Amélie Oksenberg Rorty, 171–187. University of California Press.
Sreenivasan, Gopal. 2020. *Emotion and Virtue*. Princeton University Press.
Tappolet, Christine. 2016. *Emotions, Value, and Agency*. Oxford University Press.
Van Norden, Bryan. 1997. "Mencius on Courage." *Midwest Studies in Philosophy 21* (1): 237–256.
Virág, Curie. 2017. *The Emotions in Early Chinese Philosophy*. Oxford University Press.
Yearley, Lee. 1990. *Mencius and Aquinas: Theories of Virtue and Conceptions of Courage*. SUNY Press.

3

Aristotle on Fear's Contributions to the Virtue of Courage

Andrew Culbreth

Fear and the ability to handle it well are central to Aristotle's account of the virtue of courage.[1] Aristotle claims that courage aims at the "mean with regard to fear and confidence" (*Nicomachean Ethics* [*NE*] II 7, 1107a32–33; III 6, 1115a7) and that it is concerned with fear more than confidence (*NE* III 9, 1117a30).[2] And as with other moral virtues that regulate feelings, Aristotle's courageous person feels fear in the right way, that is, in relation to the right objects, at the right time, in the right degree, and for the right reasons. The difficulty lies in explaining what exactly it means to feel fear well and the precise role that fear plays in the virtue of courage.

There are two closely related puzzles in Aristotle's treatment of courage and fear that scholars have attempted to resolve. First, there is a question of whether the brave person experiences fear while exhibiting courage.[3] On the one hand, Aristotle says that the brave person is fearless (*NE* III 6, 1115a32–33, cf. *Eudemian Ethics* [*EE*] III 1, 1228b4). On the other hand, Aristotle characterizes the brave person as someone who "will fear" frightening things in the right way, and someone who "will endure" terrifying things for the sake of the noble (*to kalon*) (*NE* III 7, 1115b11–13).

This puzzle is closely connected to a second question about the motivations and virtuous character of Aristotle's courageous person. Commentators worry that if the brave person feels fear and yet must overcome this fear in order to act virtuously, then the brave person is merely self-controlled (*enraktēs*), not virtuous.[4] Aristotle distinguishes self-control (*enkrateia*) from virtue on the basis of the self-controlled person's inner conflict between appetite and reason. Like the virtuous person, the self-controlled person abides by correct reason and chooses to act well; unlike the virtuous person, the self-controlled person must overcome a strong or bad desire that runs contrary to the rational choice (*NE* VII 9, 1151b34–1152a3).[5] If the brave person must overcome or "endure" fear in order to act as reason directs, and if fear involves the desire to avoid harm or death, then the brave person must overcome certain desires in order to act virtuously.[6] Such behavior appears to be characteristic of self-control, not virtue.

Commentators have offered various ways to resolve both puzzles—whether Aristotle's brave person feels fear and, if so, whether the brave person is self-controlled or virtuous. In this chapter, I explain the relevant debates in the literature and show that Aristotle has the resources to meet both challenges by appealing to his distinction between courageous and non-courageous fear. Fear, like most emotions for Aristotle, can be felt either well or poorly (*NE* II 5, 1105b25–1106a1). Courageous agents experience fear for their physical survival, insofar as they are human, and they must experience this fear in the right way: meaning, they fear the right things, at the right time, in the right contexts, to the right degree, and for the right reasons. Their fear, however, does not motivate them to avoid fearful situations that afford opportunities to act courageously. Instead, they can put the objects of their fear into proper perspective, taking appropriate precautions against physical harm or death while nevertheless attempting to achieve a noble goal through courageous activity. In this way, Aristotle's brave person can experience fear without having to overcome that fear as though it were contrary to the rational choice to pursue the courageous action.

First, I explain Aristotle's definition of fear. After that, I respond to the question of whether the brave person feels fear. Far from being fearless, brave people are brave because they feel fear, especially the fear of death, and they feel this fear in the right way. Finally, I show (following others) that Aristotle's brave person is not self-controlled, but rather fully virtuous and the brave person has no internal disharmony. Courageous agents can incorporate their fear into their activity as a motivation that contributes toward the accomplishment of their courageous action. While they act for the sake of the noble, their fear enables them to take appropriate precautions in pursuing that goal.[7] Proper fear thus makes an essential contribution to the achievement of a noble goal, rather than providing a motivation that must be overcome if brave people are to act well. Aristotle's account not only highlights an important relationship between fear and virtue, but it also defends a crucial intuition that people are brave because they feel fear, rather than despite their fear.

What Is Fear?

In *NE* III 6, Aristotle says that people define fear as the expectation of a future evil (III 6, 1115a9–10). His definition closely resembles Plato's definition of fear at *Laches* 198b or *Protagoras* 358d.[8] In the *Rhetoric*, when discussing the emotions relevant for persuading others, Aristotle defines fear as a kind of pain or disturbance derived from the impression (*phantasia*) of a future, painful evil (*Rhet.* II 5, 1382a21–22).[9] Moreover, the evil must appear to us to be imminent or close at hand and also to be a great pain or a harm that can cause our destruction (1382a22–30). In the *EE*, Aristotle reiterates that fear is the expectation of "pains whose nature is to be destructive to life" (*EE* III 1, 1229a39–1229b1) or of things capable of causing destructive pain, and which appear to be near and not far away (1229b14–16).

While we fear pain, we find frightening whatever can cause pain or portends it (*Rhet.* II 5, 1382a27–30). David Konstan shows that fear, for Aristotle, is not only a pain or disturbance, but it also involves a cognitive judgment or evaluation that the future evil is harmful to us: for example, in fearing a rattlesnake or the indications of one, we evaluate it as harmful (Konstan 2006, 130).[10] Such evaluations involve reasoning, sometimes including complex reasoning about social relations: for example, Aristotle mentions that we fear others whom we judge to be angry and hostile toward us and also capable of harming us (*Rhet.* II 5, 1382a33–5; see Konstan 2006, 132).

Fear is not only the anticipation of future evils that we judge to be harmful, but it also can include a desire to avoid those evils.[11] At *NE* II 3, for example, Aristotle claims that the harmful and the painful are objects of avoidance (*phugē*, 1104b30–32), and later he says that we avoid pain as an evil (*NE* III 4, 1113b1–2). In *De Anima* (*DA*), he says that "wherever [pleasure and pain] are present, there is desire, for desire is an appetite for what is pleasant" (*DA* II 3, 414b4–6). As Curzer 2012 interprets this passage, it seems plausible that fear's anticipation of pain is attended by a desire to avoid that pain.[12]

While in the *Rhetoric* and *EE*, Aristotle appears to restrict frightening things to whatever can destroy us or cause us great pain, at *NE* III 6, Aristotle widens the scope of frightening things to: "disgrace, poverty, disease, friendlessness, death" (III 6, 1115a10–11). Aristotle says that it is good to fear certain things, such as disgrace (*NE* III 6, 1115a12–13), and he suggests that it is natural to fear others, such as death (*NE* III 6, 1115a24–27). Each of the frightening things listed at *NE* III 6 amounts to the lack or loss of goods of fortune, or external goods, which are relevant for our happiness. Although Aristotle insists that virtue is necessary for happiness, and that the value of goods of fortune depends on the presence of virtue (cf. *EE* VIII 3 1248b26–34), he also claims that without certain external goods (such as wealth or friends) in addition, it is much harder—if not impossible—for us to flourish (*NE* I 8, 1099a31–b7).[13] The potential loss of these goods of fortune would result in a real harm, one that would be natural to fear.

Finally, for Aristotle, fear is not felt the same way by all people. Fear, like other emotions, can be felt either well or poorly (*NE* II 5, 1105b27–1106a1). This point is crucial, since, as we will see below, courage disposes us to feel fear *well*, that is, to fear the right things, to appropriate degree, in the right contexts, and for the right reasons. Cowards, in contrast, feel fear poorly: they fear the wrong things, or they fear excessively, or for the wrong reasons, or in the wrong situations, and so on.

Does Aristotle's Brave Person Feel Fear?

Fear, and how we handle it, is central to Aristotle's account of courage, since he claims that courage aims at the mean with respect to feelings of fear and confidence (*NE* II 7, 1107a32–33, III 6, 1115a7). Courageous action is both medial with respect to these emotions, that is, it hits the mean in feelings of fear and confidence, and courageous agents act for the sake of the noble in dangerous circumstances that elicit these emotions. Aristotle claims further that courage concerns fear more than confidence (*NE* III 9, 1117a30), because courageous action involves the pain of facing up to death.

The vice of cowardice, in contrast, is marked by the fact it disposes one to feel fear excessively and to fear the wrong sorts of things (1115b33–35).[14]

At *NE* III 6, Aristotle specifies the scope of courageous activity even further by constraining the object of fear relevant to courage and the circumstances in which brave people exhibit courage. While cowards may fear too much and fear the wrong sorts of things, the courageous person is distinguished (in part) both by fearing the right things and by not fearing the wrong sorts of things. So, with what sorts of terrifying things is the brave person concerned? As he continues his discussion in *NE* III 6, Aristotle narrows it down to serious, painful injury and especially death:

> [T1] With what sort of frightening things, then, is the brave person concerned? Or is it with the greatest ones? For no one is more disposed to stand firm against what is terrifying. Now death is the most frightening of all things; for it is an end, and nothing seems to be any longer either good or bad for the dead. (*NE* III 6, 1115a24–27)[15]

Death appears to be the proper object of the courageous person's fear, since the brave person should be concerned with the most terrifying things and death is most terrifying of all. Death is so terrifying, Aristotle claims, because there appears to be nothing either good or bad for the dead—a justification that stands in stark contrast to the views of Socrates or Epicurus, for whom this is the very reason why (if true) we ought not fear death, as Broadie 2002 observes.[16] Likewise in the *EE*, Aristotle claims that "it is thought practically the special mark of bravery to take up a certain attitude towards death and the pain of it" (1229b3–4). While there is a question in the literature about whether the courageous person must fear death alone or whether they fear some things in addition to death (such as physical pain), a charitable interpretation of these passages, taken together, would be that the courageous person fears great and destructive physical injury and especially death.[17]

Regarding the circumstances in which virtuous people exhibit courage, Aristotle restricts the scope of courageous action even further:

> [T2] But the brave person would not seem to be concerned even with death in *all* circumstances, e.g. at sea or in disease. In what circumstances, then? Surely in the noblest. Now such deaths are those in battle; for these take place in the greatest and noblest danger . . . Properly, then, one will be called brave who is fearless in face of a noble death, and of all emergencies that involve death; and the emergencies of war are in the highest degree of this kind. (*NE* III 6, 1115a28–35)

Virtuous people exhibit courage in the face of death, specifically when facing death or destruction in the greatest or noblest circumstances: namely, a noble death in battle (*NE* III 6 1115a29–31). As with all moral virtue, courage aims especially at the noble; it is not merely a matter of remaining calm in any terrifying circumstance, even ones that might spell death, such as serious illness or a shipwreck. We must face death for the sake of a noble goal or while exhibiting some prowess (1115b4–5), conditions that can be met when attempting to defend one's *polis* in battle for the sake of the common good.[18] It is not clear whether Aristotle wishes to narrow the scope of courageous action to battle alone. Are there other cases in which we face death and nevertheless act for the sake of the noble? To limit courage exclusively to acting for the noble in *battle* seems to be excessively restrictive. Perhaps Aristotle intends to emphasize that death in battle is the *most noble* way to die. We could argue that Aristotle restricts the scope of bravery to facing serious, imminent destructive pain or death in situations where there is the possibility of achieving the noble.[19] Brave people are distinguished by the ability to handle fear well in these situations: they hit the mean with respect to feelings of fear (and confidence), and they face the fear of death (and serious physical harm and loss) while acting for the sake of the noble as reason prescribes.

The Fearlessness of the Brave Person

Even though Aristotle claims that courageous people experience fear in the right way, he appears to hold at times that the courageous person is fearless. For example, at *NE* III 6, Aristotle says that, "at sea also, and in disease, the brave person is fearless" (1115a34–1115b1). This claim, however, is not a challenge for the view that the brave person experiences fear. Death at sea and in disease fall outside of the scope of courageous action, as we noticed in T2, above: namely, facing death in battle for the sake of the noble. So, it is possible for the courageous person to be fearless in the face of a sea storm or grave illness, but their fearlessness in these contexts is simply not relevant for courageous action. Similarly, just because a person is fearless in other contexts—and thus why people extend the term "brave" to shameless individuals, according to Aristotle (*NE* III 6, 1115a14–16)—it does not follow that brave people are fearless while acting courageously.[20] As Vigani 2017 notes, the relevant question is not whether the courageous person experiences fear *ever*, but rather whether the courageous person experiences fear while exhibiting courage (Vigani 2017, 316–317).

So, do courageous agents feel fear while acting courageously, that is, when facing death or serious physical injury for the sake of the noble? As we saw in T2, above, Aristotle emphasizes the brave person's *fearlessness* in exactly these situations. A similar passage in the *EE* corroborates the fearlessness of the brave person: "the brave person seems to be in general fearless, the coward prone to fear; the latter fears many things and few, great things and small, and intensely and quickly, while the opposite fears either not at all or slightly and reluctantly and seldom, and great things only" (*EE* III 1, 1228b4–9). Although Aristotle hedges his claim here slightly—that is, the brave person may fear great things only or reluctantly—his general point is that the brave person exhibits little to no fear.

Perhaps Aristotle really does think that the mark of bravery is fearlessness, as other ancient philosophers, such as Socrates, seem to have supposed.[21] Although Aristotle says that courage hits the mean with regard to feelings of fear and confidence, it is possible that the mean with respect to fear is *to feel no fear at all* in the relevant contexts.[22] Moreover, as Brady 2005 points out, even though Aristotle claims that some things, such as death, are proper objects of fear, it is not clear that the brave person is afraid of death while acting courageously (Brady 2005, 190-4). Instead, as Vigani 2017 contends, the brave person's complete focus on the noble goal might silence any ancillary fears of the personal costs of standing firm in battle for the sake of the noble (Vigani 2017, 326–7). More recently, Woolf 2022 has defended the view that Aristotle's brave person feels little to no fear when acting courageously. On his view, courageous agents will not find it fearful to face enemies in battle, since they follow reason in acting for the sake of the noble and presumably what is noble "will not be something that merits fear" (Woolf 2022, 120).[23]

Another way to explain the courageous person's fearlessness, as others have noticed, is to draw a distinction between the emotional state of fearlessness and the behavioral state of fearlessness.[24] Someone can be fearless in the sense that they lack the emotional state of fear: that is, one lacks the painful expectation of future evil and the corresponding desire to avoid it. Alternatively, someone can be fearless in the behavioral sense, meaning they do not express any of the behaviors associated with fear, such as fleeing from danger or cowering. Perhaps Aristotle means that courageous people are fearless exclusively in the behavioral sense. If that is the case, then it is possible that courageous people could feel the emotion of fear and yet exhibit fearless behavior by not avoiding truly terrifying situations. I will return to this point in the next section.

The Fears of the Brave Person

A closer look at Aristotle's remarks on courage, however, reveals that Aristotle does not remain committed to his claims about fearlessness throughout his discussions of courage in either the *EE* or the *NE*. Fear can be rational, even commendable in certain contexts. At *NE* III 7, Aristotle claims that those who fear nothing are insensible or mad (1115b24–27). At *EE* III 1, Aristotle observes that if things did not appear frightening to the brave person, then "one might say there is nothing impressive about that" (1228b11).[25] Aristotle's remark introduces an intuition that feeling fear and facing up to it are part of what makes courage so impressive.[26]

At *NE* III 7, Aristotle appears to revise his claim about the fearlessness of the brave person:

> [T3] Now the brave person is as dauntless as a human may be. Therefore, while the brave person will fear even the things that are not beyond human strength, the brave person will fear them as one ought and as reason directs, and will endure them for the sake of what is noble; for this is the end of virtue. But it is possible to fear these more, or less, and again to fear things that are not terrible as if they were. Of the faults that are committed one consists in fearing what one should not, another in fearing as we should not, another in fearing when we should not,

> and so on . . . The person, then, who endures and who fears the right things and with the right aim, in the right way and at the right time . . . is brave; for the brave person feels and acts according to the merits of the case and in whatever way reason directs . . . Therefore it is for a noble end that the brave person endures and acts as courage directs. (*NE* III 7 1115b10-24)

Aristotle's point here is crucial for his understanding of courage. He admits that courageous people feel fear but they are distinguished by their ability to feel fear in the *right way*. To feel fear in the right way involves several things. For one, we must fear the right sorts of terrifying things, including things that are beyond human capacity to face (1115b7–10). The brave person both is able to identify which things are genuinely frightening and fears these things in the right contexts, above all when facing a noble death while defending one's city in battle. Moreover, the courageous person must feel fear in the right degree, meaning in a way that hits the mean, as determined by the person of practical reason (*NE* II 6, 1106b36–1107a2). Finally, the brave person must face these fears for the right motive, namely "for the sake of the noble (*tou kalou*)." As he reiterates later in *NE* III 8, "it is the mark of a brave person to endure things that are, and appear, frightening for a human being, because it is noble to do so and shameful not to" (1117a16–17). Aristotle's considered view must be that the brave person does feel fear, but that they feel fear in the right way, meaning to the right degree, in relation to the right objects, at the right time, in the right contexts, and for the right reasons (i.e., for the sake of the noble).

How, then, do we reconcile these passages with Aristotle's claims that the courageous person is fearless? One possibility is, as Young 2009 contends, that Aristotle's remarks on the fearlessness of courageous agents are intended to highlight the contrast with excessively fearful cowards (Young 2009, 446). Others, such as Woolf 2022, argue that while brave people are in general fearless, they may feel some fear in grave and extreme situations—although even in those cases they do not feel fear to a great degree (Woolf 2022, 122–3).[27] Alternatively, some commentators explain the courageous person's fearlessness by appealing to the distinction between fearlessness as an emotional state and fearlessness as a behavioral state, mentioned above. On this view, Aristotle's brave person can experience the emotion of fear and have a corresponding desire to avoid truly terrifying things, and yet express none of the avoidance behavior associated with fear, such as fleeing from battle or cowering.[28] Perhaps, as Pears 1980 and Heil 1996 argue, Aristotle has this distinction in mind when he claims that brave people fear death *qua* human being, and yet are fearless *qua* courageous person (*EE* III 1, 1228b26–30).[29] However we interpret this passage, clearly the brave person does feel fear, at least *qua* human being.

In sum, although Aristotle's comments on courage appear to suggest that the brave person feels no fear, a more complete picture of his remarks confirms that the brave person does feel the emotion of fear although they do not shirk or avoid terrifying situations in which they act for the sake of the noble. The brave person feels fear in the right way, meaning: in the right contexts, at the right time, to the right degree, in relation to truly fearful things, especially death, and they face fearful things for the sake of the noble. Courageous agents also recognize that they risk great losses, pain, and even death. This is why fear is so central to courage: unlike trained soldiers whose experience makes them feel invulnerable (*NE* III 8, 1116b5–15), and unlike those who have nothing to lose (*NE* III 9, 1117b18–20), courageous agents recognize that the virtuous action renders them vulnerable to great losses that can harm their happiness. Situations that demand courage are so difficult, in part, because they require us to choose between competing goods and to sacrifice some goods of fortune (such as physical health) for the sake of the noble.[30] Even though courageous people may judge that it is necessary to choose the noble at those costs (1117b13–15), they still fear the harm that results from losing those goods. Indeed, courageous people have reason more than anyone to fear death, since they risk losing the greatest good for a human being, that is, a virtuous and happy life (1117b9–13). The ability to grapple with those fears and nevertheless act confidently for the sake of the noble is what makes courage so admirable. It is also this same disposition that risks diminishing courageous agents' status as fully virtuous, as we will see in the next section.

Fear, Self-Control, and the Virtue of Courage

So far, we have seen that Aristotle's brave person feels fear (especially the fear of death) and feels it in the right way, as reason directs, and for the sake of the noble. Aristotle's inclusion of fear in the virtue of courage, and his description of how the courageous person experiences fear, has led some commentators to worry that Aristotelian courage is really a case of self-control (*enkrateia*). Aristotle describes self-control in comparison with the virtue of moderation (*sōphrosunē*): the self-controlled person abides by correct reason and chooses to do the moderate action, but they must overcome their appetites for certain bodily pleasures and master desires that run counter to the correct and moderate choice (*NE* VII 9, 1151b34–1152a3, cf. VII 7, 1150a34–6). The virtuous person, in contrast, experiences no such pleasure or appetite contrary to reason and they do not need to master their desire for bodily pleasure in order to choose and act well.

Commentators have tended to locate a similar conflict in the courageous person's motivations.[31] If fear involves the desire to avoid wounds and death, and the courageous person must overcome these fears in order to do the courageous action as reason directs, then it appears that the courageous person must overcome or resist desires that are contrary to the virtuous choice and action.[32] Aristotle's language, too, appears to ascribe an internal conflict to the brave person: the brave person is one who "endures" (*hupomenei*) terrifying things for the sake of the noble, as reason directs (*NE* III 7, 1115b12, *hupomenōn* at 1115b18).[33] Hence, the brave person appears to be merely self-controlled and not fully virtuous.[34] So, we must find a way to explain Aristotle's account of courage in such a way that we do not attribute contrary desires to the courageous and do not describe them as overcoming or struggling against their inclinations.[35]

Fear's Contribution to Courage

Since it is the contrary desire to avoid what we fear that is supposed to generate the self-control puzzle in the first place, removing this desire from the courageous person's motivations would thus save them from being self-controlled. Some commentators, such as Brady 2005 and Vigani 2017, have followed this approach. Concretely, Vigani 2017 argues that the evidence of Aristotle's claims about courage suggest that the brave person simply is fearless, meaning the brave person does not feel the emotion of fear when exercising courage (Vigani 2017, 326–7).[36] Brady 2005, in contrast, has a more subtle position: brave people can feel fear, in the sense that they view physical harm, pain, or death as evil, and yet they do not have a corresponding desire to avoid these things, and therefore they do not express any avoidance behavior either (Brady 2005, 192–4).

In response to Vigani 2017, Aristotle's courageous agent does experience fear (even if not to a great degree), so it is incorrect to argue that they are fearless. In response to Brady 2005, as we have seen above, it is difficult to understand how, on Aristotle's view, someone can be pained by the prospect of death and yet not have a corresponding desire to avoid it. Curzer 2012 questions whether Aristotle accepts this separation of the anticipation of pain from the desire to avoid that pain, on the basis of *DA* 414b4–6 (discussed above).[37] It seems that, for Aristotle, wherever there is pleasure or pain, so too is there desire for pleasure or, presumably, the desire to avoid pain. So, it appears that if the brave person can view physical harm or death as something evil, as Aristotle admits, then they should likewise desire to avoid it.

Another line of interpretation, similar to Brady 2005, comes from Heil 1996, who distinguishes between a brave person's emotional and motivational states: while the brave person does feel fear as an emotion, they lack the motivation to act on that fear by avoiding the terrifying situation, and thus the brave person's motivational state is fearless (Heil 1996, 58–61).[38] While this distinction introduces a clever interpretation of *EE* III 1 (1228b26–29), it also comes at a great cost: Heil admits that courage really is like self-control.[39] More precisely, on Heil's view, courage is actually endurance (*karteria*), or "fortitude" (Heil 1996, 49; 65–8). So, courageous people must resist their emotional state of fear and they must struggle against themselves in order to act courageously. This view appears to violate Aristotle's distinction between self-control and virtue, one of his key ethical theses.[40]

A more fruitful way to resolve the problem can be found in another group of interpretations, which I call the "fear as contribution" view.[41] According to this school of thought, fear does not involve a desire to flee from battle or the circumstance in which one can achieve the noble. By removing the desire to flee as a constituent element of courageous fear, these interpreters remove the contrary desire that is supposed to generate the self-control puzzle in the first place. As Young 2009 restates the issue, while self-control presupposes that one's desire is *contrary* to one's choice to act virtuously, we need not view the courageous agent's desire to avoid death as *contrary* to the choice to achieve the noble in battle (Young 2009, 446-7). We would only have a case of contrary desires if the courageous person desires to flee battle while also choosing to go toward the noble in battle (Young 2009, 447). But desire to avoid loss of life, which is part of the fear of death, is not the same as the desire to flee from battle. So, the courageous person's desire is not *contrary* to their aim. Instead, they desire to accomplish a noble action while preserving their life in the process.[42]

Another way to state the solution is as Leighton does: courageous agents do not need to overcome their fear; instead, they harness their fear to identify and prepare for potential harms on the battlefield (1988, 91). In Leighton's terminology, the relevant passions in courage are "facilitators" of virtuous activity (1988, 91). Fear can warn the courageous person to dangers that they may wish to avoid while trying to act courageously; fear enables the courageous person to take proper stock of the potential evils in their surroundings—for example, risks of death, serious injury—and the courageous person tries to accomplish the noble in battle while avoiding these serious harms. So, we can accept that the brave person experiences fear of serious injury or death, is pained by these things, and desires to avoid them, without admitting that the brave person desires to flee battle. Their desires and their choices are not at odds, as may be the case with self-control, but rather reason and desire can work in tandem. Leighton and Young, however, still have not explained the exact way in which fear facilitates courage. How exactly does the courageous person incorporate fear into their courageous action?

Curzer 2012 attempts to explain this by arguing that the brave person desires to go into battle and to achieve the noble, while fear warns the brave person to take appropriate precautions in the process. As Curzer writes, "Fear says to the courageous person, 'since you are going to stand and fight, put on your armor'" (Curzer 2012, 60). Courageous fear neither involves a desire to shrink from courageous action, nor to run and flee from a situation where death and wounds are a risk. Instead, the courageous person takes appropriate precautions that may "keep the agent alive and functional long enough to accomplish the mission," as Curzer puts it (Curzer 2012, 61).

Curzer's elaboration of this solution to the self-control puzzle is compelling. It does, however, raise an immediate problem. What if brave soldiers are going into a situation in which death is certain, such as the Spartans at Thermopylae? Jiang 2000 raises examples like this as a criticism of the "fear as contribution" view.[43] In these cases, Jiang thinks, the desire to avoid harm results in cowardice, since the only way to avoid death in these cases is to flee from battle. Conversely, if the brave person stands firm and acts for the sake of the noble despite certain death, then they appear to be self-controlled, since they must overcome their desire to avoid death.

Curzer 2012, however, shows why the brave person's fear does not collapse into self-control or cowardice in these situations: the solution rests on the difference between non-virtuous and virtuous ways of feeling fear (Curzer 2012, 61).[44] Notice that taking *appropriate* precautions is not the same as avoiding danger or death by any means necessary, including fleeing from a fight. While cowards may flee from battle and forsake a noble goal out of fear for their lives, the courageous agents' habituation enables them to feel fear in the *right* way, as we saw above. The courageous may go into battle knowing that they will die because it is noble to do so, and fear guides them to take appropriate precautions as they face the terrors of war for the sake of the noble. As Curzer remarks, even the Spartan soldiers at Thermopylae wore armor, not to avoid death (since their death was inevitable), but rather to allow themselves to survive long enough to accomplish their mission (Curzer 2012, 61). If they had gone into battle without any armor at all, then they would have been either rash or insensibly fearless and, moreover, they would not have lasted very long. Fear contributes to their action by alerting them to potential dangers and motivating them to take the proper precautions to avoid those dangers as they attempt to achieve the noble, even at the cost of death.

Courageous Fear in the Face of Inevitable Death

The example of brave soldiers who go into a battle knowing that death is certain, such as the Spartans at Thermopylae, raises another problem: it is not clear whether Aristotle thinks that courageous people would fear death *at all* in these sorts of cases.[45] When discussing the emotion of fear in *Rhetoric* II 5, Aristotle claims that fear involves a hope (*elpis*) that survival or safety are possible:

> [T4] Nor are people afraid who consider that they have already suffered every terror and have grown coldly indifferent to the future, like those being flogged to death and already nearly dead; on the contrary, for them to be afraid there must be some hope of being saved, about which they are anxious. A sign of this is that fear makes people inclined to deliberate, whereas no one deliberates about hopeless things. (*Rhet.* II 5, 1383a3–8)[46]

In order to experience fear, it seems, we must have some hope of survival or safety, without which we cease fearing. Once we lose that hope, we no longer fear an imminent great loss or harm. Instead, we coldly resign ourselves to inevitable pain or destruction.

Based on this passage from the *Rhetoric*, it seems that soldiers who face inevitable death must not fear death, since they have no hope of avoiding it. If it is necessary to fear death to act courageously, and if they lack the hope of survival that is necessary for the fear of death, then it appears that they should not be courageous. How do we make sense of the brave person's hopes and fears in these extreme cases? Does the brave person still feel fear at all?

We can resolve this problem by reconsidering the objects of fear. So far, we have followed Aristotle in focusing on wounds and death as the main objects of courageous fear. But Aristotle also includes disgrace among the evils that people fear (*NE* III 6, 1115a10–11), and he thinks that it is good to fear disgrace (1115a12–13). Pearson 2009 has argued that ignobility or disgrace are potential objects of fear for the courageous person, and that the courageous person is motivated to avoid disgrace.[47] As Pearson 2009 contends, the courageous person's sensitivity to disgrace provides a motivation to stand firm in dire straits: they fear disgrace more than death (Pearson 2009, 132–3). Now, the courageous person should never fear voluntarily acting in a shameful way, since they are virtuous. I would like to suggest, however, that they may fear failing to achieve the noble in battle due to circumstances beyond their control: for example, being overpowered by an enemy attack. Alternatively, the courageous may fear failing to accomplish their mission, just as, according to Young 2009, they may be confident about succeeding at their mission (Young 2009, 451–2).[48]

What I am suggesting is that when courageous people face certain death, such as the Spartans at Thermopylae, they do not fear death, since they have no hope of survival (following *Rhetoric* II 5, 1383a3–8). They have coldly resigned themselves to death, as Aristotle suggests, and they do not approach death apprehensively. But these soldiers *do* still feel fear and their fear motivates them to take precautions against certain harms. The key is that instead of fearing death, they fear the evil of disgrace or failing to accomplish a noble goal. This fear motivates the courageous agent to avoid disgrace by, for example, standing firm against death for a noble cause. If we take T4 seriously, however, the brave person's fear depends on some hope of being saved. One might wonder what the self-sacrificial soldiers hope to be saved from, if not death. Pearson 2009 argues that they have the impression of being safe not from physical danger, but rather from disgrace (Pearson 2009, 131). If they fear disgrace, then they hope to be safe from it. As the fear of disgrace motivates the courageous person to avoid shame by standing firm against death, the hope for the noble inspires the confidence to press forward.[49] Indeed, this may be what Aristotle has in mind when he claims in *NE* III 7 that, "a coward, then, is a despairing (*duselpis*) person, for he fears everything. But a courageous person is the opposite, for to be confident is the mark of a hopeful person (*euelpidos*)" (*NE* III 7, 1116a2–4).

In the extreme cases we are considering, fear contributes to the courageous action in just the same ways as it would in situations where brave people fear wounds or death: they feel fear in the right way, for the right reasons, and it motivates them to take appropriate precautions to avoid the shameful outcome of failing to achieve the noble in battle. The Spartans at Thermopylae, for example, might fear that an accident or a misstep could crush them before they accomplish their self-sacrificial mission, motivating them to take appropriate precautions while fighting, despite certain death. They exhibit certain avoidance behavior, such as wearing armor, not to avoid death in battle, but rather to survive long enough to accomplish a noble goal. The advantage of this interpretation is that it reconciles fear's essential contributions to courage with Aristotle's claim that fear also requires the hope of being saved (T4, above). As I have tried to show, fear can still make essential contributions to courage even in cases when one recognizes that one will die.

Conclusion

I have tried to show that, against those who claim that Aristotle's courageous person is fearless, Aristotle's courageous person does feel fear. They feel fear in the right way, and they are habituated to feel fear toward the right things, in the right degree, at the right time, in the right contexts, and to act in the face of terrifying things for the sake of the noble. Against those who might worry that this account renders the courageous person merely self-controlled, I have tried to show, following others, that Aristotelian courage is genuinely virtuous and that it does not involve contrary desires that must be overcome or against which the brave person must struggle. Fear contributes to Aristotelian courage by motivating the brave person to avoid potential harms while attempting to achieve the noble in battle. Even in cases in which courageous fighters recognize that death is certain, their fear enables them to take appropriate precautions against potential harms, including disgrace, for the sake of achieving a noble goal.

Acknowledgments

Many thanks to Ami Harbin, Marta Jimenez, Lawrence Lengbeyer, and Aaron Colton for their helpful comments on earlier drafts of this chapter. Special thanks to Burt Howell and the Intersections Villa Faculty Writing Retreat, sponsored by Boston College's Division of Mission and Ministry, for providing the time and space required to revise and complete this chapter.

Notes

1 As with all moral virtues, Aristotle thinks that the virtue of courage is concerned with feelings and actions. Courage concerns the feelings of fear (*phobos*) and confidence (*tharros*) and acting for the sake of the noble in situations that risk death or serious physical harm, especially in battle. I explain these features of courage, below.

2 Translations of Aristotle's texts are from Barnes 1984 unless otherwise noted, with occasional modifications by me. For the Greek text, I have used the following Oxford Classical Texts editions: for the *Nicomachean Ethics* (*NE*), Bywater 1894; for the *Eudemian Ethics* (*EE*), Walzer and Mingay 1991; for the *Rhetoric* (*Rhet.*), Ross 1959, and for *De Anima* (*DA*), Ross 1956.

3 Throughout the chapter, I use the adjectives "brave" and "courageous" interchangeably to describe the courageous person (*andreios*) or courageous action, and I use the terms "bravery" and "courage" interchangeably to refer to the virtue of courage (*andreia*).

4 There is a considerable body of literature dedicated to the problem of courage and self-control, which I discuss, below. For formulations of this problem, and various attempts to resolve the problem, see *inter alia* Young 1977, 2009, Pears 1980, Leighton 1988, Heil 1996, Jiang 2000, Stohr 2003, Brady 2005, Curzer 2012, 55-62, Vigani 2017.

5 In the passage at *NE* VII 9, Aristotle distinguishes self-control from the virtue of moderation (*sōphrosunē*) in particular: the self-controlled person experiences an appetite for bodily pleasure that is contrary to reason, while the moderate person

experiences no such appetite. For the virtuous person, in general, the rational and non-rational parts of the soul should "chime in all things" (*NE* I 13, 1102bb28).

6 See, for example, Pears 1980, 174, or Young 2009, 445, for the claim that fear involves the desire to avoid wounds or death.

7 This is a solution offered by, for example, Leighton 1988, Young 2009, and Curzer 2012, 59–62. My view, below, defends this solution, which I call the "fear as contribution" view, and expands upon it by explaining the fears of the courageous person who recognizes that death is inevitable.

8 See Broadie 2002, 323 for this observation.

9 I have borrowed the translation of *phantasia* as "impression" from Konstan 2006, 130, who provides a helpful interpretation of Aristotle's treatment of fear in the *Rhetoric*. See Konstan 2006, 129–155.

10 For his discussion of the cognitive evaluations involved in fear, see Konstan 2006, 130–135.

11 Pears 1980, speculates that just as Aristotle defines the emotion of anger as the desire to return pain for pain at *DA* 403a30–31, so too fear could be "the desire to avoid harm that is judged probable" (Pears 1980, 175). See Brady 2005, 193, who agrees that, "while . . . fear is defined as pain at the expectation of loss, fear can also be understood as the corresponding desire to avoid that loss."

12 Curzer 2012, 57, uses the passage at *DA* 414b4-6 to argue that, for Aristotle, we have a desire and motivation to avoid the objects of fear. I return to this point below.

13 For an insightful explanation of Aristotle's views on the relationship between goods of the soul and external goods, or goods of fortune, see Jimenez 2018.

14 Aristotle goes so far as to say that cowards "fear everything" (1116a3), but presumably he means that they fear every danger in the relevant situations.

15 I have modified this translation from Ross and Urmson 1984, consulting primarily Rowe 2002 and Reeve 2014.

16 See Broadie 2002, 323. While Broadie does not specify any passages in which Socrates holds this view, a clear contender is the so-called "Two Things" argument at the end of Plato's *Apology*, in which Socrates argues that if death is "like nothing" (akin to a dreamless sleep), then it is a great gain, and thus we ought to be hopeful regarding death (*Ap*. 40c–e).

17 See, for example, Curzer 2012, 55 for this view, and a treatment of some of the voices in this debate, including Brady 2005 and Duff 1987.

18 See Irwin 1999, 211–212 for a similar suggestion as to what makes death in battle noble.

19 In this respect, Aristotle's account of courage is more restricted than that of Socrates. See Vigani 2017, 314.

20 Aristotle thinks that the attribution of bravery to shamelessness depends on an extension of the normal sense of "courage," since the shameless person lacks fear and "the brave person also is a fearless person" (III 6, 1115a15).

21 As a proponent of the view that Aristotle's brave person is fearless, Vigani 2017, 328, observes that Aristotle's view may seem odd to us, but this fact makes Aristotle's view an interesting and possibly useful corrective to contemporary accounts of courage. For Socrates' view of fearless courage, see, for example, *Protagoras* 359c2–e1. See Jimenez 2022 for an explanation of Socrates' view in the *Protagoras* and Aristotle's criticism of it.

22 The "mean" is not the same as the quantitative mean between two extremes; it is a qualitative mean and it is context-relative. See Urmson 1980 (especially 160–2) for a discussion of the Doctrine of the Mean; for a discussion of the mean in relation to fear and the virtue of courage, see Leighton 1988, 79 and Vigani 2017, 326–7.

23 See also Woolf 2022, 117. Although Woolf here examines Aristotle's account in the *EE*, he finds Aristotle's account to be generally consistent across the *EE* and *NE*. Woolf, however, does admit that the brave person experiences fear in extreme cases, if only to a small degree (Woolf 2022, 122–123). Woolf's overall view is that Aristotle's brave person feels "little to no fear in relation to his proprietary activities," and he argues that Aristotle aims to remove the painful aspect of fear as much as possible from courageous activity in order to reconcile the virtue of courage (which involves painful fear) with his view that the life of virtue is a pleasant one (Woolf 2022, 115).

24 See, for example, Pears 1980, 178: "A man may behave fearlessly because he lacks the appropriate fear or because, although he has it, he behaves like a man who lacks it." See Brady 2005, 193 for a restatement of this view and 193 n.11 for a survey of these views in the literature.

25 Translation from Inwood and Woolf 2013. Woolf 2022 contends that Aristotle's remark at *EE* 1228b11 is dialectical and not necessarily his definitive view (Woolf 2022, 126 n.19).

26 Konstan 2006, 134–136, shows that writers across the tradition of ancient Greek literature share this intuition.

27 While Woolf 2022 aims to downplay this fact as a "fairly narrow point" (Woolf 2022, 122), I contend that the fact that Aristotle admits that brave people feel some fear is an important qualification.

28 For examples of this view see, for example, Young 1977, 197: "courageous agents do not experience the possibly disabling *symptoms* of fear"; Pears 1980, 178-179; Broadie 1991, 91: the courageous person's distress is not "expressed in avoidance behavior"; and Heil 1996, 58-61. See Brady 2005, 193 (esp. n.11) for a survey of these views.

29 For this view, see Pears 1980, 178-179, and Heil 1996, 58-61.

30 At *NE* II 3, 1104b30-1105a1, Aristotle says that the virtuous person chooses correctly concerning objects of choice: namely, the pleasant, the advantageous, and the noble. As Jimenez 2018, 157–158, explains, the virtuous person can correctly grasp the hierarchy and relations of dependency between these objects of choice and can recognize that the noble is preferable over the advantageous or the pleasant in cases where these objects may come apart.

31 See, for example, Brady 2005. Young 2009 argues, based on *NE* VII 4, 1148b9–14, that, "[although] Aristotle restricts the sphere of self-control, properly speaking, to the sphere of temperance, it is clear that he envisages analogous of self-control for the other virtues. See e.g. VII.4 1148b9–14" (Young 2009, 444).

32 See Pears 1980, 174 for the claim that fear involves the desire to avoid wounds or death. See also Young 2009, 444–445, who shows how self-control is manifested by contrary desires, and that courage could be similarly construed.

33 Perhaps the puzzle about self-control could be side-stepped by appealing to the fact that self-control concerns bodily pleasures, whereas courage concerns pain (*NE* III 9). In the passages on self-control, Aristotle introduces "endurance" (*karteria*) as the

condition of resisting bodily pains (*NE* VII 7 1150a13–14). This condition, however, is not virtue either. Aristotle thinks that courage is either pleasant or at least painless, and that courageous agents are supposed to act without any internal conflict (*NE* II 3, 1104b7–8). Later in *NE* VII 7, Aristotle appears to cast endurance as a resistance to bodily pleasures *and* pains, and claims it is worse than self-control, which involves overcoming or mastering them (1150a33–36). See Broadie 2002, 397, for a note on the ambiguity of this passage.

34 For a formulation of this problem, and various proposed solutions, see inter alia Young 1977, Leighton 1988, Heil 1996, Jiang 2000, Stohr 2003, Young 2009, Curzer 2012, 55–62, Vigani 2017.

35 In what follows, I treat a few of the proposed solutions to this problem outlined in the literature. For a helpful summary of some of these positions, see Curzer 2012, 55–62, although I include additional authors in the relevant debates, such as Young 2009 and Vigani 2017.

36 Woolf 2022 also defends the view that the brave person feels little to no fear. I leave his view out of this debate since he explains Aristotle's views of fear in relation to a different problem—namely, how to reconcile the exercise of courage, which involves facing pains and fear, with Aristotle's contention that the life of virtue is a pleasant one. Woolf also dismisses the possibility of an enkratic counterpart to courage (see Woolf 2022, 127–129).

37 As Curzer 2012, 57, points out (mentioned above), *DA* 414b4–6 suggests that pleasure and pain are connected with desire and aversion, respectively. So, if the courageous view death as evil, then they should have a desire to avoid death. Moreover, we may worry that Brady's solution, by making the courageous person into someone who is not motivated to avoid death at all, risks rendering the courageous person into someone who is insensibly fearless.

38 We find a similar view in Pears 1980, 179, who distinguishes between fears that contribute to the action and behavioral fearlessness.

39 See Heil 1996, 49, for his statement of this view; see Curzer 2012, 57–58, who shares this worry about Heil's view.

40 Moreover, Heil's view risks attributing inner turmoil to the courageous person. At *NE* II 3, 1104b7–8, however, Aristotle says that brave people are pleased or not pained by standing their ground against terrifying things.

41 Here I am thinking of Leighton 1988, Young 2009, and Curzer 2012, 59–62. Pears 1980, 178, introduces the notion of "contributory fear," which contributes to the courageous action.

42 For his elaboration of this solution, see Young 2009, 446–447, and Curzer 2012, 59–62, for a similar solution.

43 See Jiang 2000, 25–26. Jiang takes aim at Young 1977's articulation of the "fear as contribution" view.

44 See especially Curzer 2012, 61–2, for his response to Jiang 2000's objection to the "fear as contribution" view.

45 Cases like these may not have been far from Aristotle's mind, since the *NE* includes examples of people choosing to die for their city-state (1169a18–29).

46 Translation from Reeve 2018 with slight modifications by me.

47 See Pearson 2009, 130–132, who argues that brave people have an impression that they are safe from disgrace, which is an evil that they fear. Vigani 2017, 324–325,

however, disagrees with Pearson's account, since (she argues) acting shamefully would never be a risk for a truly virtuous person. Curzer 2012, 22, excludes disgrace from the potential objects of courageous fear on the grounds that disgrace properly belongs to the learner's proto-virtue of shame. For a recent and more complete treatment of shame as a proto-virtue of the learner, see Jimenez 2020.

48 Vigani 2017, 325–326, raises the possibility that the courageous person can fear missing the target of virtue. But Vigani rejects this possible interpretation on the grounds that the courageous person is fearless (Vigani 2017, 326). I disagree with Vigani's view, however, because she denies that the courageous person feels fear.

49 Pearson 2009, 134, contends that his interpretation of the courageous person's confidence and fear can explain why the courageous agent is hopeful even in the face of certain death. See Pearson 2009 for a full discussion. For more on the hopes of Aristotle's courageous person, see Gravlee 2000.

Bibliography

Barnes, Jonathan (ed.). 1984. *The Complete Works of Aristotle.* 2 vols. Bolingen Series. Princeton: Princeton University Press.

Brady, Michelle. 2005. "The Fearlessness of Courage." *Southern Journal of Philosophy* 43, no. 2: 189–211.

Broadie, Sarah. 1991. *Ethics With Aristotle*. New York: Oxford University Press.

Broadie, Sarah, and Rowe, Christopher. 2002. *Aristotle: Nicomachean Ethics*. Philosophical introduction and commentary by Sarah Broadie, translated by Christopher Rowe. New York: Oxford University Press.

Bywater, J. (ed.) 1894. *Aristotelis Ethica Nicomachea*. Oxford: Clarendon Press.

Cooper, John M., and Hutchinson, D. S. 1997. *Plato: Complete Works*. Indianapolis: Hackett.

Curzer, Howard J. 2012. *Aristotle and the Virtues*. New York: Oxford University Press.

Duff, Antony. 1987. "Aristotelian Courage." *Ratio* 29, no. 1 (Jun.): 2–15.

Fortenbaugh, W. W. 2002. *Aristotle on Emotion* (2nd ed.). London: Duckworth.

Gravlee, G. Scott. 2000. "Aristotle on Hope." *Journal of the History of Philosophy* 38, no. 4: 461–477.

Grimaldi, William M. A. 1980. *Aristotle Rhetoric I: A Commentary*. New York: Fordham University Press.

Grimaldi, William M. A. 1988. *Aristotle Rhetoric II: A Commentary*. New York: Fordham University Press.

Heil, John Ferguson. 1996. "Why Is Aristotle's Brave Man So Frightened? The Paradox of Courage in the Eudemian Ethics." *Apeiron* 29, no. 1: 47–74.

Holberg, Erica. 2019. "Aristotle on the Pleasure of Courage." *Polis: The Journal for Ancient Greek and Roman Political Thought* 36, no. 2: 289–312.

Inwood, Brad, and Woolf, Raphael (tr. and ed.). 2013. *Eudemian Ethics*. Cambridge: Cambridge University Press.

Irwin, Terence (tr. and ed.). 1999. *Nicomachean Ethics* (2nd ed.). Indianapolis: Hackett.

Jiang, Xinyang. 2000. "Courage and the Aristotelian Unity of Action and Passion." *Philosophical Inquiry* 22, no. 1: 23–45.

Jimenez, Marta. 2018. "Aristotle on Enduring Evils While Staying Happy." In *Evil in Aristotle*, edited by Pavlos Kontos, 150–169. New York: Cambridge University Press.
Jimenez, Marta. 2020. *Aristotle on Shame and Learning to Be Good*. New York: Oxford University Press.
Jimenez, Marta. 2022. "Aristotle and Protagoras against Socrates on Courage and Experience." In *Socrates and the Socratic Philosophies: Selected Papers from Socratica IV*, edited by Claudia Marsico, 361–376. Baden-Baden: Academia Verlag.
Konstan, David. 2006. *The Emotions of the Ancient Greeks*. Toronto: University of Toronto Press.
Leighton, Stephen. 1988. "Aristotle's Courageous Passions." *Phronesis* 33: 76–99.
Pears, David. 1980. "Courage as a Mean." In *Essays on Aristotle's Ethics*, edited by Amélie Oksenberg Rorty, 171–187. Berkeley: University of California Press.
Pearson, Giles. 2009. "Aristotle on the Role of Confidence in Courage." *Ancient Philosophy* 29: 123–137.
Reeve, C. D. C. (tr.). 2014. *Nicomachean Ethics*. Indianapolis, IN: Hackett.
Reeve, C. D. C. (tr.) 2018. *Rhetoric*. Indianapolis, IN: Hackett.
Roberts, W. Rhys (tr.). 1984. "*Rhetoric*." In *The Complete Works of Aristotle*, vol. 2, edited by J. Barnes, 2152–2269. Princeton, NJ: Princeton University Press.
Rogers, Kelly. 1994. "Aristotle on the Motive of Courage." *The Southern Journal of Philosophy* 32, no. 3: 303–313.
Ross, W. D. (ed.). 1956. *Aristotelis De Anima*. Oxford: Clarendon Press.
Ross, W. D. (ed.). 1959. *Aristotelis Ars Rhetorica*. Oxford: Clarendon Press.
Ross, W. D., and Urmson, J. O. (tr.). 1984. "Aristotle, *Nicomachean Ethics*." In *The Complete Works of Aristotle*, vol. 2, edited by J. Barnes, 1729–1867. Princeton, NJ: Princeton University Press.
Smith, J. A. (tr.). 1984. "Aristotle, *On the Soul*." In *The Complete Works of Aristotle*, vol. 1, edited by J. Barnes, 641–692. Princeton, NJ: Princeton University Press.
Solomon, J. (tr.). 1984. "Aristotle, *Eudemian Ethics*." In *The Complete Works of Aristotle*, vol. 2, edited by J. Barnes, 1922–1981. Princeton, NJ: Princeton University Press.
Stohr, Karen E. 2003. "Moral Cacophony: When Continence Is a Virtue." *The Journal of Ethics* 7, no. 4: 339–363.
Striker, Gisela. 1996. "Emotions in Context: Aristotle's Treatment of the Passions in the *Rhetoric* and His Moral Psychology." In *Essays on Aristotle's Rhetoric*, edited by Amélie Oksenberg Rorty, 112–127. Berkeley: University of California Press.
Urmson, J. O. 1980. "Aristotle's Doctrine of the Mean." In *Essays on Aristotle's Ethics*, edited by Amélie Oksenberg Rorty, 157–170. Berkeley: University of California Press.
Vigani, Denise. 2017. "Aristotle's Account of Courage." *History of Philosophy Quarterly* 34, no. 4: 313–330.
Walzer, R. R., and Mingay, J. M. (eds.). 1991. *Aristotelis Ethica Eudemia*. Oxford: Clarendon Press.
Woolf, Raphael. 2022. "Courage and Pleasure in Aristotle's Ethics." In *Psychology and Value in Plato, Aristotle, and Hellenistic Philosophy: The Ninth Keeling Colloquium in Ancient Philosophy*, edited by Fiona Leigh and Margaret Hampson, 114–133. Oxford: Oxford University Press.
Young, Charles M. 1977. "Aristotle on Courage." In *Humanitas: Essays in Honor of Ralph Ross*, edited by Howe Jr., Quincy, 194–203. Claremont, CA: Scripps College Press.
Young, Charles M. 2009. "Courage." In *A Companion to Aristotle*, edited by Anagnostopoulos, Georgios, 442–456. Malden, MA: Wiley-Blackwell.

4

Do the Brave Master Their Fears—or Avoid Them?

Lawrence Lengbeyer

Much effort goes into imbuing military personnel with the excellent character trait of courage or bravery. But what exactly is this virtue at which such efforts aim? Is the ultimate virtue-development goal warfighters who face the threats, cope with and surmount their resulting fears, and persevere in performing their duties? Or warfighters who encounter such situations without experiencing fear, and hence without needing to cope with it?

According to what I will call *the Classical View of character*, originally bequeathed to us by Aristotle and still prevalent today (including in parts of the current volume), the virtue of courage is interpreted as involving the withstanding and overcoming of reasonably experienced fear. It is a disposition to master or rise above one's ongoing fear when confronting circumstances that are fearsome, that is, properly provoking of fear.[1] On this standard conception, courage does not allow, let alone require, an absence of fear in the face of fearsome circumstances. One must face up to these circumstances and stay the (right) course *despite* the presence of fear. To lack fear altogether is to be of unsound mind, or at least rash or out of control.

I maintain, however, that this tradition of thinking about courage is mistaken—that the only persons properly regarded as unqualifiedly brave are those who experience *no* fear while handling fearsome circumstances. However much we rightly praise, and are impressed by, those who overcome their fears, these persons are not exemplars of true courage but occupy an imperfect state that is somewhat defective.

After some brief ground clearing, I will survey the central reasons that undergird the widespread support for the Classical View of courage as requiring both the experiencing and overcoming of fear. I will then attempt to rebut those reasons, offering an alternative virtuous ideal of courage as fearlessness and explaining that this is enabled by a process of 'shallow cognizing' whereby the truly brave person prevents the arousal (or perhaps continuation) of fear, while yet neither losing the benefits of alertness and physiological response nor suppressing the knowledge or ongoing awareness that is needed for rational practical reasoning and action. Before concluding the chapter, I will contrast alternative philosophical accounts of fearlessness and address some critical objections to conceiving of courage as involving avoidance of fear.

Fear

For my purposes, it suffices to take fear to be the unpleasant, aversive apprehension of a danger that threatens one (or someone or something with which one strongly identifies). The threat is to something that one cares about and so would not want to lose.[2] (Thus, someone who longs for escape from life need not feel fear upon apprehending a threat to her life.) The full-blown experience of fear includes a cognitive component (the perception or thought of the danger), an affective component (the unpleasant feeling), and a physiological component (bodily arousals of various sorts, though fainting is possible, too).

So, is courage better understood to be a stalwartness in the face of trepidation-inducing dangers, as the Classical View maintains, or an intrepid stoutheartedness that recognizes dangers without fear and gamely confronts them?

Five Arguments for the Classical View

There is a battery of reasons that support the widespread belief that courage requires fear.

1. For one thing, the authority of Aristotle carries substantial weight, and Aristotle is widely read as claiming that the virtue of courage in facing the dangers of battle (which is his focus) involves the mastery or use, rather than elimination, of fear.

   > [T]he man who does not fear the things he should, and neither when nor as he should, is foolhardy. (EE 1221a15–20)[3]
   >
   > [I]f he is afraid of nothing at all and goes to face everything, he becomes rash. (NE 1104a20–23)
   >
   > The person who is excessively fearless . . . would be some sort of madman, or incapable of feeling distress, if he feared nothing, neither earthquake nor waves, as they say about the Celts. (NE 1115b25–30)
   >
   > [S]tanding firm against what is painful makes us call people brave; that is why bravery is both painful and justly praised. . . . [T]he brave person will find death and wounds painful, and suffer them unwillingly, but he will stand firm against them because that is fine or because failure is shameful. (NE 1117a30–b9)[4]
   >
   > [I]t is quite possible for brave people not to be the best soldiers. Perhaps the best will be those who possess no other . . . [virtues, and hence find less value in life and therefore less pain (fear) at the prospect of death, making them willing] to sell their lives for small gains [in war]. (NE 1117b17–20)

2. More important than the mere fact that Aristotle apparently regards fear as present in bravery is that Aristotle's view, it is commonly thought, is true and

well-supported by his broader view of character traits, namely, his so-called Doctrine of the Mean.

> [V]irtue of character . . . aims at the intermediate condition in feelings and actions. (NE 1109a20–25)
>
> We can be afraid, e.g., or be confident, or have appetites, or get angry, or feel pity, . . . both too much and too little, . . . ; but [having these feelings] at the right times, about the right things, towards the right people, for the right end, and in the right way, is the intermediate and best condition, and this is proper to virtue. Similarly, actions also admit of excess, deficiency and the intermediate condition. (NE 1106b18)
>
> In feelings of fear and confidence the mean is bravery. (NE 1107a30+–b5)

The Doctrine of the Mean, which remains influential to this day, seems to require that courage involve fear; fearlessness would appear to be a non-virtuous excess.

3. The Classical View seems supported also by ordinary intuitions about familiar cases. Surely we regard the person who strides across a busy highway—or a busy battlefield—without experiencing fear as unhinged, do we not? This is not bravery, a character excellence, but something like irrational foolhardiness, recklessness, rashness, excess of daring, or obliviousness.
4. Manifold researchers, and not only in philosophy,[5] have emphasized the utility of emotions like fear. In many cases, emotions are functional, leading those who experience them toward better practical choices. Fear, for instance, is the product of conscious and subliminal monitoring of our environment, and feeling it commonly causes us to become both more perceptually alert to dangers and more physiologically aroused—hence stronger and faster, better equipped for 'fight or flight.' It makes sense that an excellence of character like courage would not forgo such advantages.
5. If we require fearlessness for courage, then we may be setting the virtue bar unrealistically high. Courage will not then be found 'in the wild.' Is it not unrealistic to think that humans can operate in highly dangerous circumstances, such as intense combat, without experiencing fear? Combat veterans often attest to the virtual universality of fear among themselves and their comrades,[6] the central challenge that they have faced being to cope with that fear in order to perform their duties.

Courage as Fearlessness

On the alternative conception that I propose, the (fully) brave person habitually engages in mental manipulations that manage to prevent the arousal (or perhaps continuation) of fear yet do not suppress the knowledge or ongoing awareness that is needed for rational practical reasoning and action. For example, on the battlefield, brave warrior W sees the enemy soldiers, their proximity, their large weapons, their fevered eagerness to kill her and her comrades, and the dangers posed by those snipers over there. W is not unaware that there might be others waiting to pounce from behind those bushes, and that her own gun has jammed. She factors all of these circumstances into her choices of behavior and into her planning. Yet she feels no fear as she does so.[7]

How is this psychologically possible? By cognizing the potential fear-inspiring data 'shallowly'—as one cognizes, for instance, the information that one's doctor presents about dire test results, maybe indicating a life-threatening disease, while nevertheless proceeding to discuss intellectually with the doctor what one's options are, what actions one ought to take or not take, and so on. One does not yield to the temptation to redirect one's attention elsewhere, toward alternative topics that will avoid all emotional disquiet. But neither does one allow oneself to experience the unrestricted, unregulated, full-blown emotion that could be caused by the new information; specifically, one does not activate (i.e., accept from memory and employ in occurrent mental activity) imagery that would likely cause disgust, nausea, grief, or panic. One does not allow oneself to think of the implications and consequences of one's death, or, therefore, of the imagery that pertains to these. The extra information would not be relevant to the immediate task at hand—it would not significantly enhance one's discussion and planning in the doctor's office. (In other contexts, such as conversations with one's romantic partner, children, or business associates, more of the information could be properly admitted, though again probably without the attendant imagery.) On the other hand, its presence to mind could very well be distracting or debilitating in a way that would undermine the current activity. At the very least, it would demand a great effort of will to maintain one's composure and focus adequately—effort that could otherwise be directed in more productive directions. Consequently, one keeps one's engagement with the issues on a purely intellectual plane, and a topically constrained one at that, thereby reproducing neither the cognitive aspect of fear nor the exact affective and physiological aspects that accompany it.[8]

And how are these mental manipulations to be accomplished? By way of the deeply and thoroughly compartmentalized nature of human cognition, a feature that is visible in many settings. It seems evident that humans employ in any particular instant of occurrent cognizing only a subset of the full network of representational resources that are stored in their long-term memories, with the activation—and thus deactivation, or *temporary forgetting*—of resources shifting from moment to moment in response to the perceived pragmatic task or situation that they take themselves to be facing.[9] Situations that call specifically for shallow cognizing can be met by directing cognitive activations toward the resources needed for merely intellectual engagement, omitting to the extent possible those that are likely to prompt emotional responses. In the case of courage, one is to avoid a full, image-rich and fear-inspiring, cognitive confrontation with the prospects of loss or suffering that one recognizes as being present.[10]

These descriptions of the mental manipulations involved in fearless bravery may seem to suggest, implausibly, processes that are explicitly and even consciously directed. But such suggestions derive from the limitations of language and need to be resisted. The key cognitive processes, like attending to certain matters while avoiding engagement with others, are executed subconsciously. They are typically also *initiated* subconsciously, the results of habitual mental practices and policies.[11]

Ordinary experience shows unmistakably that people are capable of shallow cognizing to control their emotions, though this phenomenon has gone unremarked in the philosophical literature.[12] It offers a potential route—if perhaps not the only route—to the attainment of fearlessness in the face of fearsome circumstances.

Note that the shallow cognizing process of emotion management involves keeping fear-arousing representations from being occurrently cognized; it does not require a denial of the value of what one cares about (like one's own life, in the case of combat) or a cessation of caring about those things. One avoids full activation of one's knowledge of the threat that one is facing[13] rather than of one's knowledge about the value or importance of what is at stake. One need not be assessing, or concerned with, the latter matter at all.

And yet, might it be psychologically possible to focus *here* in order to obtain a second potential route to fearlessness? In theory, at least, one might suppress (that is, inactivate, within one's compartmentalized cognitive system) one's cognitions regarding the value of what is threatened. So, in the case of combat, one would elude fear by temporarily forgetting about the special, unique importance of one's own imperiled life and limb. Perhaps this bit of temporary forgetting is psychologically possible; this is not clear. But even if it is, the *forgetting* obviously would not amount to *believing* that one's life has no real importance. Nor need it cause a parallel forgetting or neglect of the value of other persons or their entitlements to proper treatment. Thus, one might be fearless toward the dangers to self, while still rationally being scrupulously avoidant of unjustly harming other parties, like innocent noncombatants.

Alternative Philosophical Conceptions of Fearlessness

An advantage of the shallow cognizing approach to courage is that it provides for the direct elimination of fear. Some alternate defenses of the possibility of fearlessness during encounters with danger struggle to provide this in a plausible manner and so need to enlarge the scope of the mental factors that need to be managed. This makes them less convincing as means of attaining fearlessness.

Brady's (2005) effort, for example, pictures courageous soldiers as achieving fearlessness through the reeducation of their desires: after the right moral education into virtue, they "do not feel the desire to avoid death" when the "larger, communal good" of the *polis* is at stake (194, 201); "the preservation of the *polis* will take priority," and these brave souls will be "no longer moved by the desire for self-preservation" (202). Hence, they will serve unstintingly in the noble cause of battle, even though they may experience feelings of fear as they contemplate the harms that may be in store for them.

But, besides stipulating a rather radical redefinition of "fearlessness"—one that allows painful feelings of terror—and a major shift in what is required to preserve the virtue-continence (self-control) distinction—from a harmony, under the guidance of reason, of action with *feelings* to a harmony of action with *desire*[14]—Brady's conception seems to ask that people pursue a more, and maybe impossibly, arduous path to virtue. The transformation of desire whose outcome is that "the courageous person is moved wholly by a desire for the noble, . . . [which] *replaces* the desire for safety" (197, emph. added) seems a wildly ambitious undertaking. Surely, of the actual warfighters who have faced death fearlessly on the battlefield, only a minuscule proportion, if any, have managed to eliminate their desires to avoid death. And why ought they? Why eliminate a perfectly rational desire—and think that Aristotle would counsel this? Even those who are 100 percent committed to a fight, who have an "eagerness . . . to face a threat" (197) by, say, fending off a heinous attack on their precious children, can still reasonably desire to avoid death. To overcome action-inhibiting fear in such cases by direct management of emotional states (utilizing shallow cognizing) would seem more achievable, and more advantageous, than by the indirection of expunging rational desires for safety.[15]

Brady's impulse to find the solution to the puzzle of courage within practical reasoning rather than emotion management is given voice also by Pears (2004), whose route to fearlessness is somewhat more psychologically plausible and more aligned with the commitment to rationality as a core, unremitting requirement of virtue.

Pears' way of preserving the valuable contrast between virtue and self-control, so that the brave need not be thought to fight against their fears, is through what he terms the "discounting" of these fears. The brave fighter indeed feels fear when contemplating the probabilities and magnitudes of possible negative outcomes (wounds and death, but maybe also other consequences of defeat, like humiliation and enslavement); not to feel fear would be pathological, in Pears' view, as he does not contemplate a process like shallow cognizing, nor does he believe, with Brady, that desires to avoid these outcomes can be educated away. But her deliberation about how to act encompasses also the probabilities and magnitudes of *positive* outcomes (victory for her *polis*), and she calculates that the latter outweighs the former. Once this mental Rubicon has been crossed, the brave soldier thereupon "discounts" the fearsome outcomes, no longer feeling fear about them. Having already been digested within the larger whole of deliberative processing, taken proper rational account of, they can be set aside psychologically. Thus they no longer trigger feelings of fear, allowing subsequent courageous action to be "frictionless" (2004, 8).[16]

Pears, however, does not explain this crucial "setting aside." He seems, perhaps, to be analogizing to cases such as where, for instance, one experiences a feeling of aversion or despondency when contemplating dragging oneself out of bed to do unpleasant chores, but after then considering the reasons in favor of this and finding them dispositive, one just gets on with it and doesn't look back, putting the negatives out of mind (at least if one is virtuous about meeting one's responsibilities). One proceeds to carry out one's chores without brooding about them or attending to their unpleasant aspects any more than is necessary to maintain rational control over one's actions.

It is not clear just what cognitive processes are supposed to underpin fears-discounting. Perhaps shallow cognizing might itself play some role. But even if so, the discounting account has some disadvantages compared to the one presented in this chapter. For one thing, the person who experiences terror prior to coming to a deliberative resolution in favor of courageous action is vulnerable to having that deliberative process distorted and disfigured by the fear. This cost is readily avoidable on the shallow cognizing account of bravery. Second, discounting appears to involve pushing the fear-inspiring information (about death, wounds, etc.) entirely out of mind, whereas shallow cognizing allows it to be thought about for purposes of effective action, merely severing the link to fearful feelings.[17] Finally, it is not clear how pre-activity discounting can preclude the return of negative emotion during later encounters with particularly unpleasant or painful experiences or prospects. As one performs one's chores, one's muscles ache painfully, or a vile odor presents itself, or one is made to play endless, unproductive phone tag. Similarly, on the battlefield, one's weapon fails; an enemy force suddenly appears; communications with the leadership are frustrated. What prevents the fearsome possible outcomes from coming to mind, undoing the poised resolve that was achieved by discounting? For discounting to have a plausible chance of succeeding, it needs to be supplemented by something like shallow cognizing—but then it is not clear what there is left for discounting to do.

Responding to the Five Arguments

1. The first challenge is to provide a convincing interpretation of Aristotle's statements that portrays him as accepting that courage does not require fear. Naturally, this is the least important task facing a challenge to the Classical View, as the challenger can always concede that Aristotle simply got courage wrong. This is a large task to be left for another time, but it is possible to point to a few sources of evidence in favor of reading Aristotle as imagining brave warriors to be fearless though they make rational, accurate appraisals of the dangers facing them.

   First, and most crucial, Aristotle insists as a general principle that possession of a moral virtue comprises right, situationally appropriate behaviors that are accompanied by proper, concordant feelings, rather than by improper, resistant feelings that need to be controlled by a struggle of willpower. And courage is one of his particular exemplars of this general principle.

   > But [actions are not enough [for virtue]]; we must take as a sign of someone's state his pleasure or pain in consequence of his action. For if someone who abstains from bodily pleasures enjoys the abstinence itself, then he is temperate, but if he is grieved by it, he is intemperate. Again, if he stands firm

> against terrifying situations and enjoys it, or at least does not find it painful, then he is brave, and if he finds it painful, he is cowardly. (NE 1104b3–8)

Fear is painful as experienced, and Aristotle apparently regards it as such,[18] which thus implies that bravery involves not feeling fear.

> Now, it is possible to dispute this reading of Aristotle, to argue that the conception of consonant action and feeling was Aristotle's position in the earlier *Eudemian Ethics*, and was even imported into the *Nicomachean Ethics*—hence the quotation just cited—but that Aristotle then realized that courage is an exceptional case, demanding a qualification to the general account: "Hence it is not true that the active exercise of every virtue is pleasant; it is pleasant only in so far as we attain the end" (NE 1117b15).[19]

However, it seems noteworthy that Aristotle did not revise the *Nicomachean Ethics* account throughout to incorporate this apparent revision of general principle that appears in his bravery discussion. Perhaps he left this qualification in the text as a problematic anomaly to be revisited later (perhaps by his successors) for eventual reconciliation into the general account—presumably with the theoretical outcome that those exercising courage do not suffer the pain of fear. If Aristotle did choose this route, he would simply have been taking the reasonable approach to anomalous counterexamples that is routine in the practice of 'normal science': gradually work on reanalyzing these so that they become supporting instances of the prevailing paradigm or core theory.[20] Of course, modern scientific norms and standards cannot be complacently projected onto inquirers in ancient Greece; but the charge of anachronism is weakened where what is being imputed seems consistent with basic (cross-cultural) rational practice, and where Aristotle evidently did choose to leave the blatant inconsistency within his text.

Further supporting the view that Aristotle was not 'all in' on conceiving of bravery as including fear are several passages (one in the *Eudemian Ethics*, but also one in the *Nicomachean Ethics*) in which Aristotle suggests that the brave person is in fact fearless, or nearly so: "[C]ourage makes a man fearless, and . . . fearlessness consists in fearing nothing, or else few things, and those slightly and reluctantly" (EE 1228b1–20); "[S]omeone is called brave to the fullest extent if he is intrepid in facing a fine death and the immediate dangers that bring death—and this is above all true of the dangers of war" (NE 1115a30–35).

For some who remain skeptical, courage as fearlessness might perhaps be squared with Aristotle's texts by following the lead of those commentators who construe Aristotle as understanding courage as an unusual emotional hybrid, a matter of both fear *and confidence*.[21] It could be thought, then, that the courageous warrior is the one whose tendencies toward experiencing fear are fully and effectively counteracted and negated by rationally experienced confidence.

2. Courage as fearlessness can be reconciled with the Doctrine of the Mean. Fearlessness is neither a deficiency nor an excess when beneficial alertness, arousal, and stalwart behavior are still achieved even in the absence of fear. Rather, courage as fearlessness is itself a mean, beyond which lies a further, vicious extreme: irrational heedlessness of dangerous realities that need to enter into effective practical reasoning about how to act. Rash, foolhardy, or oblivious persons do not even take proper cognitive account of the relevant fearsome circumstances in choosing their actions. Fearlessness, though, does *not* entail this, because fear is not the only route to such awareness. Courageously fearless persons are cognizant of these circumstances and take them into account; they simply do not allow these realities to scare them, to get them off their game, to provoke them into improper behavior, or to distract or terrorize them.

   If vigilant fearlessness is thus the mean, and heedlessness of relevant realities the excess, the deficiency is experiencing action-inhibiting fear—cowardice—just as in the Classical View. But what then of the Classical View's ideal, of being disposed to experience, yet overcome, fear? Well, this overpowering of fear by willpower or self-discipline is surely a greatly superior state to simple cowardice, but it is only an intermediate, and ideally temporary and transitional, point on the path to complete courage. In this, it is parallel to other not-quite-virtues where individuals reliably display the proper conduct, yet (prior to achieving the full virtue) without having their feelings in harmonious sync with such conduct.

   Consider temperance, which Aristotle addresses immediately after courage, as these two "are the virtues of the non-rational parts" (NE 1117b20). Virtuous temperance is, Aristotle insists, not painful: "someone is temperate because he does not feel pain at the absence of what is pleasant, or at refraining from it" (NE 1118b30). Thus, while the *striver* for temperance struggles to overcome the temptation to inappropriate bodily pleasures, the *fully* temperate person—in a parallel to courage as fearlessness—seemingly feels no such tug that then needs to be resisted and overcome. Her reason has shaped her desire into a fine shape, so that she need not face the painful feelings of misguided appetite (NE 1119a5) in the course of conquering it.[22]

   Similarly, consider generosity. The truly generous person's giving is done "with pleasure or [at any rate] without pain" (NE 1120a 25–30). She need not overcome a self-concerned reluctance to give, which indeed could be painful; rather, she never feels such reluctance. Still once more, with the virtue of good temper, the excellence consists in feeling appropriate anger, and also *not feeling* inappropriate anger—as opposed to experiencing but conquering this painful emotional state.
3. The pathological irrationality on display in certain examples of fearlessness is readily erased when the individual possesses a rational heedfulness of relevant circumstances. It is unnecessary to resort to fear to provide this responsiveness, and thus it is a false dichotomy to suggest that the only alternatives are irrational fearlessness and rational fear. If people have good reasons to undertake actions (and so are not unreasonable in their choices of ends or their aimless lack of ends) and are alert to the dangers and their proper weights (and so are not

unreasonable in their practical-instrumental reasoning), then they can be both fearless and entirely rational. Their internal mental manipulations do not involve irrationally forgetting about the dangers to be avoided[23] or convincing themselves that the dangers are nonexistent. Rather, they involve only a lack of emotionally affecting vividness, because they are cognized shallowly and intellectually without making contact with the mental states that would lend them emotional power and attentional magnetism.

Furthermore, do we really regard as pathologically incompetent the soldier who does not feel fear as she wades into battle, as suggested in the earlier argument for the Classical View? Or is this person actually an enviable paragon of bravery, albeit one whom most of us cannot hope to emulate?

4. Courage as fearlessness does not actually forgo the perceptual and bodily advantages that are provided by experiences of fear. Fearlessness does not mean inattentiveness, or slackness, or lack of energy. Consider that one may grow out of a child's fear of being burned by the stove while retaining a practically effective awareness of the danger it presents and a strong rational motivation to avoid touching it when it may be hot. Or consider the mental and physical state of a basketball player who, despite knowing that her teammates and fans are counting on her to help the team prevail in the Big Game, is undistracted by fear or anxiety. Perceptually, she is highly alert to all threats, opportunities, and other circumstances, and she has complete command over her rational capacities. Moreover, she walks onto the court ready for a physical challenge and is then able to meet the demands of banging her body against others for rebounding or shooting position, blanketing an opponent, or jumping out to help a teammate on defense. She may be experiencing strong competitive feelings, yet she keeps a cool head. This is the sort of 'passion' that is demanded on the battlefield, only with the stakes immeasurably higher. As Aristotle notes, "brave people are . . . full of emotion"; "their emotion cooperates with them," by contrast with those (like animals) whose distress and emotion "drives them in an *impulsive* rush to meet danger, *foreseeing none of the terrifying prospects*" (NE 1116b35, emph. added).

   In addition, fear actually is often a performance *degrader*, not an enhancer. Scientists now commonly refer to fear as leading to a response of fight, flight, *or freeze*[24]—the last of these having potential value in certain kinds of settings, but also being dysfunctional in many, probably most, others. Fear-produced performance impairments include cognitive confusion, distraction, and panic.

   So if the benefits of arousal can be obtained without fear, then fearlessness would appear to be a superior state for someone to be in when facing dangers, on the battlefield or elsewhere. Eradicating one's fear of public speaking is surely better than standing fast in the face of it; and when faced with a life-threatening crisis, it is better to have nothing interfering with one's coolheaded response than to feel fear that one then needs to control. Consistent with this, there are reports of selectors of military personnel for special forces assignments (e.g., Navy

SEALs) having a preference for those whose psychological profiles reveal that they have somewhat reduced emotional reactions.[25]

5. As for whether fearlessness actually currently exists "in the wild," one kind of relevant evidence might be drawn from instances of so-called *moral courage*, where the fearsome dangers concern not physical harm or annihilation, or psychological suffering, but all else, including serious social, material, and career costs. Occasions for the exercise of moral courage are many, including in the military, even on the battlefield. But surely it is not controversial to claim that there are individuals who are fearless when encountering such challenges, proceeding to choose the morally elevated option notwithstanding great foreseen costs. So why think it beyond the resources of rational humans to be fearless about grave *physical* dangers?

   Still, it is conceivable that exercising physical bravery in highly dangerous circumstances, including mortal combat, is more difficult than exercising moral bravery, possibly because the fear of physical harm may have qualitatively unparalleled strength and be more deeply embedded in the human psyche (perhaps placed there by evolutionary forces). Senior military personnel, in my own experience teaching at a military academy, tend to claim that fear is inescapable, for example, when landing a jet on the tiny deck of an aircraft carrier, in the rain, and at night—but at the same time, they do grant that training and experience make enormous differences in reducing the fear reaction.[26] And stories of battlefield heroism often seem to leave no place for fear; the heroes are absorbed in their extraordinary activities without debilitating thoughts of the perils. The typical report from the front lines seems to paint a similar picture: *of course*, everyone is scared . . . and yet maybe some are not. For example, here is Richard Holmes, in his *Acts of War: The Behaviour of Men in Battle*.

   > Fear is the common bond between fighting men. The overwhelming majority of soldiers experience fear during or before battle: what vary are its physical manifestations, its nature and intensity, the threat which induces it, and the manner in which it is managed. Only a tiny percentage of soldiers never know fear at all. (2003, 204)

   We ought to be studying the intrepid few, to see whether, in fact, they experience no fear (rather than merely suppress it, leading to a later breakdown) and, if so, what we might learn about how to manufacture this state in those who are not already inclined toward it.

Two Objections

OBJECTION: Fear need not be debilitating, and thus fearlessness might not be the superior state for incorporation within virtue. Arguably, much that is salutary in human behavior is effectively driven by *unconscious* fears—for example, exercise regimens are in many cases driven by fears of aging, infirmity, and death[27]—and thus there is no good case for deeming fear elimination as productive of more excellent states of the soul.

RESPONSE: The objection seems to suggest that every case of choice aiming to avoid some undesirable or painful state of affairs ought to be characterized as driven by fear. Such an approach effaces valuable distinctions. It would attribute a fear-of-death-or-injury motivation both to the white-knuckled driver navigating a winding mountain highway at night during a blizzard and that same driver practicing normal care during a routine daytime driving errand. The latter ascription is not convincing; vastly expanding the realm of fear to allow for it seems a high theoretical cost to pay for defending the position that courage involves fear.[28] It can be acknowledged that much fear is experienced below the level of self-awareness—and that there is certainly more to be said about just how to distinguish such phenomena from true fearlessness[29]—without throwing the door wide open to ascribing fear even when thoughts of danger are far distant from occurrent reasoning.

OBJECTION: If warriors manage to dispense with fear, as this chapter's ideal of courage as fearlessness advocates, then they will also be losing certain other-regarding emotional capacities that are crucial for ensuring, or at least facilitating, ethical conduct on the battlefield. Without knowing what it feels like to be afraid of injury or death, how will warfighters be able to feel the sympathy, empathy, or compassion for their adversaries or, especially, innocent noncombatant bystanders that they need in order to treat them with the respect and care that they are due?[30] If warfighters have no vivid, emotionally affecting sense of their own physical fragility and vulnerability—a situation that is, arguably, already present given the increasing deployment of long-range, stand-off weaponry, but would be exacerbated by a broader elimination of fear—then how can they be expected to have any such sense of the vulnerability of the civilians whom they need to safeguard as much as possible?

That is, if shallow cognizing distances warriors from confronting the emotional force of their own potential losses and sufferings, might it make them insensitive also to the losses and sufferings that their actions might bring to *other* parties? Even if they might rightly wish to maintain a good measure of such insensitivity toward their combat *adversaries*, surely this does not extend to the innocent parties who are liable to be caught in the crossfire. And yet, fearlessness seems likely to breed detachment, alienation, callousness, and hence brutality in warfare. Surely nothing claiming to be the virtue of bravery can have such a consequence.

RESPONSE: There is no good reason to think that the moral insensitivity of warriors to their fellow humans is psychologically implied by the fearlessness generated by shallow cognizing. It is possible to have an unmistakable awareness of one's own physical fragility and vulnerability—and those of other persons—without this being mediated by *fear*. Indeed, one had better maintain a vibrant and vigilant intellectual awareness of one's vulnerability throughout one's service on the battlefield, because without that awareness one will be incapable of rationally choosing maximally effective courses of action.

Warriors who have a proper rational, intellectual appreciation for, and principled commitment to, the ethical constraints and demands upon them will be very wary of inflicting injury upon innocent parties, and will never allow such considerations to stray far from the center of their practical reasoning about how to act. Just as they will place a high priority in their rational calculations upon maintaining their *own* safety, despite shutting themselves off from fear-inflaming cognitions about their own death or injury, so too will they care for the well-being of innocent third parties and take appropriate account of them in their reasoning. It seems not to be the case that experiencing fear, let alone experiencing it *in the moment* during combat, is indispensable for conducting oneself honorably with regard to innocents. It may even be counterproductive, undermining states of mind more conducive to rational, virtuous conduct.

Aristotle does assert that those who enjoy prosperity to the degree that they "think that they cannot possibly suffer evil" cannot feel pity for those who suffer undeserved adversities (Rhetoric 1385b).[31] The former are "insolent" (*ibid.*) as well as "contemptuous" and "rash" (1383a). But fearlessness that is rational is *aware* of perils and risks that might be suffered, and is compatible even with a sober consciousness of the tragic. So there is no cause here for an Aristotelian worry about the pity connection to others being short-circuited.[32]

Conclusion

Why has there been so much resistance to, or at least lack of interest in, the notion of courage as fearlessness? Beyond the appeal of the reasons offered at the outset, we can speculate that the main sticking point might be a matter not of logic, or philosophical analysis, or textual exegesis, but simply a widespread everyday intuition that those who overpower their fears are to be greatly admired—they are achieving something that most of us believe is far beyond ourselves—making it jarring and unattractively unappreciative to suggest that these paragons are actually beset by *vice* and at best only *progressing toward* virtue.

But this suggestion deserves to be accepted without antagonism, as it is compatible with intuitive admiration for the fear-overcoming striver for virtue. Why not concede that, while persons possessing fully virtuous traits are rightly to be celebrated as our role models, admiration is also called forth by strenuous efforts to fight through obstacles and move in the direction of virtue? Why deny the laudable, impressive achievements of those who experience and overcome fear, or that they deserve recognition for their trait of imperfect courage (or maybe of some distinct related virtue involving determination, fortitude, or willpower)? In sum, why can there not be a second, distinct warrant for admiration in the realm of character?

It is not even clear that true courage as fearlessness ought to be deemed as impressively heroic as this arduous fear-overcoming. Consider a different trait that bears some relation to courage: selflessness. Selflessness sometimes involves a *deliberate* choice to set aside one's own self-interests: despite full awareness of the stakes for oneself, one makes the tough call. Selflessness can also be *unthinking*, however—spontaneous acts done out of concern for others, with neglect for self.[33] This latter variety is arguably a purer, more ideal strain of selflessness, as the stakes for self are never even taken notice of. It may also be easier to attain, as the outcome of training aimed at focusing attention on certain situations rather than mainly at absorbing ideals of honor and exemplars of selfless choice to be effortfully emulated. Yet the former variety, of the deliberate sort, may therefore be, precisely because of its imperfection, more awe-inspiring and meritorious due to the difficulty brought by the awareness involved, and the consequent need for direct strength of will.

Courageous conduct may, similarly, be reachable by two roads—confronting the dangers mentally, feeling the fears, yet still choosing to persevere, on the one hand; and the less conscious courage as fearlessness, avoiding a full psychological confrontation with the fearsome dimensions of one's situation, on the other. Some people might be better suited to one than the other. Training might differ for each, and the latter may possess great untapped potential at this point. It may also represent a higher, more desirable ideal for humans to strive for. Still, though, the former—courage as fear-overcoming—may be a more demanding and toilsome achievement, and in that respect more praiseworthy. The perfectly brave, or generous, or temperate person arguably has it easy. With reason permeating her soul, her behaviors and choices naturally, habitually, follow the right courses. Perhaps she needs to beware of lapses caused by systemic weaknesses like illness or fatigue—lapses that might possibly undermine her virtuous habit, multiplying or snowballing on subsequent occasions of choice—but this job of virtue maintenance ought not be taxing, and therefore seems unlikely to elicit much admiration. On the other hand, the person who faces strong subjective headwinds in facing dangers, or bodily temptations, or calls for parting with things of value, earns widespread esteem for making an effort to persist in the face of their relentless force.

So we ought to keep distinct in our minds two issues: what exactly constitutes the human perfections that particular virtuous character traits represent, and what moral evaluations are appropriate for those who demonstrate either these virtues or the imperfect states that resemble them. Let us certainly honor and applaud the strivers for courage, especially those who not only fight the good fights against terror but even prevail. But let us not allow this commendable impulse to lead us to distort and dilute our conception of courage. If we can accept a modestly enriched notion of the possible individual achievements in the realm of virtue, we will encounter no inconsistency between rightly lauding those who overcome fear and still remaining steadfast to an understanding of courage as fearlessness.

Acknowledgments

I am grateful for the insightful feedback provided on an earlier version of this chapter by, among others, Julia Driver, Chris Eberle, Shannon French, Bob Fullinwider, P. J. Ivanhoe, Iddo Landau, George Lucas, Ariel Meirav, Martha Nussbaum, Danny Statman, and Roger Wertheimer. The views expressed in this document are those of the author(s) and do not reflect the policy or position of the U.S. Naval Academy, Department of the Navy, the Department of Defense, or the U.S. Government.

Notes

1 Talk of "mastering" or "overcoming" one's feelings of fear may strike some as inconsistent with Aristotle's emphasis on the consonance between action and feeling in the virtuous person. The more Kantian notion of struggling against, and overpowering, fear has certainly come to infuse common understandings of courage, and for good reason. It is difficult to see any overall constructive role for ongoing fear on the battlefield or in other dangerous circumstances. Hence what might have seemed the Aristotelian ideal, a person who is animated by some sort of productive, well-tuned fear, has yielded somewhat to *control*-of-fear conceptions.

2 Some commentators emphasize this as a distinctively *evaluative* element of the emotion (e.g., Nussbaum 2001).

3 Citations to "EE" are to Aristotle's *Eudemian Ethics*, with section references drawn from Michael Woods' (1992) translation of books I, II, and VIII, and from the Harris Rackham (1981) translation.

4 Citations to "NE" are to Aristotle's *Nicomachean Ethics*, with section references drawn from Terence Irwin's (1985) translation.

5 For biologists, "The main function of fear and anxiety is to act as a signal of danger, threat, or motivational conflict, and to trigger appropriate adaptive responses" (Steimer 2002, 233); "Fear is commonly thought to have adaptive functions in terms of both cognition and behavioral response" (Adolphs 2013, R85). In psychology, fear's functionality exemplifies the textbook principle that "emotions normally help us function efficiently and in a way that increases our chances of survival" (*Principles of Social Psychology* 2015, 92); see also, Paul Ekman Group (n.d.).

6 I have personally heard such attestations from colleagues at the U.S. Naval Academy. See also Urmson 1988, 66 ("Any sane man is going to be afraid from time to time in battle"). But there is scholarly support for this conventional wisdom. See, for example, Ranson 1949 ("The trite saying 'everybody is afraid in combat'" captures the "extreme, repeated, and continued battle fear" that produces the "normal battle reaction"); Miller 1999, 256 ("No one . . . doubts that soldiers are afraid. . . . Commanders have always assumed the fearfulness of their soldiers"); Miller 2002, 130 ("fear is ubiquitous in battle"); Keegan 1983, 70–71 (attributing to "the leading historian of the European Theatre, General S.L.A. Marshall," the core view "that the battlefield is a place of terror," that "fear is general among men" in battle).

7 Vigani (2017, 326–27), at one point in her wide-ranging analysis, conjectures, similarly, that fearlessness might be attainable through the controlled direction of

attention away from the potential personal harms that one faces, while one still maintains some sort of background awareness of these risks. She does not develop in any detail her insight that, for at least one kind of brave person, during an episode of exercising that virtue, "[t]he focus is on the task at hand; in the moment there is not head space, so to speak, for fear of the potential costs." The account provided in this chapter can be seen as a substantially more elaborated and specific set of claims about the mechanism by which fear can be eluded via what can be described as the management of attention.

8 The concept of shallow cognizing deployed in this chapter is drawn from "Shallow Cognizing for Self-Control over Emotion & Desire" (St Cross Special Ethics Seminar public presentation, Oxford University, Jan 2023) and "Shallow Cognizing and Virtue" (European Society for Philosophy & Psychology, Sep 2021). Its conception of mental mechanics dovetails with some theoretical approaches that are current in psychology, including neuropsychology. For instance, Joseph LeDoux's influential conception (see, e.g., 2020) shares the fundamental idea, traceable back to the Stoics, that emotion activation is predicated upon cognitive perception and reasoning. It also shares the view that these cognitive processes are generally subconscious and selectively employ subsets of memory-stored representational resources (including not only propositional knowledge but also imagistic reaction patterns developed in the course of prior experience) that get activated by the world situation as construed in the moment. In LeDoux's model, the collection of cognitive assets employed in producing an emotional response comprises the active 'object in context' schema, the active emotion schema, and the active self schema. (LeDoux contends that this cognitive processing gives rise along mostly distinct pathways to both subjective feelings and behavioral responses, as opposed to first producing feelings that then secondarily provoke behaviors; but that debate is not relevant to the concerns of this chapter.) In LeDoux's terms, the shallow cognizing that permits the bypassing of fear in displays of courage would seemingly occur via limitations in the fear *emotion schema* that would be activated and used in producing both feeling and behavior upon encountering a stimulus that is recognized as dangerous based upon the individual's prior experience. The phenomenon of shallow cognizing reveals that a person's fear schema is not a unitary whole, all of which is always activated; parts of it can be productively kept dormant by the capable shallow cognizer. At the same time, her 'object in context' and self schemas can be uncompromised, allowing her to maintain the fully rational understanding of the situation and of her place in it that facilitates a courageous response.

9 This "perspect" model of cognition is elaborated in, for example, Lengbeyer 2007.

10 This shallow cognizing avoidance of disturbing ideas should be more difficult when one is faced perceptually with inescapable disturbing sensory inputs. It is one thing to think, say, about the prospects of torture if one should be captured by the enemy—shallow cognizing seems readily available here—and something very different once one has been not only captured but also is being connected to the torture apparatus. Courage as fearlessness might be unattainable in such circumstances, except for perhaps the most exceptional practitioners of shallow cognizing. Indeed, this distinction might offer a way of making new sense of Aristotle's claim that humans cannot be asked to be fearless in the face of earthquakes and tidal waves (NE 1115b25–30).

11 Though it seems possible to initiate them *occasionally* with conscious awareness, an initiation that is chosen intentionally or perhaps merely observed knowingly.

12 A comparable, but distinct, phenomenon of emotion management that has been termed "emotion compression" by Olúfẹ́mi Táíwò (2020) involves managing "the manner and intensity with which emotions are expressed," rather than the emotions themselves.

13 For the combat situation, for example, one might leave dormant one's knowledge about the torture that awaits one if captured, or the torment of being hit by the enemy's flamethrower, or the devastation that is in store if the enemy prevails.

14 Pears, too (2004, 10), attributes to Aristotle a "conviction that in a truly virtuous life there must be complete harmony between desires and actions."

15 Brady (2005, 192) is blocked from seeing possibilities like shallow cognizing by her reasoning that (i) reacting rationally to a dangerous situation (as required for virtue) demands "recognition of the likelihood of harm"; that (ii) this cannot be a "simply intellectual" understanding, "[g]iven the role of emotion in judgment"; and hence that (iii) it entails "feeling fear as the emotional recognition of the likely loss." Even if (i) is true, (ii) appears to be false, and thus (iii) does not follow. She goes on to reason, incorrectly, that "Aristotle has already ruled out the possibility that the courageous person can simply avoid the pain of expecting death, when he counts the fearlessness of the experienced and hopeful as merely imitations of courage" (193). If, as I contend, there are ways to avoid this painful fear other than eliminating awareness of the danger, then Aristotle's dismissal of those two examples of pseudo-courage due to their lacking full awareness of the danger does not warrant the conclusion that his view blocks the virtuously brave from avoiding the fear of death. Finally, it is not even clear that eliminating the desire for safety suffices for brave action if one's feelings of fear cannot be conquered. Miller (1999, 247–48; 2000, 110–11) recounts an affecting report from a union officer in the U.S. Civil War who encountered a soldier who was apparently wholehearted in his desire to risk his life in battle, but whose repeated struggles to move ahead were undermined by his disobedient, fear-enfeebled legs.

16 Pears (2004, 11) does allow that the brave person might subsequently gain new knowledge that prompts a revised deliberation, reviving the fear-arousing calculation of negative outcomes. But this wrinkle seemingly does not alter the basic picture or what it says about whether courage entails fearlessness.

17 Pears is sensitive to this potential problem for his account: the person encountering danger "discounts the counter goal [death and wounds, for example], but *not as an irrelevance—he might act more cautiously because of it*—he discounts it only as something that is going to have any further effect on his general response to his predicament" (2004, 10–11, emphasis added). Unfortunately, this attempt to stipulate away the difficulty is not supported by Pears with any explanatory argument.

18 See NE 1105b20+: "By feelings I mean appetite, anger, fear, confidence, envy, joy, love, hate, longing, jealousy, pity, in general whatever implies pleasure or pain."

19 I am indebted to Martha Nussbaum for this suggestion.

20 This is the influential conception of philosopher-historian of science Thomas Kuhn, presented most famously in *The Structure of Scientific Revolutions* (1962). A very similar account of this particular feature of scientific practice, but cast in terms

of the "positive heuristic" to be followed by scientists working within a "research programme," is given by Imre Lakatos (for instance, in his 1978).

21 For example, Pears 1980.

22 This explanation fits the Brady (2005) template for explaining the virtue of courage, in that it contemplates the refinement, and even elimination, of desire. By contrast, an explanation of temperance paralleling the account offered in this chapter would allow for bodily desires to persist, yet the yearnings that come from them to be purged by shallow cognizing of the desires' objects. A desire-modification account might be superior for temperance, though still inferior for courage, in light of the more central place of desire, strictly speaking, in the vices that are overcome by temperance compared to the vices that are overcome by courage: the pains of (imperfect) temperance typically come from resisted, unfulfilled desires, while those from (imperfect) courage typically come from the emotion of fear.

23 This statement is a simplification. The stream of cognizing is continually producing periods of temporary forgetfulness about matters that are not relevant to the immediate pragmatic context at hand, even if those matters sometimes rapidly return to awareness afterward. (See Lengbeyer 2007.) The point in the text ought to be taken in the more macro sense used in everyday conversation: our rationally aware warfighter is conventionally said to remain aware of the enemy gunfire throughout the firefight episode, even though, when more finely sliced, that awareness can be seen to be temporarily interrupted by periods where attention is fully absorbed elsewhere (for instance, on navigating treacherous terrain or assisting an injured comrade).

24 For example, Schmidt et al. 2008.

25 Dr. Brad Johnson, Professor of Psychology, Department of Leadership, Ethics, & Law, United States Naval Academy, personal communication, April 22, 2024. See also NATO Research and Technology Organisation 2012, 4–2 ("SOF needs individuals who can cope with extreme stress. The goal of selection is to identify individuals whose limits are higher than those of other people"). Researchers are working on teasing out the contributions of the various components of psychopathy—fearlessness generally thought to be among these—to combat-related behaviors and dispositions, such as decreased vulnerability to PTSD or depression. See, for example, Bowes et al. 2021; Kavish et al. 2021, 471; Anestis et al. 2017; Landay and Frieder 2018.

26 Training and real-life experience ought to reduce fear in multiple ways: (1) letting one learn how to practice shallow cognizing effectively; (2) instilling precedent action routines that become so habitual that they get activated and reenacted automatically even before fear-provoking cognizing can gain momentum; (3) providing situational familiarity that removes fear of the unknown and indicates less cause for fear than had previously been thought, thereby partly undermining the cognitive basis for the fear.

27 This suggestion is due to Martha Nussbaum.

28 Similarly, it seems hardly plausible to suppose, in my own case, that unconscious fears (of infirmity or earlier death) play a significant role in motivating my exercise runs when there is a far more present and pressing *contrary* fear that I experience, of the extended physical and psychological suffering that each run will bring. Of course, this is no *proof* that those unconscious fears are not operative—it could be

alleged that it is only with their assistance that my pressing fears of suffering can be overcome—but why multiply these highly speculative unconscious entities when there seem to be sufficient explanatory resources in the standard folk-psychological motivations toolbox that contains desires, values, ideals, plans, and such like?

29 One possibility here might be to develop an account parallel to the one offered in Lengbeyer 2005.

30 To approach this from a different angle, if soldiers were to learn to experience no fear by coming to evaluate their own lives or bodily health as nothing worth caring about all that much, then how much less would they think of others' well-being, and how much less motivated would they be to protect that well-being and to restrain themselves from violating it?

31 Citations to "Rhetoric" are to the J. H. Freese translation (1926) of Aristotle's *Rhetoric*.

32 Further, it seems that even if it were the case that the fearless could not draw upon feelings of compassion, they would still be able to act scrupulously and compassionately toward others, guided by their ethical principles, habits, and commitments.

33 See Lengbeyer 2005.

Bibliography

Adolphs, Ralph. 2013. "The Biology of Fear." *Current Biology* 23: R79–R93.

Anestis, Joye C., Tiffany M. Harrop, Bradley A. Green, and Michael D. Anestis. 2017. "Psychopathic Personality Traits as Protective Factors against the Development of Post-Traumatic Stress Disorder Symptoms in a Sample of National Guard Combat Veterans." *Journal of Psychopathology and Behavioral Assessment* 39: 1–10

Aristotle. 1926. *Rhetoric*. Translated by John Henry Freese. Cambridge: Harvard University Press; London: William Heinemann.

Aristotle. 1981. *Eudemian Ethics*. Translated by Harris Rackham. Based upon *Aristotle in 23 Volumes*, Vol. 20. Cambridge, MA, Harvard University Press; London, William Heinemann. http://www.perseus.tufts.edu/hopper/text?doc=Perseus:text:1999.01.0050.

Aristotle. 1985. *Nicomachean Ethics*. Translated by Terence Irwin. Indianapolis: Hackett.

Aristotle. 1992. *Eudemian Ethics*. Translated by Michael Woods. 2nd ed. Oxford: Clarendon Press.

Bowes, Shauna M., April L. Brown, William W. Thompson, Martin Sellbom, and Scott O. Lilienfeld. 2021. "Do Psychopathic Traits Statistically Protect against PTSD? A Retrospective Study of Vietnam Veterans." *Journal of Personality Disorders* 35: 127–144.

Brady, Michelle E. 2005. "The Fearlessness of Courage." *Southern Journal of Philosophy* 43: 189–211.

Holmes, Richard. (1985) 2004. *Acts of War: The Behaviour of Men in Battle*. 2nd ed. Formerly *Firing Line*. London: Weidenfeld & Nicolson.

Kavish, Nicholas, Danielle Boisvert, Eric M. Cooke, Richard H. Lewis, Matthias Woeckener, Jessica Wells, and Todd A. Armstrong. 2021. "Further Evaluation of the Associations Between Psychopathic Traits and Symptoms of PTSD and Depression in a Nonclinical Sample." *Journal of Personality Disorders* 35: 469–480.

Keegan, John. 1983. *The Face of Battle: A Study of Agincourt, Waterloo and the Somme*. London: Pimlico.
Kuhn, Thomas. 1962. *The Structure of Scientific Revolutions*. Chicago: University of Chicago Press.
Lakatos, Imre. 1978. *The Methodology of Scientific Research Programmes: Philosophical Papers, vol. 1*. Cambridge: Cambridge University Press.
Landay, Karen, and Rachel E. Frieder. 2018. "Cold-Blooded Killers? Rethinking Psychopathy in the Military." In Peter D. Harms & Pamela L. Perrewé, editors, *Occupational Stress and Well-Being in Military Contexts* (Research in Occupational Stress and Well Being, vol. 16), pp. 23–47. Leeds: Emerald Publishing.
LeDoux, Joseph E. 2020. "Thoughtful Feelings." *Current Biology* 30: R617–R634.
Lengbeyer, Lawrence. 2005. "Selflessness and Cognition." *Ethical Theory & Moral Practice* 8: 411–435.
Lengbeyer, Lawrence. 2007. "Situated Cognition: The Perspect Model." In David Spurrett, Don Ross, Harold Kincaid, & Lynn Stephens, editors, *Distributed Cognition and the Will: Individual Volition and Social Context*, pp. 227–254. Cambridge, MA: MIT Press.
Miller, William Ian. 1999. "Fear, Weak Legs, and Running Away: A Soldier's Story." In S. A. Bandes, editor, *The Passions of Law*, ch. 9, pp. 241–264. New York: New York University Press.
Miller, William Ian. 2002. *The Mystery of Courage*. Cambridge, MA: Harvard University Press.
NATO Research and Technology Organisation. 2012. "Psychological and Physiological Selection of Military Special Operations Forces Personnel." *Final Report of Task Group HFM-171*.
Nussbaum, Martha C. 2001. *Upheavals of Thought: The Intelligence of Emotions*. Cambridge: Cambridge University Press.
Paul Ekman Group. n.d. "Fear." https://www.paulekman.com/universal-emotions/what-is-fear/.
Pears, David. 1980. "Courage as a Mean." In Amélie Rorty, editor, *Essays on Aristotle's Ethics*, pp. 171–187. Oakland, CA: University of California Press.
Pears, David. 2004. "The Anatomy of Courage." *Social Research* 71: 1–12.
Principles of Social Psychology. 2015. University of Minnesota Libraries.
Ranson, Stephen W. 1949. "The Normal Battle Reaction: Its Relation to the Pathologic Battle Reaction." *Bulletin of the U.S. Army Medical Department* 9 (suppl.): 3–11. Reprinted in Frederick R. Hanson, ed., *Combat Psychiatry: Experiences in the North African and Mediterranean Theaters of Operation, American Ground Forces, World War II*, ch. 1. Washington, DC: U.S. Government Printing Office. https://achh.army.mil/history/book-wwii-combatphsych-section1-1.
Schmidt, Norman B., J. Anthony Richey, Michael J. Zvolensky, and Jon K. Maner. 2008. "Exploring Human Freeze Responses to a Threat Stressor." *Journal of Behavior Therapy and Experimental Psychiatry* 39: 292–304.
Steimer, Thierry. 2002. "The Biology of Fear- and Anxiety-Related Behaviors." *Dialogues in Clinical Neuroscience* 4: 231–249.
Táíwò, Olúfẹ́mi O. 2020. "Stoicism (as Emotional Compression) Is Emotional Labor." *Feminist Philosophy Quarterly* 6.
Urmson, J. O. 1988. *Aristotle's Ethics*. Oxford: Blackwell.
Vigani, Denise. 2017. "Aristotle's Account of Courage." *History of Philosophy Quarterly* 34: 313–330.

5

Moderating Fear After Trauma?

An Aristotelian Analysis

Lily M. Abadal

While the last decade has generated an increase in research into Aristotelian virtue ethics, there is a notable lack of work that considers how trauma impacts character development. As Nancy Snow (2020) puts it, there is a need for "deep and nuanced studies of various kind of trauma, how they can undermine capacities for virtue development, how moral repair can take place, and what virtues might be available to members of different groups who have been traumatized" (Snow, 2020, 31). Essentially, the scholars at the center of contemporary investigations into virtue ethics have been largely silent on these topics. The first reason for this, of course, might be because the notion of trauma itself is a modern construct which would have been foreign to ancient philosophical discourse. Thus, those relying on an Aristotelian framework of the virtues would need to heavily extrapolate from Aristotle's framework to conduct such an investigation. Second, any exploration into trauma requires some familiarity with the relevant psychological literature on trauma and a basic understanding of the neuroscience which informs it.

This chapter will aim to begin this conversation as it specifically relates to the moral psychology of fear post trauma given the assumption that habituation and the exercise of virtue require moderation of emotion. In other words, this chapter explores how the moral psychology of fear is impacted by trauma, preventing either the acquisition of virtue or the development of virtue. It specifically considers the kinds of neurological changes those who have endured trauma can experience and how these changes can impact judgments about moral objects. These changes, which can result in automatic, heightened sensitivity to detect and respond to fear-inducing threats, will be synthesized into the framework of Neo-Aristotelian virtue ethics. At the culmination of this chapter, I will have merely scratched the surface of two philosophical questions that merit much further exploration. First, how can trauma affect virtue development? Second, how can models of virtue do justice to the experiences of individuals whose lives have involved trauma? Central to answering both these questions lies a nuanced understanding of fear and why the moderation of it is essential for character development.

This chapter will be divided into four parts. First, I must outline, albeit briefly, Aristotle's account of virtue acquisition as outlined in the *Nicomachean Ethics*. Next, I will present some relevant psychological and neurological research on trauma. Third, I will aim to synthesize the Aristotelian account outlined with the neurological research presented and how this synthesis bears weight on the two central questions I just outlined above. Finally, I will draw conclusions and present some further questions for investigation.

Before beginning this inquiry, however, it is necessary to further justify it. It seems to me that responsible Aristotelians ought to take into account recent research on those events that pose some threat to virtuous character development seriously as it is part of the naturalist enterprise to consider new knowledge gained from empirical investigation and integrate it into existing theories accordingly. This present chapter is an attempt to do so.

Aristotelian Account of Virtue Development

The Aristotelian understanding of character development has three central themes relevant to our discussion of trauma. The first of these is the emphasis placed on habituation. Virtue development requires the exercise of virtue-like behavior. Over time, and with the right intentions, this practice should yield the development of virtuous dispositions—the proclivity to think, feel, and act like a virtuous person. The aspiring acolyte begins this journey in an akratic state, desiring to be virtuous and not yet having the strength to behave like a virtuous person (NE VII.8, 1151a5–25). This is followed by the practiced, yet merely continent, pupil who can fulfill the demands of virtue without the proper or corresponding affections (NE VII.9, 1151a30–1151b30). Finally, the student of virtue can be so aptly called "virtuous" once she exhibits virtuous behavior and enjoys carrying out that virtuous behavior. This is often described in the literature as seeking "virtue for virtue's sake."[1] All of this describes a process. In other words, virtue is not natural or innate. Instead, it is developed and acquired over time. Throughout this developmental process, a person learns how to temper their emotions, carefully attuned over time by the guidance of practical reason.

This leads us to the second theme, which is often characterized as a unique feature of Aristotelian virtue ethics when compared to both Kantian deontology and utilitarianism: the important role of right feeling or emotion. In other words, virtue is found in the mean between two extreme states of feeling (NE II.6, 1106a15–25). Courage, for instance, denotes a mean between rashness and cowardice—when someone acts rashly it means they do not have enough fear to act well, while cowardice implies that they have too much fear to act well (NE II.7, 1104b20). As a result, the virtuous person has a practiced and appropriate emotional response to various stimuli in their environment. They are not overwhelmed with anxiety when asked to speak in front of a crowd spontaneously. Similarly, they do not become excessively flustered when challenged by a peer.[2] They would experience the emotion that allows them to act well in that given scenario—fearful enough to be careful with their words but not so fearful that they recoil at the request to speak. This is precisely why the virtues must be developed over time. This ideal emotional state that makes way for it cannot simply be commanded at will. Judiciousness alone is far from virtue.

Understanding that virtuous action requires right judgment, the ability to temper desire, and the practiced feeling and expression of emotion, it is no wonder that Aristotle held what is known as the "unity of the virtues" thesis.[3] In other words, a person could not be courageous if they are lacking in temperance or prudence. Similarly, they could not be temperate or prudent if they are lacking in courage. Absence of one virtue will denote the absence of the other. As a result, and if Aristotle is correct, the virtues would develop in tandem. Courage cannot be developed without practical reason nor practical reason without courage. While this is widely accepted as a feature of Aristotelian ethics, there is debate in the secondary literature about whether Aristotle is accurate in positing such a unity—a debate we don't have the space in this chapter to engage.[4]

Nonetheless, we can imagine how this plays out by considering a trite example. Suppose Peter is a professor and is getting ready to deliver a guest lecture at a very prestigious university. As he opens his laptop to project his slides and pull up his notes, he realizes that his computer has died. He has no notes or slides for the lecture and is woefully unprepared to give his talk off the cuff. Discerning what to do next, exercising practical reason, will be quite difficult for Peter if he is overwhelmingly fearful about his present circumstance and how bad he may look in front of his peers. Here, the experience of fear, particularly if it is overwhelming, will have a direct impact on whether Peter can think through his next steps and exercise his best judgment about how to handle his mistake. Even if Peter were able to temper his fear enough to think about and judge the best course of action, courage would still be required to carry out that action. All of this is to say, it would take a great deal of courage to admit the mistake, collect oneself, and deliver the lecture well despite the fear that it would go poorly due to not having the materials. On the contrary, a person lacking courage might exercise poor judgment in this scenario—deciding to fake a sudden illness and back out of the lecture.

PTSD, DTD, and Trauma's Impact on the Brain

Now that I have outlined the basic themes of Aristotle's ethics relevant to our discussion on trauma, we can further explore trauma itself and how trauma changes normal neural processing. When people speak of trauma in ordinary language, they include a wide array of experiences. It would not be odd for a high school student to describe their breakup with a romantic partner as "traumatic" or for a person working under a toxic manager in corporate America to describe the experience as "traumatizing." In this section, I make an intentional choice to align with the clinical usage and understanding, which employs a much narrower use and appropriation of the term.[5] Our exploration of trauma will begin there.

According to the DSM-V's diagnostic criteria for post-traumatic stress disorder (PTSD), traumatic stress involves exposure to "actual or threatened death, serious injury, or sexual violence."[6] This exposure need not be firsthand; individuals can be negatively impacted by events they witness. In other words, trauma can result from third-party exposure. For instance, a child who witnesses violent acts against their mother could experience trauma. Even the revelation of physical abuse suffered by their mother could trigger traumatic stress. The use of "could" in this example is significant. While experiencing a traumatic event, whether firsthand or as a bystander, is a necessary condition for PTSD, it is not sufficient. There are instances where exposure to such events does not lead to subsequent psychological distress. However, if the traumatic event does induce physiological distress, it manifests through intrusion symptoms, avoidance, negative alterations in cognition and mood, and changes in arousal and reactivity.[7] Let's look at these symptoms more closely.

Intrusion symptoms include unwanted and unannounced recollections of the traumatic event; they can present as dreams, flashbacks, or involuntary thoughts (Contreras, 2024). As Contreras explains, these memories could manifest as images, sounds, smells, or any sensory aspect of the experience (Contreras, 2024, p. 155). These intrusions often lead victims to feel as though they are reliving the trauma they suffered—like they are unable to escape it. Many victims report that intrusive memories can disrupt daily functioning, causing distress and impairing the individual's ability to concentrate or engage in everyday activities. Moreover, the persistent recurrence of these intrusive symptoms can further exacerbate feelings of helplessness and anxiety, perpetuating the cycle of trauma-related distress. In addition to inescapable, intrusive thoughts, traumatized individuals may also become avoidant of the pain inflicted by the trauma. We can understand avoidance in two different respects. First, avoidance can be physical. Individuals could physically avoid situations and circumstances that engender reminders of past trauma. For instance, if someone was physically assaulted in the parking lot at their university, they might avoid that parking lot or avoid going back to school altogether. However, the avoidance can also be psychological. Fear of facing the trauma again or feeling the pain from that experience can result in dissociation, which "allows individuals to temporarily protect the mind from experiences that overwhelm their capacity for cognitive processing through a passive disengagement from reality and a compartmentalization of behaviors, thoughts, memories, and feelings related to trauma" (Schimmenti, 2018, p. 553). Dissociation can result in feeling disconnected from one's body or in having difficulty recognizing, naming, and understanding bodily sensations. Someone with dissociative symptoms, for example, may experience intense stress and anxiety—marked by an increase in heart rate, heightened startle reflex, and so on—but appear calm.

Victims of trauma may also develop persistent and exaggerated cognitive distortions, including negative beliefs about themselves or the world. These beliefs may include pervasive mistrust toward others and a distorted sense of self-worth, hindering their ability to form meaningful connections and pursue personal fulfillment. For instance, trauma victims may come to believe that "no one can be trusted" or that they "will never experience happiness again." This sometimes results in what clinicians refer to as "moral injury," which is often comorbid with PTSD. As Carey and Hodgson define it,

> Moral injury is a trauma-related syndrome caused by the physical, psychological, social, and spiritual impact of grievous moral transgressions, or violations, of an individual's deeply-held moral beliefs and/or ethical standards due to: (i) an individual perpetrating, failing to prevent, bearing witness to, or learning about inhumane acts which result in the pain, suffering or death of others, and which fundamentally challenges the moral integrity of an individual, organization or community, and/or (ii) the subsequent experience and feelings of utter betrayal of what is right caused by trusted individuals who hold legitimate authority. (2018, 2)

Ultimately, moral injury reflects a profound rupture in an individual's sense of moral integrity and trust in others, exacerbating the psychological toll of trauma.

Furthermore, victims of trauma may find themselves consistently experiencing negative emotional states like anger, fear, or horror. These mood changes are closely linked with heightened arousal and reactivity, especially if the individual experiences intense fear following the trauma. According to the DSM-V (2013), notable alterations in this regard may include hypervigilance, an exaggerated startle response, and difficulties with concentration. From this, it is evident that individuals who have experienced trauma are more prone to perceiving the world as inherently unsafe, leading to a heightened propensity for fear and a persistent need to vigilantly monitor their surroundings for potential threats to their well-being.

This is especially the case when children experience trauma, leading to the distinction of developmental trauma disorder (DTD). As Daniel Cruz explains:

> the DTD diagnosis is intended to classify the complex and pervasive exposure to life-threatening events that (1) occur during sensitive periods of infant and child development; (2) disrupt interpersonal attachments; (3) compromise an individual's safety and security; and (4) alter cognitive, behavioral, and emotional control (Ford, 2017, 2021; Spinazzola et al., 2018). The diagnosis directly pertains to complex neurobehavioral disturbances, referring to the broad range of changes to the nervous system that occur in children who have been exposed to recurrent episodes of life-threatening events, such as violence in the home or prolonged separation from primary caregivers. (2023, 23)

Ultimately, DTD is characterized by ongoing and persistent exposure to adverse childhood experiences during critical periods of development. These adverse experiences fundamentally alter the child's sense of security and safety in the world, which may lead to perpetual feelings of fear and the same negative physiological responses that accompany that exaggerated experience of fear—hypervigilance, increased startle response, and difficulty concentrating, and distorted cognition or perception (Cruz, 2023). While PTSD can manifest at any age following a traumatic event, primarily focusing on specific symptoms triggered by the trauma, DTD encompasses broader developmental disruptions, including pervasive attachment difficulties (Spinazzola, 2021). As a result, they each necessitate tailored approaches to diagnosis and intervention.

We can see from what we have reviewed so far that most of these effects of traumatic stress relate to fear. This is because trauma, either developmental or acute, fundamentally changes neural activity in response to environmental stimuli. We can appreciate how drastic these changes are by comparing them to normal neural processes. As Bessel van der Kolk explains:

> Living creatures more or less automatically respond to incoming sensory information with relatively stable neuronal and hormonal activation, resulting in consistent action patterns: predictable behaviors that can be elicited over and over again in response to similar input. Under ordinary conditions the executive and symbolizing capacities of the prefrontal cortex can modify these behaviors by providing the ability to observe, know, and predict by inhibiting, organizing, and modulating those automatic responses. This allows people to manage and preserve their relationships with their fellow human beings on whom they so profoundly depend for meaning, company, affirmation, protection, and connection. (2006, 278)

These processes allow people to be flexible, take into account context, detail, and novelty, enabling them to produce normal appropriate responses to their environment. Victims of trauma experience a disruption in these normal processes. In traumatized individuals, the executive capacities of the prefrontal cortex give way to the fight, flight, or freeze response of the amygdala. As Van der Kolk notes:

> Exposed to traumatic reminders, subjects had cerebral blood flow increases in the right medial orbitofrontal cortex, insula, amygdala, and anterior temporal pole, and a relative deactivation in the left anterior prefrontal cortex, specifically in Broca's area, the expressive speech center in the brain, the area necessary to communicate what one is thinking and feeling. [. . .] When people are reminded of a personal trauma they activate brain regions that support intense emotions, while decreasing activity of brain structures involved in the inhibition of emotions and the translation of experience into communicable language. (2006, 277)

One important thing to note about these neurological impacts of PTSD and DTD is that they are beyond conscious control. As Van Der Kolk explains, "emotions occur not by conscious choice, but by disposition: limbic brain structures, such as the amygdala tag incoming stimuli and determine their emotional significance" (2006, 277). Ultimately, reminders of the past automatically activate certain neurobiological responses beyond the realm of conscious comprehension. As a result, these limbic brain structures cannot be directed at will. The readiness of the limbic system to tag certain stimuli is informed by past experiences and the significance of those past experiences, particularly ones that threatened safety and survival.

Trauma's Impact on the Virtues

Now we are positioned well enough to consider the first question posed at the start of this chapter: how can trauma affect virtue development? There are three symptoms of trauma, which we covered above, that I argue, pose an especial threat to the virtues: (1) avoidance (2) changes in arousal and reactivity (3) negative alterations in cognition and mood. Let's consider each of these in turn and how they impact the exercise and development of the virtues.

I will begin by considering avoidance symptoms. If we recall our brief outline of the Aristotelian framework earlier, virtues are not innate qualities but are rather cultivated through deliberate practice and habituation. To develop courage, a student of virtue must undergo repeated exposure to situations that evoke fear, striving to embody virtuous behavior despite internal struggles. This process eventually leads to the development of a habitual disposition toward courageous action. However, individuals who have endured trauma may grapple with avoidance tendencies, which in some cases could curtail their opportunities for moral growth. Such individuals consciously evade circumstances reminiscent of their traumatic past and may extend this avoidance to environments perceived as generally dangerous or intimidating. Consequently, their ability to cultivate courage and engage in virtuous conduct may become restricted. Without exposure to situations that induce fear, there isn't an opportunity to act well despite it.

We can see how this process plays out by exploring why exposure to fearful situations is necessary for moral formation. Imagine a scenario in which a parent strives to shield their child from any situations in which their child will feel fearful or anxious. If the child is afraid to take a difficult test, the parent allows them to stay home to avoid taking the test. If the child is afraid to perform in the school play, the parent calls their teacher saying the child is sick. By shielding the child from opportunities to feel fear, they also limit their child's character development. The child will not have opportunities to practice feeling fear—to habituate their thinking and feeling in circumstances that make them afraid. As a result, they might continue into their adult lives being avoidant of situations that induce that same sort of fear, stress, or anxiety and be incapable of acting courageously when they inevitably do encounter situations that evoke those emotions. A much more exaggerated, but similar, scenario unfolds for victims of trauma who have avoidance symptoms following a traumatic experience. By shielding themselves to avoid the painful reminders of past wounds or feelings that are reminiscent of their trauma response, they can minimize or even eliminate opportunities that could help train their fear and build courage. Thus, learning to moderate fear after trauma can be complicated by avoidant coping mechanisms.

While avoidance can preclude opportunities to cultivate and maintain the virtue of courage, changes in arousal and reactivity can make it more likely for victims of trauma to experience excessive fear. For example, hypervigilance results in an increased proclivity to scan and find perceived threats in one's environment. Hypervigilant people may be more likely than others to see threats where they do not exist or to construe circumstances and individuals as threatening when they are not. Similarly, an exaggerated startle response heightens sensitivity to potential dangers, increasing the likelihood of reacting defensively or impulsively in situations perceived as hazardous. Consider a woman who has experienced domestic violence; her husband would frequently throw hard objects at her during heated arguments, resulting in significant injuries. Now, envision this woman engaging in a challenging discussion with a colleague. As her colleague reaches for a ceramic coffee cup during the conversation, the woman, because of her hypervigilance, is likely to automatically perceive this action as potentially threatening. In this scenario, her colleague had no indication that he would throw the cup, nor does he have a history of that sort of violence. In other words, he was just planning to drink coffee from the cup. However, her body has been trained to be extra sensitive to someone picking up hard objects during a conflict. It developed this sensitivity to protect her from dangerous threats to her safety. Consequently, when she picks up on this cue, her body enters fight or flight, she abruptly ends the conversation, and exits the room. The fear she experiences is automatic and overwhelming. Putting all of this together, the woman's trauma response may make it difficult to practically discern how to handle confrontation with her colleagues and to act accordingly.

Furthermore, hypervigilance can also cause cognitive distortions or exaggerated beliefs about what those perceived threats mean for them and how they should act in response. These beliefs shape personal narratives and the lens through which one interprets the world and others in it (Zare, 2019). We can imagine how exaggerated beliefs would manifest in everyday social interactions. For example, a hypervigilant person may interpret ambiguous social cues as signs of rejection or hostility, leading to exaggerated beliefs such as "everyone is out to get me" or "I am always being judged negatively." In a romantic relationship, this could manifest as an individual interpreting minor disagreements or moments of distance as evidence of impending abandonment or betrayal. This may lead to exaggerated beliefs such as "my partner doesn't really love me" or "they are going to leave me for someone else," despite lack of concrete evidence supporting these conclusions.

In both of these scenarios, we can see how cognitive distortions can give rise to fear and vice versa, both of which impact practical decision making.[8] As a result, individuals may display various behaviors that reflect their heightened perception of threat and their distorted interpretation of reality. For instance, someone who believes "everyone is out to get me" in social interactions may become overly defensive or withdrawn, avoiding social situations altogether to protect themselves from perceived threats. Similarly, in a romantic relationship, someone who believes "my partner doesn't really love me" may exhibit clingy or controlling behavior due to excessive fear of losing the relationship. As a result, they may constantly seek reassurance or become excessively jealous in response to imagined threats to the relationship. Ultimately, practical reasoning can become difficult when the situation being evaluated is filtered through these cognitive distortions.

Putting all of this together, we can conclude this section by saying that those who have experienced trauma may find it more difficult to develop and exercise virtue when they experience an automatic and exaggerated fear response. This can impair practical reasoning and complicate the possibility of acting courageously.

There are three important qualifications to make following this conclusion. First, it is important to note that fear is not always or necessarily an impediment to virtuous behavior or the cultivation of virtuous dispositions. In fact, feeling fear is an important part of acting courageously. If we consider Aristotle's virtue of the mean, the courageous person is not one who never feels fearful. Instead, they feel the right amount of fear appropriate to the circumstance. For if dangers or threats are legitimate ones, the right amount of fear will make one ready to take the appropriate course of action. For example, a firefighter who feels a healthy level of fear before entering a burning building is better prepared to respond effectively to the situation. This fear serves as a signal of the potential dangers present, motivating the firefighter to proceed with caution and follow proper safety protocols, ultimately enabling them to perform their duties courageously while minimizing unnecessary risks. Bringing all of this together, the point I have made above isn't that fear is an impediment to virtue. Rather, *excessive* fear and its corresponding hypervigilance and distorted cognitions are, by definition, impediments to virtuous behavior.

Second, when a person develops hypervigilance and avoidance as a result of trauma, these effects should not be thought of as static tendencies thereafter. Hypervigilance, avoidance, and the like are rather dynamic effects of trauma that may be experienced more or less intensely during different periods of a person's life. Different contexts, circumstances, and relationships can quell them or make them manifest. For instance, time and distance from the event in question may considerably mitigate the expression of hypervigilance.

Finally, if it is true that, in some cases, the effects of trauma may complicate the cultivation of virtue, this does not mean that the development of virtue is impossible, nor even that it is less available, all things considered, to those who have experienced trauma compared to those who have not. The fact that trauma effectively rewires the autonomic nervous system in ways that privilege a reactionary response from the amygdala should raise questions about how we conceive of frameworks for understanding virtue in general and about whether a classical Aristotelian conception of virtue is a helpful one in light of how many people experience trauma. Are there alternative ways to understand the exercise of virtue that do not demand unscathed neural circuitry or a miraculous upbringing?

How Can Victims of Trauma Become Virtuous?

Having acknowledged the challenges victims of trauma may encounter in exercising virtue due to heightened fear responses, it leads us to explore avenues for the post-traumatic development of virtues in the Aristotelian sense. In this section, we will consider how the path to virtue for victims of trauma may look a bit different. However, before outlining this path, we should first be reminded of the fact that, for Aristotle, the threshold for virtuous behavior is high—arguably unrealistically so—and there are several necessary conditions for it to take hold. One must have considerable monetary resources, excellent friends, adequate time for leisurely activity, and exemplary mentors, among many other things. This already makes the pool of potentially virtuous people quite small. I can imagine that Aristotle, particularly during his own time and context, would render it impossible for victims of tragedy to become virtuous in the strict sense, just like he would consider it impossible for those without monetary resources to become virtuous. That being said, I will suggest here that the pathway to virtue is much wider than Aristotle envisioned. So, while we will be exploring this through an Aristotelian lens, we will arrive at an answer that Aristotle himself would not give.

The pursuit of virtues in the aftermath of traumatic stress or developmental trauma may diverge from the path outlined by Aristotle. While numerous points of departure could be examined, I will focus our discussion here on an essential additional step: caring for the neurological processes that increase activity in the brain structures allowing for regulation of extreme emotions and deliberation. For those who have experienced trauma, and perhaps also for those who have not, accessing conditions which support practices of, and capacities for, emotional regulation can be a key building block in developing virtue. I will note two examples of methods that support emotional regulation in post-traumatic recovery here below; however, it is worth noting that these examples are not the only therapeutic supports that could be successful.

The first is prolonged exposure therapy (PE), which is in some cases used as a treatment for PTSD. Grounded in principles of cognitive-behavioral therapy (CBT), PE aims to alleviate the distress associated with some forms of traumatic memories by systematically confronting and processing them (Lewis et al., 2020). Through repeated exposure to feared stimuli or memories in a safe and controlled environment, individuals gradually habituate to the distressing material, fostering desensitization and emotional processing. Therapists guide clients through recounting their traumatic experiences in detail, encouraging them to confront avoided situations or triggers that evoke distress (Fao et al., 2007). Though not suitable for all contexts or cases, by facilitating the retrieval and reprocessing of traumatic memories, PE endeavors to promote cognitive restructuring and facilitate emotional regulation (Fao et al., 2007).

Eye Movement Desensitization and Reprocessing (EMDR) is also a widely utilized therapeutic approach in trauma treatment, offering a unique and effective method for addressing distressing memories and symptoms associated with traumatic experiences (Trentini et al., 2015). Founded on the premise that trauma-related distress stems from unprocessed memories, EMDR aims to facilitate adaptive processing of traumatic material through bilateral stimulation, typically achieved through eye movements or other forms of rhythmic stimulation (Shapiro, 2018). During EMDR sessions, individuals are guided to recall distressing memories while simultaneously engaging in bilateral stimulation, allowing for the reprocessing of traumatic experiences in a safe and controlled manner (Carlson et al., 1998). Through this process, EMDR seeks to foster the integration of fragmented traumatic memories into the individual's broader cognitive framework, ultimately promoting resolution of trauma-related symptoms and facilitating psychological healing. Both PE and EMDR attempt to restore neural circuitry by scaffolded exposure to traumatic memories. As a result, should be helpful in reducing negative, exaggerated moods and cognitive distortions.

Let me be clear that these are only two potential therapeutic approaches in the support of emotional regulation, which can be part of the picture of the development of post-traumatic virtue. They are not universally endorsed by all practitioners, nor need they be. My broader point is simply to begin to point to the need for a richer, empirically informed account of post-traumatic experiences that can begin to do justice to the emotional supports that can be valuable in the cultivation of virtue.

Conclusions and Questions for Future Exploration

My line of reasoning for this chapter has been to establish that virtuous activity requires moderation of fear—to exercise both prudence and courage. Traumatic stress and the hypervigilance, cognitive distortions, and avoidance symptoms it creates can complicate emotional lives, and with them, our paths to the cultivation of virtue. While Aristotle's own account did not address these realities clearly enough, we now have access to empirical information on some approaches to support those who have experienced traumas and can use this information to shape an account of virtue development more responsive to our actual conditions.

Notes

1 I use the "she" pronoun her for inclusivity. However, Aristotle would not have regarded women capable of virtue in the strict sense.

2 There is significant debate in recent virtue ethics literature surrounding situationism, questioning if virtue does truly carry across all contexts as I suggest here. For more on this, see Snow, Nancy E., and Franco V. Trivigno. *The Philosophy and Psychology of Character and Happiness*. New York: Routledge, 2014.

3 See: Halper, Edward, 1999, "The Unity of the Virtues in Aristotle," *Oxford Studies in Ancient Philosophy*, 17: 115–144, for a more detailed account of the "unity of the virtues" thesis in Aristotle.

4 Elizabeth Tefler (1989), for example, argues that Aristotle is mistaken in arguing for a unity of the virtues.

5 It would be worthwhile to conduct an extended philosophical treatment of trauma, but I don't have the space in this chapter to do so.

6 American Psychiatric Association. 2013. Diagnostic and Statistical Manual of Mental Disorders. 5th ed. Washington, DC: American Psychiatric Association.

7 As noted in Zukerman, Gil, Michal Pinhas, and Michal Icht. "Hypervigilance or Shutdown? Electrophysiological Processing of Trauma-Unrelated Aversive Stimuli after Traumatic Life Events." *Experimental Brain Research* 241, no. 4 (2023): 1185–97, some victims of PTSD experience dissociative symptoms as opposed to hypervigilance. In those victims, we would not see the same sort of automatic cue reactivity.

8 We can think of the relationship between excessive fear and cognitive distortions as a positive feedback loop. In other words, this relationship is not causally linear. Instead, heightened fear leads to the development of cognitive distortions, and cognitive distortions lead to people being more fearful, and so on.

Bibliography

American Psychiatric Association. 2013. *Diagnostic and Statistical Manual of Mental Disorders*. 5th ed. Washington, DC: American Psychiatric Association.

Battaglia, Simone, C. Nazzi, and J. F. Thayer. 2023. "Heart's Tale of Trauma: Fear-Conditioned Heart Rate Changes in Post-Traumatic Stress Disorder." *Acta Psychiatrica Scandinavica* 148, no. 5: 463–66.

Carey, L. B., and T. J. Hodgson. 2018. "Chaplaincy, Spiritual Care and Moral Injury: Considerations regarding Screening and Treatment." *Frontiers in Psychiatry* 9: 619.

Carlson, John G., Claude M. Chemtob, Kristin Rusnak, Nancy L. Hedlund, and Miles Y. Muraoka. 1998. "Eye Movement Desensitization and Reprocessing (EDMR) Treatment for Combat-Related Posttraumatic Stress Disorder." *Journal of Traumatic Stress* 11, no. 1: 3–24.

Contreras, Antonieta. 2024. *Traumatization and Its Aftermath : A Systemic Approach to Understanding and Treating Trauma Disorders*. New York, NY: Routledge.

Cruz, Daniel. 2023. *Developmental Trauma: Theory, Research and Practice*. New York, NY: Routledge.

Foa, Edna B., Elizabeth Ann. Hembree, and Barbara Olasov. 2007. *Prolonged Exposure Therapy for PTSD: Emotional Processing of Traumatic Experiences: Therapist Guide*. Oxford: Oxford University Press.

Grasser, Lana Ruvolo, Bassem Saad, Celine Bazzi, Hiba Abu Suhaiban, Dalia F. Mammo, Ragda Izar, Noor Abou Rass, et al. 2023. "The Fear That Remains: Associations between Trauma, Related Psychopathology, and Fear-potentiated Startle in Youth Resettled as Refugees." *Developmental Psychobiology* 65, no. 4: e22385-n/a.

Hodgson, Timothy J., and Lindsay B. Carey. 2017. "Moral Injury and Definitional Clarity: Betrayal, Spirituality and the Role of Chaplains." *Journal of Religion and Health* 56, no. 4: 1212–28.

Hughes, Daniel. 2017. "Dyadic Developmental Psychotherapy (DDP): An Attachment-focused Family Treatment for Developmental Trauma." *Australian and New Zealand Journal of Family Therapy* 38, no. 4: 595–605.

Lewis, Catrin, Neil P. Roberts, Martin Andrew, Elise Starling, and Jonathan I. Bisson. 2020. "Psychological Therapies for Post-Traumatic Stress Disorder in Adults: Systematic Review and Meta-Analysis." *European Journal of Psychotraumatology* 11, no. 1.

Leighton, Stephen. 2019. "Aristotle on Fear's Expression." *Philosophical Inquiry* 43, no. 1: 225–39.

Lloyd, Sarah. 2023. "An Innovative Approach to Working with Children Who Have Experienced Developmental Trauma: An Introduction to the Building Underdeveloped Sensorimotor Systems (BUSS®) Model." *Adoption & Fostering* 47, no. 2: 157–73.

Lorenz, Hendrik. 2014. "Aristotle's Analysis of Akratic Action." In *The Cambridge Companion to Aristotle's Nicomachean Ethics*, 242–62. New York: Cambridge University Press.

Miller, Patrick Lee. 2014. "Finding Oneself with Friends." In *The Cambridge Companion to Aristotle's Nicomachean Ethics*, 319–49. New York: Cambridge University Press.

Schimmenti, Adriano. 2018. "The Trauma Factor: Examining the Relationships among Different Types of Trauma, Dissociation, and Psychopathology." *Journal of Trauma & Dissociation* 19, no. 5: 552–71.

Shapiro, Francine. 2018. *Eye Movement Desensitization and Reprocessing (EDMR) Therapy: Basic Principles, Protocols, and Procedures*. Third edition. New York: The Guilford Press.

Shatrova, Daria, Pablo F Cáncer, and Jose Manuel Caperos. 2024. "The Role of Interoception in Reducing Trauma-Associated Distress: A Feasibility Study." *European Journal of Psychotraumatology* 15, no. 1: 2306747.

Snow, Nancy E. 2020. *Contemporary Virtue Ethics*. Cambridge: Cambridge University Press.

Spinazzola, Joseph, Bessel der Kolk, and Julian D. Ford. 2018. "When Nowhere Is Safe: Interpersonal Trauma and Attachment Adversity as Antecedents of Posttraumatic Stress Disorder and Developmental Trauma Disorder." *Journal of Traumatic Stress* 31, no. 5: 631–42.

Spinazzola, Joseph, Bessel Kolk, and Julian D. Ford. 2021. "Developmental Trauma Disorder: A Legacy of Attachment Trauma in Victimized Children." *Journal of Traumatic Stress* 34, no. 4: 711–20.

Trentini, Cristina, Marco Pagani, Piercarlo Fania, Anna Maria Speranza, Giampaolo Nicolais, Alessandra Sibilia, Lucio Inguscio, Anna Rita Verardo, Isabel Fernandez, and Massimo Ammaniti. 2015. "Neural Processing of Emotions in Traumatized Children Treated with Eye Movement Desensitization and Reprocessing Therapy: A hdEEG Study." *Frontiers in Psychology* 6: 1662.

Turri, Maria Grazia. 2015. "Transference and Katharsis, Freud to Aristotle." *International Journal of Psychoanalysis* 96, no. 2: 369–87.

Zare, Zahra, Homayoun Sadeghi-Bazargani, Diana Stark Ekman, Fatemeh Ranjbar, Robert Ekman, Mostafa Farahbakhsh, and Hemmat Maghsoudi. 2019. "Cognitive Distortions as Trauma-Specific Irrational Beliefs Among Burn Patients." *Journal of Burn Care & Research* 40, no. 3: 361–67.

Zukerman, Gil, Michal Pinhas, and Michal Icht. 2023. "Hypervigilance or Shutdown? Electrophysiological Processing of Trauma-Unrelated Aversive Stimuli after Traumatic Life Events." *Experimental Brain Research* 241, no. 4: 1185–97.

6

Anselm on Fear, Duty, and Moral Motivation

Parker Haratine

This chapter addresses the problem of fear and motivation for duty-based ethics in dialogue with Anselm of Canterbury.[1] Contrary to many medieval philosophers who subscribed to eudaemonistic ethics, Anselm of Canterbury maintained that a moral obligation does not necessarily correspond to actions that make one happy. Rather, an agent can be required to act for the sake of justice alone. This position implies that an agent may be required to act against his interests despite being fearful for his happiness or well-being. While Anselm's type of position captures the intuition that some moral duties require us to put aside our self-interest, his position also generates the problem of how to explain the moral motivation of agents when they are afraid and must put aside their own interests. A common explanation for motivation is that the agent sees something as good for oneself; while the Eudaemonist can claim this motivation, Anselm cannot. This chapter explores how Anselm addresses the apparent explanatory gap in moral motivation in situations where an agent fears for his well-being.

While some authors have discussed Anselm's view of moral motivation and the will, and others have discussed to what extent happiness and morality coincide, contemporary authors have not discussed Anselm's view of moral motivation primarily in the context of a rational agent being fearful for his well-being.[2] Rather than mainly addressing these former debates, this chapter addresses the upshot of Anselm's separating morality from happiness for his account of moral motivation, especially for cases in which a rational agent is fearful and their moral motivation does not coincide with their happiness. This chapter thus addresses a question that arises from the claim that Anselm separates morality from happiness.

As will become clear below, for Anselm, the term "happiness" casts a wide net and does not necessarily coincide with one's physical well-being. Rather, on my reading of Anselm, happiness involves satisfying the innate inclination for happiness with what one perceives will make them happy (more below). Nevertheless, happiness can also refer to one's physical well-being and livelihood, and this chapter will focus on the latter cases of happiness to address the question of fear for one's well-being rather than merely concern for one's interests.

I shall proceed by detailing a standard construal of eudaemonistic ethics for medieval philosophers. I shall then detail one of its shortcomings, namely, its failure to account for cases in which an agent may be morally obligated to act against his self-interest and when afraid. This will provide a helpful contrast to understand Anselm's position. I shall then turn to examine Anselm's account of moral motivation and how Anselm explains one's motivation when one is afraid for their happiness or well-being. Specifically, I show how Anselm's theory of the two wills and his view of justice and happiness can account for different motivations. While Anselm's theory does not stand in for duty-based ethics *simpliciter*, his position provides an interesting historical example of how an agent is motivated to act when fearful for their happiness or well-being.

Medieval Eudaemonistic Ethics and a Problem

In this section, I shall address several aspects of Eudaemonism that are relevant to the present discussion. While there are perhaps additional theses to this way of thinking, and while each medieval author might take these claims up in different ways, the following rough sketch of Eudaemonism will suffice to provide background and relief for Anselm's position.[3] These are:

> *Eudaemonist Principle*: That everything we will, we ultimately will for the sake of our own happiness;
>
> *Realization of Kind-Nature*: That happiness/flourishing is coextensive with fulfillment or realization of one's kind-nature;
>
> *Moral Obligation*: That the fulfillment of one's kind-nature is coextensive with fulfilling one's moral obligation.

A word on each of these. The first thesis, that all individuals only will their own happiness, is generally known as the "Eudaemonist principle."[4] The *Eudaemonist Principle* is not merely the claim that everyone desires to be happy at some point in time and in some fashion. This much is uncontroversial. The *Eudaemonist Principle* rather claims that everything a rational agent wills, it wills for the sake of its own happiness. There is exactly one final end for which to act, and that end is one's happiness. Other objects might be willed as a means to some further end, such as food for health. Yet, on pain of regress, there must be some ultimate or final end for which to act. Happiness is just such an end that is willed for its own sake.[5] Whether it be food, sex, play, or study, each of these activities or objects is eventually willed for the sake of the individual's happiness. On this view, it is hard to imagine that someone could act because he believes that the action is right or because he loves another individual for that same individual's sake.

The second thesis, *Realization of Kind-Nature*, clarifies the content of happiness. On this view, all created individuals are members of a kind and exemplify a kind-nature. Exemplifying a kind-nature implies that one has a certain end or telos associated with being a member of the kind. Additionally, one has corresponding capacities to achieve the prescribed end. When an individual actualizes his capacities and reaches the prescribed end, this is understood as fulfilling his kind-nature. So, to use a standard example, a token knife exemplifies the kind-nature of being a knife. It exemplifies this by having a purpose or end, to cut things, and has corresponding capacities to achieve this end, such as the capacity to be sharp. When this knife is sharp, it exemplifies its kind-nature well and achieves its end to a certain degree. Crucially, an entity can exemplify a kind-nature to a greater or lesser degree. A sharp knife will exemplify its kind-nature and achieve its end well, whereas a dull knife will fail to achieve its end as well. The same applies to human beings. When a human acts rationally and pursues happiness and virtue (for example), the human realizes his kind-nature better than a human who is irrational and full of vice. The human being has corresponding capacities, such as the intellect and will, to achieve this end. In actualizing the capacities properly, the human being realizes his kind-nature. On this view, then, to truly pursue one's happiness and flourishing is coextensive with pursuing one's self-actualization.

An important implication of the first two theses is that true happiness is not subject to the whims of desire or reducible to personal preference. While each individual only ever wills something for the sake of happiness, this individual might be mistaken about what will genuinely contribute to his happiness. For example, one might believe that eating several pints of ice cream in one sitting will contribute to his happiness, though she is objectively mistaken. The criterion for any object or activity to contribute to one's happiness is whether the object or activity will contribute to one's overall flourishing or well-being (*Realization of Kind-Nature*). One may very well be mistaken, but in being mistaken, she is still willing something for the sake of happiness.

Finally, the third thesis claims that fulfilling one's kind-nature exhausts one's moral obligations. There is exactly one moral obligation, and that moral obligation supervenes upon fulfilling one's nature and the actions that promote one's happiness and self-actualization. One could make this thesis a bit milder and maintain that all other moral obligations (if there are any) are fulfilled only if the agent simultaneously fulfills this moral obligation to actualize one's kind membership. This weaker position would allow room for the view that God is the *summum bonum* while claiming that one can will God and will the actualization of one's kind-nature. However, to provide a stark contrast, *Moral Obligation* will presently involve the stronger claim. Much like the *Eudaemonist Principle*, *Moral Obligation* also makes it difficult to imagine someone acting exclusively or even primarily for the love of another or the sake of duty.

With these above theses in mind, we have a clear picture of what Anselm may take to be the problem with the eudaemonistic picture of ethical obligations. Eudaemonism does not capture cases in which one is required to act for duty, and it does not capture cases of love of another individual for their own sake. These are both cases that at least require an individual to put aside one's flourishing as the end of action and act for another end. More strongly, there may be cases of moral duties in which one is required to *deny* one's flourishing, such as the duty to care for and love others, the duty to keep promises, and even perhaps the duty to self-sacrifice.[6] One might, for example, have the duty to care for ailing family members at a cost to oneself. To fulfill these moral obligations requires individuals to not focus on but deny their flourishing. In short, some moral duties seem to require us to act in spite of our fear and either neglect or deny our happiness and flourishing. Eudaemonism, on the contrary, maintains that one's moral obligation coincides with one's flourishing.

The problem is that the eudaemonistic picture does not capture relevant ethical cases and our intuitions about those cases. When one attempts to build a theory of the good life and what actions count as right and wrong, one is building a theory—the *explanans*—to explain certain data—the *explananda*. Should an *explanans* not capture an *explanandum* well, the *explanans* must be revised, expanded, or objected.

It is not my purpose here to advance a knockdown argument against Eudaemonism. It is also not my present aim to claim that Eudaemonism was off the mark in every respect. For one, notice that Eudaemonism excels at explaining why individuals are motivated to act morally in circumstances that do not involve fear and self-abnegation. It does not permit indulgence of just any desire but rather easily provides an account of moral motivation in daily cases. What is right for an individual to accomplish will eventually align with one's flourishing. Rather, my present aim in discussing Medieval Eudaemonism and some possible weaknesses is to provide the relevant conceptual background for Anselm's ethical view and to further provide some motivation for Anselm's view. There are, of course, possible responses that one may make on behalf of Eudaemonism, but I shall presently set these aside.[7]

I shall now turn my attention to an alternate view of ethics. This alternative view is Anselm's, and it aligns more with what is called "duty-based" ethics. I shall discuss Anselm's view of the will and how his view supports a version of duty-based ethics that still helps itself to different aspects of Eudaemonism. Anselm's picture captures the above cases of moral obligation that may require a sacrifice of one's flourishing. While Anselm may explain the above cases of duty and sacrifice, he must now explain moral motivation in circumstances when doing what is morally right requires one to set aside—and possibly deny—one's happiness.

Anselm on Motivation and Moral Obligation

To address Anselm's position about moral motivation when one is fearful, I shall first address Anselm's general views on motivation and obligation. Addressing these aspects of Anselm's thought will provide the relevant conceptual background to Anselm's answer to the present question. Anselm distinguishes between the will for happiness (*commodum*) and the will for justice (*iustitia*). There is some discussion of whether the will for justice merely moderates the will for happiness, or instead, whether it provides a distinct end for which to act. I cannot fully enter into this secondary discussion here, though I will presently maintain that the will for happiness and the will for justice provide the created agent with distinct ends for which to act.[8] For Anselm, there are two basic *affectiones* (dispositions) of the uncorrupted will: one for happiness (*commodum*), and one for justice (*iustitia*) (*DC* 3.11). The will for happiness is the disposition to will goods that will serve to increase the agent's happiness (whether perceived or actual). The will for justice, also known as rectitude or uprightness, is the disposition to will rectitude of will for its own sake and the will that one ought to follow. The wills orient an agent toward an end—they provide a reason for action—and exhaust the agent's motivational dispositions. A created rational agent acts only if it is for the sake of happiness or for the sake of justice.

In *DC* 3.11, Anselm articulates that there are three senses to the term "will": the faculty, the *affectiones* or dispositions, and the specific volitions or uses of the will. The faculty is the power and instrument by which the agent moves, just as reason is the instrument for reasoning and sight the instrument for seeing. We use these respective instruments when we see, reason, and will. The *affectiones* are the basic inclinations and motivations toward particular ends. These dispositions allow us to have volitions (the uses of the instrument). Anselm writes, "The affection (*affectio*) of this instrument is that by which the instrument itself is so disposed to will something—even when it is not thinking about what it wills—that if the thing comes to mind, the instrument wills it just then or in the proper time" (*DC* 3.11; SII, 279). These dispositions are not occurrent desires for any particular object; rather, they are basic desires toward an end which dispose an individual to have volitions and respond to specific objects of desire. For Anselm, one can ultimately explain every action or motivation in terms of these basic inclinations. Like the power of the will, these dispositions are present even though a person does not have a specific volition. Anselm uses the example of a just person sleeping who is still disposed to will justice. Finally, the use of the will is a specific volition that arises from a disposition and aligns with the disposition's end. When one acts upon the disposition for happiness or justice, this is a volition or use of the will.[9]

The above sketch illuminates how Anselm does not avail himself of the standard Eudaemonist picture, not least because it means that rational creatures do not always act for happiness. As I have argued elsewhere, Anselm maintains that the will for justice and the will for happiness provide two separate ends for which to act.[10] The will for justice does not merely moderate the will for happiness. If this were the case, the agent could only ever will something for the sake of happiness and choose to will something for happiness justly or unjustly. Rather, for Anselm, the will for justice provides a separate end for which to act. Anselm conducts a thought experiment about God creating an angel part by part. Anselm first imagines that God only gives the angel the will for happiness, and then he imagines that God only gives the angel the will for justice. *Ex hypothesi*, since we can conceive of God creating an angel with only the will for justice and further conceive of this angel acting for the sake of justice, Anselm maintains that the will for justice provides a distinct end for which to act (*DCD*, 14), even if these ends may eventually or accidentally coincide.[11] This position means that Anselm denies the *Eudaemonist Principle*, that everything we will, we ultimately will for the sake of our own happiness.

Anselm also maintains that rational creatures are morally obligated to follow the will for justice, a further departure from the Eudaemonist picture. To put the claim in Anselm's terminology, to will justly means that the agent wills "rectitude" or "uprightness" of will for its own sake (*DV* 12). Anselm distinguishes between the *what* of the volition (the object) and the *why* of the volition (the end). In *De Veritate* 12, the teacher and student agree that willing what is right is not sufficient to praise a thing. When a horse willingly grazes grass, the horse wills what it ought to will. However, the horse does not do so for the right reason, not least because the horse does not have the intellect to distinguish right from wrong (*DV* 12).

To be morally praiseworthy, the rational creature must preserve rectitude of will for its own sake. A person who wills what is right, but wills it for some reason other than justice, is not morally praiseworthy. To use Anselm's example, the individual who gives food to a starving person for the sake of vain glory is not morally praiseworthy. So, too, if someone is compelled or bribed to will justly. The individual whose volitions are morally praiseworthy is the one who wills what is just for the sake of justice alone. Because the will for happiness and the will for justice provide distinct ends for which to act, it follows that a person may be morally required to act in a circumstance that would result in harm or loss to themselves. Thus, Anselm would also generally deny *Moral Obligation*, the claim that fulfilling one's kind-nature is coextensive with fulfilling one's moral obligation. As the reader will see in the following section, this claim that justice may be a disinterested affair raises the question of how an agent is motivated to act when fearful for his well-being.

Anselm essentially maintains that an act is morally right if and only if the individual wills rectitude of will for its own sake. Anselm reasons in *DV* 12 that an action is called just on account of the will and not merely because of some property the action exhibits. He writes, "Rectitude of action is called justice, but only if the action proceeds from a just will" (DV 12; SI, 194).[12] And, whenever an individual wills rectitude of will for its own sake, the individual is just. Anselm strengthens this position by arguing that, even when an individual fails to bring about their intention, having willing rectitude of will for its own sake is still praiseworthy (*ibid.*). Willing this rectitude of will for its own sake is thus necessary and sufficient for being just and morally praiseworthy.[13]

With this claim laid out, Anselm is careful to maintain that the agent must, in principle, have the capacity to *spontaneously* will justice for justice's sake to be morally praiseworthy. To will something spontaneously is to will something freely and from oneself, as opposed to willing under a type of compulsion or necessity. In Anselm's thought experiment about the angel under construction (*DCD* 12–14), the angel is neither praiseworthy nor blameworthy when it is created with only one will. When God only gives the angel the will for happiness, the agent is limited to willing everything for the sake of happiness (*DCD* 13). Like a horse that has a will for happiness and wills to eat grass, the rational creature couldn't do otherwise, whether this is because the belief that "x is happiness-promoting" or because the action is mainly explained in terms of its disposition and nature that God has given it. This same point applies to the angel that only has the will for justice—whenever the one-willed agent wills justice for its own sake and wills under the belief "x is just," the actions are under a type of necessity.[14] Once the angel has both the will for justice and the will for happiness, it can choose between the two inclinations and be morally praiseworthy or blameworthy. When the angel makes this self-initiated action, Anselm calls the action spontaneous. The point, for Anselm, is much like the point that the rational agent must have an intellect to know and will justice—the agent must have the capacity of will to will free and morally relevant actions.[15] With this qualification in mind, the morally praiseworthy rational creature is the one who wills rectitude of will for its own sake.

For Anselm, a rational will ought to be just, and justice is not found outside of a rational will (*DCV* 3). Since justice exists only in a rational will, so too can injustice only exist in a rational will. But injustice is not technically a thing that exists—injustice is the lack of justice that ought to be present in the rational creature. For Anselm, this justice is what is due to God, and to be just in will is to be subject to God's will (*CDH* I.11). So, to be unjust in some respect means that one fails to submit to God in that respect. Inversely, being just means that one submits to God and, in one sense, fulfills their rational nature.[16] Rational nature was so made, according to Anselm, to be just. God gave rational nature the two inclinations of the will—along with the intellect to discern right from wrong—so rational creatures might fulfill this duty and be just. Elsewhere Anselm describes this as loving God (*Mon* 68; *CDH* II.1). So, God has equipped rational creatures with the capacity to be just, and when they are just, they are doing what they ought to do.

Let us conclude this section by reflecting on how to classify Anselm's position. Doing so will allow us to apply Anselm's general view on moral motivation and obligation to the specific question of acting for what is right when one is fearful for one's happiness or well-being. First, Anselm's picture of the two-willed agent highlights that he subscribes to a type of voluntarism. Voluntarism is best understood in contrast to intellectualism, the latter of which roughly maintains that the right kind of belief will necessitate the agent's will to move. A voluntarist maintains that the will is a type of power of choice, and the will retains a causal or explanatory priority over the intellect and its reasons.[17] Anselm's voluntarism is best seen with an example quite relevant for our purposes, which he proposes in *DLA* 7. Even when the morally just agent is tempted to lie out of fear of death, the will can overcome this temptation and fear. The will may be overcome at times by temptation and fear, though it can in principle always overcome these situations. To elaborate on this point, Anselm invokes his distinction between the instrument of the will and the specific volition or use of the will. He reasons by analogy that, if you see a strong man pin down a bull at one point and then later see a ram escape from the same strong man, you do not generally conclude that the man is any less strong at the later point. Rather, you would conclude that the man did not use his strength well. (*DLA* 7) *Mutatis mutandis*, the will is strong enough to overcome the fear of death and the temptation to lie, even though it sometimes does not.

Notice that Anselm also maintains that moral statements are true or false. That is, statements of the form "X is right" and perhaps "Y is good" (as well as their denials) have a cognitive value. Additionally, Anselm maintains that the truth of these kinds of statements does not depend upon a subjective psychological state such as an attitude, belief, or preference about the world. The truth of these statements rather depends upon the rational subject's willing rectitude of will for its own sake, something that translates to submitting to and obeying God. To put Anselm's position in contemporary terminology, Anselm is a cognitivist and an objectivist—in this regard, Anselm's position is standard for medieval philosophers.[18]

One might dispute the claim that Anselm is an objectivist and argue that, because a proper intention is required for an act to be just (i.e., morally right), Anselm is instead a subjectivist. Along these lines, one could suggest that what is morally right is dependent upon a psychological state, namely, an intention. However, willing rectitude of will for rectitude's sake does not imply that the subject's attitude or preferences determine the truth of the moral claim. While willing rectitude of will requires the subject to have the proper intention and psychological state, the fact that the subject ought to will justice for its own sake is independent of the subject's attitude or preference. For this reason, Anselm is an objectivist.

For present purposes, we must examine what moral motivation looks like in cases in which one's happiness is at stake. Recall that Anselm's splitting apart of the two affections implies that he denies happiness is the sole end for which one ever acts (*The Eudaemonist Principle*). Anselm has already expressed discontent with this principle by positing that the will for justice, and the associated beliefs, can independently motivate an agent. In short, Anselm maintains that sincere beliefs of the sort "x is happiness-promoting" and "x is just" both motivate a rational agent to act. And, since the will for happiness and justice provide two distinct ends for which to act, it follows that holding a belief "x is just" is at least conceptually distinct from the belief "x is happiness-promoting." Furthermore, because the will for justice is the one which an individual is morally required to follow, Anselm denies the above thesis *Moral Obligation*.

Anselm's Position Applied: Fear and Motivation

We are now in a position to apply Anselm's understanding of motivation and moral duty to the original question. Recall that the original question is how Anselm, as opposed to a Eudaemonist, would address an agent's motivation when that agent is fearful for their happiness. Specifically, how does Anselm account for motivation and fulfilling one's moral duty when one may need to put aside and possibly deny their happiness?

Before I address this question according to Anselm, recall that Anselm's term "happiness" casts a broader net than the Eudamemonist view which maintains that happiness coincides with one's well-being. While Anselm does not thoroughly specify the material content of happiness and leaves it at the general level of happiness (*commodum*) and well-being (*bene esse*) (cf. *DCD* 12 and *DC* 3.12), it is clear that willing justice may at times require one to sacrifice their happiness. In general, for Anselm, someone follows the inclination for happiness only if they think the object will promote their happiness and is advantageous to that individual. So, the belief that something will bring happiness is a necessary condition for being happy.[19] In *DCD* 13, Anselm maintains that if the angel that only has the will for happiness cannot pursue greater and nobler goods for the sake of happiness, it will pursue lesser goods that it can make use of, even goods that are fit for irrational animals. Nevertheless, if the angel can, it would will the object that would produce the greatest happiness for it.[20] In both cases, the one-willed angel pursues happiness and what is advantageous to it. While pursuing justice may require one to put aside all kinds of happiness, for Anselm, I shall presently limit the discussion to cases in which an agent must put aside happiness understood as one's natural well being, as in Anselm's above case of lying for fear of one's life. Thus, the question is not how an agent can be motivated when concerned for or interested in his general happiness, but specifically how an agent can be motivated when fearful for, and possibly required to deny, his happiness or well-being.

Anselm's first answer is that justice can be intrinsically motivating for the rational creature. Since an agent can will what is just for its own sake, having the belief that "x is just/right" can provide the agent with an intrinsic motivation to act. Moreover, the value of justice does not necessarily depend upon the benefits that one may receive. This means that Anselm denies a desire-based account of value and motivation. Since the two wills provide distinct ends, pursuing justice is a generally disinterested affair.[21]

While this first claim formally distinguishes the two types of motivation, Anselm does not comment upon the felt experience of the motivation to pursue happiness or to discharge one's duties. We might say on behalf of Anselm that, for beliefs of the kind "x is just/right" to provide different motivation than beliefs of the kind "x happiness-promoting," the former type of belief may compel, bind, or convict the agent to an extent.

Even if Anselm were to maintain that an agent may feel convicted or morally bound to discharge a duty, this position would not require the further claim that Anselm's rational agents act justly out of necessity. As we saw in Anselm's thought experiment about the angel under construction, this was not the case. Moreover, if such a sincere belief that "x is right" were to necessitate a just action, then some of the good angels would not have fallen from God's presence. According to Anselm, the angels before the fall knew what was right and yet fell (*DCD* 22). So, we can also conclude that beliefs of the kind "x is right" do not, in all cases, necessitate the agent's action.

Now, despite Anselm's voluntarism, Anselm consistently maintains that rational creatures cannot be just and fulfill their moral duties by their own means. Anselm states repeatedly that humans do not have justice from themselves but from God. This is so for the first humans (*DCV* 1–2), the first angels (*DCD* 3), and any other rational creature (*DV* 12). Once unjust, human beings cannot make themselves just again without divine grace (*DCV* 2). For Anselm, this claim ensures that people cannot be just on their own and need God to be just, a point that plays a large part in his theology of salvation and atonement found primarily in *Cur Deus Homo*.

Rather than self-made moral agents, the rational creature receives justice from God and wills justice as its own simultaneously. The reception of justice and the willing of justice occur at the same time, and God's gifting of justice is logically prior to the creature's willingness to preserve it (*DV* 12 & *DCD* 3). To drive home his point about rational creatures receiving justice, Anselm asks his student to consider why the first angel fell. Was it because God didn't give the angel the will to persevere in justice and, consequently, because God was the cause of the angel's fall in some significant sense? Surely not! God gave the angel the will to persevere in justice, and the angel failed to receive it (*DCD* 3).[22] God's giving justice to the angel is logically prior to the angel willing it, and the angel later denied what he had initially received. Though we might say that the angel didn't "receive" justice, this would be true only because the angel denied what was given to it.

This thought experiment and the claim that justice is always given highlight that justice is a gift given to rational creatures. Humans can lose the will for justice when they sin and fail to be just, and they must have divine aid to regain their justice. Indeed, in *DC* 3.12, Anselm remarks that the will for justice is "separable" from rational creatures, though the will for happiness is "inseparable." In other words, rational creatures can lose the disposition for justice, but not lose the disposition for happiness.

Anselm would thus provide different answers to the question of an agent's motivation and duties when one is fearful for one's happiness. If the agent is just, then they would have this motivational disposition to act for what is just and could choose to act for what is just, even at personal cost. This motivation and justice would be a grace from God, and the recognition of the value of justice would intrinsically motivate (though not necessitate) the rational creature to act justly. It would not necessitate the action, for Anselm is a voluntarist (see above). If the agent is unjust, then either God gives them the motivation to act justly in the moment, or the agent will act for what promotes their happiness. In this latter scenario, the unjust rational creature would overcome the fear of losing happiness only by still acting for the sake of happiness in some fashion.[23]

Anselm's position stands as a historic example of duty-based ethics that offers an answer to the question of how agents may be motivated to act when fearful for their happiness. Where it was not obvious that Medieval Eudaemonism could account for certain cases of moral duty, Anselm's system provides a straightforward answer—the rational agent can be motivated by justice for its own sake, and this is due to two separate inclinations of the will. Anselm's duty-based approach to ethics thus diverges from Medieval Eudaemonism in significant ways and fares better with respect to addressing certain ethical cases and intuitions.[24] Nevertheless, Anselm retains elements of Medieval Eudaemonism when he maintains that an agent has certain ends and associated capacities to achieve those ends. For Anselm, the rational agent is made to be just and has the associated capacities to achieve this end (albeit, with divine aid); the end of happiness is also natural and inseparable for rational creatures, and rational creatures have a relevant capacity for achieving this happiness. These two claims about the will retain elements of *Realization of Kind-Nature*. For this latter Eudaemonist thesis also, generally, maintains that rational agents have relevant capacities for achieving certain ends. While I must presently leave aside the question of whether Anselm's system of ethics is defensible, Anselm's duty-based approach captures cases of ethical obligations when one must set aside or deny his happiness, and it provides a picture of how this works in terms of a rational agent's motivation.

Acknowledgments

Some portions of the present chapter were originally published in Haratine 2024. I am grateful to the American Catholic Philosophical Quarterly for permission to republish portions of this chapter.

Notes

1 For Anselm's texts, I use Schmitt 2002. The texts and abbreviations are as follows: *De casu diaboli* (*DCD*), *De conceptu virginalis et pecatto originalis* (*DCV*), *Monologion* (*Mon*), *De veritate* (*DV*), and *De concordia* (*DC*). All translations of Anselm's texts are my own.

2 Ekenberg, Barnwell, and Rogers are examples of scholars engaging in the debates about the will/to what extent happiness and morality coincide (Ekenberg 2016; Barnwell 2010; K. Rogers 2022). Sweeney's work and that of Goebel and Hösle show more attention to Anselm's view of the affections and emotions (E. C. Sweeney 2012; Goebel and Hösle 2005). However, neither of the latter works addresses fear and moral motivation. For further literature on these debates, see below.

3 For an overview of this system and some adherents, cf. (Kent 2003; Steele 2018; Brower 2004).

4 (Kent 2003, 235).

5 Eudaemonists will also normally maintain that happiness is "complete" and cannot be willed for another end. Such a qualification is not salient presently. Cf. (Steele 2018, 128–29).

6 This may be an exception since one could regard it as a morally supererogatory action (one that goes beyond the call of duty).

7 One need look no further than Foot for a contemporary defender of Eudaemonism. Cf. (Foot 2001).

8 For the most recent discussion of this debate, cf. (Haratine 2024; Ekenberg 2022; E. Sweeney 2022; K. Rogers 2022).

9 It is a standard consensus that Anselm also deploys this distinction in his famous thought experiment about the angel being created part by part in *DCD* 12. Cf. (Visser and Williams 2009, 180; K. A. Rogers 2012, 192).

10 See Haratine 2024. Anselm maintains a distinction between natural happiness and beatitude that is not entirely relevant for present purposes. While Anselm hints at this distinction, this is not to say that he subscribed to an Aristotelian sense of natural happiness in which happiness requires the cardinal virtues, for example. Rather, Anselm describes the will for happiness as something that all sentient creatures possess, which lends itself to the claim that happiness is something like gratification or inclination-satisfaction in accordance with sentient nature. For more on this distinction, cf. *DCD* 12, *Mon.* 68, *CDH* II.1, and *DC* 3.11–13.

11 For alternative views, cf. (K. Rogers 2022; Ekenberg 2022; K. Rogers 2008).

12 "Dicitur enim rectitudo actionis iustitia, sed non nisi cum iusta voluntate fit actio." Anselm also discusses this in *DCV* 4.

13 For more on this, cf. Boler 2014, Quinn 1988. Boler maintains that Anselm doesn't necessarily deny that actions are morally right or wrong, but that it is only proper to speak of rational subjects as "having justice" or "being just." Quinn maintains that, for Anselm, the intentions alone are morally relevant. Where one lands on this interpretive debate will only be of minor importance for the present discussion.
14 Anselm's interpreters debate the type of necessity the angel is under when it only has the will for happiness (and, *mutatis mutandis*, when it only has the will for justice). However, we can presently set this debate aside. Cf. Ekenberg 2016; Haratine 2024; Visser and Williams 2009, 152. The language of an action being "happiness-promoting" in this paragraph follows Ekenberg.
15 *Per* Anselm, though fallen rational creatures cannot will justice without grace, they are still under the same obligation to be just as the original creatures made with justice (*DCV* 1–2).
16 For a good discussion of these two views of the goodness of the will, cf. (Visser and Williams 2009, 198).
17 Anselm does not distinguish between ethical and psychological voluntarism, where ethical voluntarism means that the action must originate from the agent's will and not be necessitated to be morally significant. However, it is clear that Anselm at least subscribes to something like ethical voluntarism.
18 For a similar gloss, cf. (Brower 2004, 224–25).
19 Anselm applies this same reasoning to the case of Christ in *CDH* II.12. Anselm argues that Christ, despite experiencing the infirmities of being human, was not unhappy, for wise people can happily undergo infirmities (i.e., the infirmities weren't against Christ's will for happiness).
20 Indeed, Anselm claims that an agent wills happiness (*beatitudo*) only because the agent thinks it is advantageous (*commodum*). He writes, "*At eum qui vult beatitudinem solam, commoda tantum velle posuimus,*" *DCD* 13, SI, page 257.
21 Others suggest that willing justice, because it is valuable, is convertible with willing justice as a benefit. Cf. (Ekenberg 2022) However, this would result in awkward and clumsy translations—it would require us to translate "willing rectitude of will for its own sake" as "for the sake of (willing) (appropriately tempered) happiness," something Anselm doesn't seem to have in mind (Normore 2002, 39). While the two types of values may offer different motivations, this is not to say that Anselm is a value pluralist, an important though separate conversation from Anselm's account of motivation given that Anselm denies the desire-based accounts of value.
22 One might contest that this discussion pertains to persevering in the will for justice, and not justice itself. In response, notice that the point can apply to willing justice to completion and God's gifting of justice being logically prior. But Anselm also seems to maintain that perseverance is nothing above and beyond willing justice to completion. He writes, "quoniam sicut eam non servamus nisi cum illam volumus, sic non est quando eam velimus et non servemus." *DV* 12; SI, 195.
23 This is not to say, however, that all actions done for happiness are unjust. Rather, it is to say that only the actions done for the sake of justice are just. Anselm does appear to maintain that there are some morally permissible actions when he claims that the will for happiness is not always bad, just bad when it is contrary to justice. (Cf. *DC* 3.13) For a contemporary discussion of this, cf. (Leftow 2022).

24 Thus, Anselm's view diverges from Aristotle and Aquinas, who generally maintain that happiness coincides with one's natural flourishing, and his view is a forerunner to Scotus's position, who, like Anselm separates happiness from morality. For additional historical context, cf. (Kent 2003; Boler 2014).

Bibliography

Barnwell, Michael. 2010. *The Problem of Negligent Omissions: Medieval Action Theories to the Rescue*. Vol. 1. Investigating Medieval Philosophy. Leiden: Brill.

Boler, John. 2014. "The Inclination for Justice." In *The Cambridge History of Medieval Philosophy*, edited by Robert Pasnau and Christina Van Dyke, 484–92. Cambridge: Cambridge University Press.

Brower, Jeffrey E. 2004. "Anselm on Ethics." In *The Cambridge Companion to Anselm*, edited by Brian Davies and Brian Leftow, 222–56. Cambridge: Cambridge University Press.

Ekenberg, Tomas. 2016. "Voluntarism, Intellectualism, and Anselm on Motivation." *Philosophical Topics* 44 (1): 59–74.

Ekenberg, Tomas. 2022. "Anselm and the Place of Happiness in Ethics." In *New Readings of Anselm of Canterbury's Intellectual Methods*, edited by Eileen Sweeney and John T. Slotemaker, 6:166–79. Anselm Studies and Texts. Leiden: Brill.

Foot, Philippa. 2001. *Natural Goodness*. Oxford: Oxford University Press.

Goebel, Bernd, and Vittorio Hösle. 2005. "Reasons, Emotions, and God's Presence in Anselm's Cur Deus Homo." *Archiv Für Geschichte Der Philosophie* 87 (2): 189–210.

Haratine, Parker. 2024. "How Anselm Separates Morality from Happiness." *American Catholic Philosophical Quarterly* Online First (June). https://doi.org/10.5840/acpq2024531290.

Kent, Bonnie. 2003. "The Moral Life." In *The Cambridge Companion to Medieval Philosophy*, edited by A. S. McGrade, 231–53. Cambridge: Cambridge University Press.

Leftow, Brian. 2022. "What Is Sin?" *Faith and Philosophy: Journal of the Society of Christian Philosophers* 39 (2): 243–71.

Normore, Calvin G. 2002. "Goodness and Rational Choice in the Early Middle Ages." In *Emotions and Choice from Boethius to Descartes*, edited by Henrik Lagerlund and Mikko Yrjönsuuri, 29–47. Dordrecht, Netherlands: Kluwer Academic Publishers.

Quinn, Philip L. 1988. "In Adam's Fall, We Sinned All." *Philosophical Topics* 16 (2): 89–118.

Rogers, Katherin. 2008. *Anselm on Freedom*. Oxford: Oxford University Press.

Rogers, Katherin. 2022. "St. Anselm of Canterbury on God and Morality." *The Monist* 105 (3): 309–20.

Rogers, Katherin A. 2012. "Anselm on the Ontological Status of Choice." *International Philosophical Quarterly* 52 (2): 183–97.

Schmitt, F. S., ed. 2002. *S. Anselmi: Opera Omnia*. Electronic. Vol. 1–5. 6 vols. Charlottesville, Virginia: InteLex Corporation.

Steele, Jeff. 2018. "Happiness." In *The Cambridge Companion the Medieval Ethics*, edited by Thomas Williams, 127–49. Cambridge Companions to Philosophy. Cambridge: Cambridge University Press.

Sweeney, Eileen. 2022. "Anselm on Evil and Eudamonism." In *New Readings of Anselm of Canterbury's Intellectual Methods*, edited by Eileen Sweeney and John T. Slotemaker, 6:180–92. Anselm Studies and Texts. Leiden: Brill.

Sweeney, Eileen C. 2012. *Anselm of Canterbury and the Desire for the Word*. Washington, D.C.: Catholic University of America Press.

Visser, Sandra, and Thomas Williams. 2009. *Anselm*. Great Medieval Thinkers. Oxford: Oxford University Press.

7

Fear as a Reactive Attitude

Robert Pál-Wallin

In the wake of Peter Frederick Strawson's landmark essay *Freedom and Resentment* (1962), much of the theorizing about moral responsibility has centered around the reactive attitudes—with a particular emphasis on guilt, resentment, and indignation. Although philosophical interest in previously unexamined reactive attitudes has grown rapidly in recent years,[1] remarkably little has hitherto been said about fear as a candidate reactive attitude.

The aim of this chapter is to explore the phenomenon of fearing other human agents *qua* agents. Drawing on P. F. Strawson's seminal work on the reactive attitudes, I aim to develop an account of agent-directed fear as a distinct reactive attitude (which I refer to as *reactive fear*). In order to pave the way for such an account, I shall, in the first part of this chapter, consider a potential objection to the central claim that people can fear other agents. The objection has its roots in a propositionalist view of mental states, according to which fear is a propositional attitude and thus essentially about potential events or state of affairs (something that is, was, or will be the case). I will provide reasons for why we should reject such a restrictive view of fear, and more specifically, why we need to embrace the idea that fear can be directed toward other human agents.

In the second part of the chapter, I contrast my proposed account of reactive fear to some existing views of fear, according to which fear is seen as reactive in a very general sense, as a reaction to any number of objects. On the account I propose, reactive fear is a distinct fearing attitude vis-à-vis human agents *qua* agents. As I aim to show, this kind of attitude is a particular mode of engagement that reflects an underlying concern of the fearing agent not to have her practical identity harmed by the feared agent. I will conclude by discussing the upshot and importance of recognizing fear as a *bona fide* reactive attitude.

Before turning to the propositionalist objection, a few methodological remarks are necessary. First and foremost, I will not attempt to establish a set of necessary and sufficient conditions for when a mental attitude qualifies as fear. Rather, the aim of developing an account of fear as a reactive attitude should be seen as an attempt to establish a family resemblance concept of fear. Second, the philosophical literature on emotions is ripe with divergent accounts of what emotions are—and what fear is—and it would simply take us too far afield to consider all these approaches, let alone trying to vindicate any of them. I will thus remain as neutral as possible with respect to what fear *consists in*, and only assume a very minimal understanding of fear as an affective reaction to a perception of some potential threat (or danger).[2,3] Third, like most emotion terms, the term "fear" (and its cognates) can be used to denote either an *affective disposition* or an *affective episode* (see Davis 1987; Deonna and Teroni 2012).[4] For example, consider the following sentences:

(1) Alex fears alligators.
(2) Alex fears the approaching alligator.

While (1) seems to express the thought that Alex has a general tendency to experience fear whenever he thinks of alligators, or sees them, or finds himself in their presence, and so on, (2) expresses the thought that Alex is, right now, in a *state of fear* because of the approaching alligator. Put differently, we can say that (1) refers to a fearing *disposition* (or *dormant* fear), while (2) refers to a particular fear *episode* (or *occurrent* fear). I will focus on fear in the episodic sense—as an occurrent mental attitude—in the remainder of this chapter. Finally, I shall assume that all episodes of fear are *intentional* mental phenomena (see Scarantino and De Sousa 2021; Teroni 2007). This does *not* mean—as one might suppose—that episodes of fear are deliberately brought about, that is, formed *with intention*, or *at will*. It means that fear exhibits *intentionality*, *viz.* a feature of mental states by which they are *directed at* or *about* things in the world (Searle 1983). Alex's fear of the alligator is intentional in the sense of being *about,* or *directed toward,* the alligator. It is common to speak of the object toward which a token emotion is directed as the emotion's *intentional object* (Massin 2021), or *particular object* (Teroni 2007).

I shall now turn to the issue of propositionalism and consider whether fear always concerns potential events or state of affairs and never individual agents.

Propositional Accounts of Fear

Propositionalism is the view according to which every intentional mental state or attitude either *is* a propositional attitude or *involves* a relation to a proposition (see Grzankowski 2012, 2013; Montague 2007). Typically, propositional attitudes are characterized as mental states that take propositions as their objects. Or, as Grzankowski puts it, propositional attitudes are "two-place relations holding between subjects and propositions" (2018, 134). In turn, propositions are ordinarily considered to be the primary bearers of truth and falsity (see e.g., Merricks 2009) and are often expressed with sentences containing a "that-clause." For example, to believe that there is an alligator in the backyard is to have a mental attitude—a *belief*—toward a proposition—that *there is an alligator in the backyard.*[5]

Propositionalism is a complex view, and it can be spelled out in different ways. Following Grzankowski (2012), we can distinguish between at least two versions of propositionalism—which I shall here refer to as *Strong Propositionalism* and *Weak Propositionalism.*[6]

Strong Propositionalism

What I call *Strong Propositionalism* is the version that holds that all putative non-propositional attitude relations (e.g., *Alex fearing the alligator*) are fully analyzable or reducible to a propositional attitude relation. On this view, if Alex is said to fear the alligator, then his fear must be fully analyzable in terms of some propositional attitude concerning the alligator—for example, Alex fears that the alligator will harm him. In effect, *Strong Propositionalism* seems to imply that, strictly speaking, our fears are never about physical objects or persons, but rather always about propositions—or about the events or state of affairs picked out by the proposition in question.

Robert Gordon (1980) seems to have endorsed something along these lines regarding fear. He explicitly states that "all fears are fears that something is (or was, or will be) the case" (1980, 560), and although he recognizes that we often communicate our fears in ways that do not display a propositional form, he contends that all such expressions are "essentially nothing more than abbreviated sentences" (ibid., 561). Thus, Gordon claims that:

> [T]o be afraid of an explosion, a reprisal, or a third world war is just to be afraid that *there will be* an explosion, a reprisal, or a third world war. (ibid., 561, italics in original)

Weak Propositionalism

In contrast, *Weak Propositionalism* allows that there can be intentional relations between a subject and a non-propositional object, but only *in virtue of* there being some propositional attitude relation between the subject and the non-propositional object. To illustrate, take the case of Alex fearing the alligator again. *Weak Propositionalism* does not require that Alex's fear of the alligator be *fully analyzable in terms of* some propositional attitude concerning the alligator. However, the view does hold that insofar as there is a fearing relation between Alex and the alligator, that relation must be *grounded in* some intentional relation between Alex and a proposition (e.g., Alex fears that the alligator will harm him).

Wayne Davis (1987) seems to espouse *Weak Propositionalism* with respect to one of the kinds of fear he identifies, namely *reactive fear.*[7] Davis' conception of reactive fear denotes a fearing relation between a subject and a non-propositional object which holds precisely *because* the subject fears *that* the object will cause harm. The object of reactive fear, so understood, can be all sorts of things—even immaterial objects (Davis 1987, 304).

Although Davis' account of reactive fear is more nuanced and flexible than Gordon's, it is still a propositional account since all non-propositional fearing relations are claimed to be grounded in propositional fearing relations. However, since the account does not exclude the possibility that fear can be about objects other than propositions (or state of affairs), it does not pose an immediate problem for the aim of this chapter.

For present purposes, *Strong Propositionalism* (henceforth *SP*) is the main villain.[8] In order to see just how *SP* poses a threat to the aim of developing an account of fear as a reactive attitude, we can sketch a potential argument that a proponent of the view may put forth. The argument would go something like this:

P1: All reactive attitudes are essentially agent-directed attitudes.

P2: Fear can only be a reactive attitude if it can be directed towards agents.

P3: Fear is always directed towards potential events or state of affairs, never individual agents.

C: Therefore, fear is not a reactive attitude.

I think we should accept P1 and P2, and at any rate, P3 is the real troublemaker. It is implied by *SP*, and if true, it would undermine the project of advancing an account of fear as a reactive attitude. I shall now provide reasons for why we should reject such a restrictive view of fear.

Fearing Agents (Against Strong Propositionalism)

I will utilize the concept of *reactive fear*, but I will do so in a narrower sense than Davis does. On my account, reactive fear refers to an agent's fearing attitude directed toward another agent *qua* agent. One archetypical example is that of the schoolyard outcast hiding in fear of his tormenting bully, or the mistreated wife fearing her drunken and violent husband. In cases such as these, the subjects' fears do not appear straightforwardly propositional, as concerning something that *is, was,* or *will be the case* (i.e., some state of affairs). The schoolyard outcast is seemingly afraid *of* the tormenting bully, and the mistreated wife is afraid *of* her violent husband. Their respective fears appear to be episodic reactions vis-à-vis these particular agents. In other words, the intentional object of reactive fear (in the intended sense) seems to be a particular *agent* and not some state of affairs.

To my mind, this type of fear is not only a familiar phenomenon in the lives of many people, but also common enough to raise legitimate misgivings as to why anybody would call it into question. At the very least, the *experience* of fearing agents is undoubtedly real, and it would be odd if proponents of *SP* refused to admit that much. However, they might argue that despite appearances and when properly analyzed, reactive fear is wholly reducible to propositional fear, the content of which merely involves a reference to the agent in question. Thus, it might be argued that in all putative cases in which an agent *A* reactively fears agent *B*, the proper analysis would reveal that what *A* in fact fears is that "*B* will perform some action φ," or that "*X* will be brought about as a result of *B's* φ-ing" (where *X* is a placeholder for some event or state of affairs). How can we respond to this line of reasoning?

One way of responding is to argue that propositional analyses of non-propositional attitudes fail to capture the relevant phenomenon. For example, some theorists have persuasively argued that such analyses are subject to *the displacement problem*, according to which the original object of the attitude is simply displaced (Forbes 2006; Grzankowski 2012). To illustrate, consider again the case in which agent *A* reactively fears agent *B*. If *A's* reactive fear of *B* is an intentional attitude, then according to *SP*, *A's* fear must be fully analyzable in terms of some proposition concerning *B*. *A's* fear-*of* must be captured in terms of fear-*that*. Accordingly, it might be suggested that *A's* reactive fear of *B* should be analyzed in terms of *A* fearing that "*B* will perform some action φ" (or some other relevant proposition). But the problem with this suggestion is that the intentional object of *A's* fear (i.e., agent *B*) now appears to have been displaced and replaced by something entirely different, namely *the event* of *B's* φ-ing. Agent-directed fears and fears concerning events are simply not equivalent. This is clear when we consider that from the fact that *A* fears that *B* will perform some action φ, it simply does not entail that *A* fears *B*. *B* might be held at gunpoint by *C*, who threatens *B* to give up crucial information that will seriously harm *A*, and so *A* might fear that *B* will reveal the information, but that certainly does not entail that *A* fears *B*.[9] As Grzankowski succinctly remarks:

> By aiming to capture, for example, liking in terms of liking-that we predict that what is liked is a state of affairs rather than, say, an individual. (2012, 382)

There is a related argument to be made here that builds directly on the displacement problem. We can call it *the normative displacement problem*,[10] and it runs as follows: As in our previous example, the suggestion is to analyze *A's* fear of *B* in terms of *A* fearing that "*B* will perform some action φ." Now, let's assume that there are normative reasons for *A* to fear that "*B* will perform some action φ." If *A's* fear of *B* can be captured in terms of *A* fearing that "*B* will perform some action φ," and there are normative reasons for *A* to fear that "*B* will perform some action φ," then that would seem to imply that *A's* fearing *B* is supported by normative reasons as well. But that implication does not hold. Again, *B* might be held at gunpoint by *C*, who threatens *B* to give up crucial information that will seriously harm *A*, and so *A's* fear that *B* will reveal the information may be supported by normative reasons, but that certainly does not entail that *A's* fearing *B* is supported by normative reasons. Here we have a case of normative displacement.[11]

What these arguments aim to show is basically that any attempt at analyzing non-propositional attitudes in terms of propositional ones results in unsatisfactory accounts of the phenomena that the analysis was supposed to account for. *A* fearing that *B* will φ does not imply that *A* fears *B*, and thus, the latter cannot be analyzed in terms of the former. The phenomenon of *A's* fearing *B* is left entirely unaccounted for, and that suggests that we must allow that fearing relations can hold between subjects and individual agents if we want to do justice to our commonplace experiences.[12]

Relatedly, insofar as an emotional reaction is symptomatic or expressive of the underlying cares and commitments of the emoting subject, the propositionalist reasoning seems to suggest—in line with Grzankowski's previous remark—that what people care about, or perhaps ought to care about, is what *state of affairs* or *events* are realized in the world. But people care deeply about many things other than state of affairs, and for very good reasons. An obvious example is, of course, how profoundly concerned we are with other people and how they relate to us. We care about their characters, their attitudes and motivations, we care about how they see things and their general orientations in life. These observations were explicitly articulated by Strawson, who stressed the "very great importance that we attach to the attitudes and intentions towards us of other human beings" (1962, 3).[13]

The propositionalist line of reasoning thus represents a major distortion of our lived human experience, suggesting that what people fundamentally care about, or even worse, *ought* to care about, is what state of affairs the world contains. People care about other people, and insofar as they do, they will engage—and will have reasons to engage—emotionally vis-à-vis particular agents in various ways. Occasionally, such emotional engagement will manifest itself in the mode of reactive fear, *viz.,* fear of other agents *qua* agents.

But perhaps one wants to insist that if it is the case that an agent *A* fears another agent *B*, it must be warranted to ask *A* why she fears *B*, and consequently, that it is warranted to expect some kind of answer that will reference something about *B* in propositional terms. Perhaps one might think that it would be odd if no such answer was available.[14] It does indeed seem perfectly warranted to pose such a question, and it would not be odd to expect some kind of answer that will reference something about the feared agent in propositional terms. But it does strike me as odd to think that the fearing agent *must* have an answer available. It is a familiar fact that our mental states can be rather opaque, and that we don't always have access to (or awareness of) the reasons in light of which we have them. That does not mean that we do not *respond* to the relevant reasons. People can indeed be highly sensitive to various facts about other agents—facts that elicit various attitudes and behaviors—without being able to articulate those facts.[15]

Reactive Fear: A Strawsonian Reactive Attitude

We noted earlier that according to Wayne Davis, not all instances of fear are propositional. In particular, his notion of reactive fear denotes a type of fear that can be directed toward any kind of non-propositional object. On Davis' view, the examples below would all count as instances of reactive fear:

1. Jenny fears the forest behind her house.
2. Walter fears the dark.
3. Alex fears the alligator.
4. Orin (the schoolyard outcast) fears Billy (the bully).

The sense of reactive fear that I am interested in here is exemplified by (4). In contrast to (1)—(3), (4) illustrates a fearing relation between a subject and a *human agent*, and thus delineates a narrower sense of reactive fear than Davis' broad conception. I shall now show how cases of the kind illustrated by (4) can be seen as involving fear understood as a Strawsonian reactive attitude.

In *Freedom and Resentment*, P. F. Strawson drew attention to what he took to be a central commonplace of our human lives, namely:

> [. . .] the very great importance that we attach to the attitudes and intentions towards us of other human beings, and the great extent to which our personal feelings and reactions depend upon, or involve, our beliefs about these attitudes and intentions. (1962, 3)

In essence, Strawson stressed our natural human commitment to participate and engage in ordinary interpersonal relationships (ibid, 7), and the evident fact that we—within the framework of such relationships—typically demand or expect "some degree of goodwill or regard on the part of those who stand in these relationships to us" (ibid, 3–4). It is in connection to these critical observations that Strawson's notion of a reactive attitude gains a foothold since the kind of goodwill that we expect of other people is *reflected in* or *expressed through* these "natural human reactions" (ibid, 6). Strawson writes:

> The personal reactive attitudes rest on, and reflect, an expectation of, and demand for, the manifestation of a certain degree of goodwill or regard on the part of other human beings towards ourselves; or at least on the expectation of, and demand for, an absence of the manifestation of active ill will or indifferent disregard. (ibid, 8)

The reactive attitudes are thus not simply reactions to any kind of pleasing or displeasing object, event, or state of affairs. Rather, these attitudes and feelings are responses directed toward persons in virtue of their displayed good or ill will. Reactive attitudes bear a special kind of interpersonal significance since they function as ways of expressing our expectations of people with whom we engage in various kinds of relationships. It is through the reactive attitudes that we convey our interpersonal concerns and commitments, in particular, those relating to how we care to be treated and regarded. How then does fear fit into the mosaic of reactive attitudes?

The beginnings of an answer can be sought, I believe, in Strawson's remarks concerning our human proneness and commitment to participate in ordinary interpersonal relationships. According to Strawson, this commitment is "part of the general framework of human life" (1962, 8), and "being involved in interpersonal relationships as we normally understand them precisely is being exposed to the range of reactive attitudes and feelings that is in question" (1962, 7). These remarks seem to suggest that, by their very nature, human beings are inescapably prone to experience reactive attitudes—in some form or other.[16] They express our interpersonal expectations and demands, and in turn, these expectations and demands seem to constitute the very condition for there being interpersonal relationships at all. Adding to this picture, I want to stress what to me seems a fundamental fact of the human condition: our *vulnerability*. Human beings are vulnerable beings. The moment we enter into a relationship of any kind, we run the risk of being exploited, manipulated, and offended. To participate in ordinary human relationships is to open oneself up to being hurt and harmed by others, and if Strawson was right to contend that our commitment to engage in human relationships is "part of the general framework of human life," then individual vulnerability must be part of that framework as well.

We can now begin to see how fear fits into the picture. In light of our commitment to participate in human relationships and the vulnerability that seems to entail, it is not surprising that humans would be prone to fear other agents. Human agents can undoubtedly be threatening. And as an emotional reaction to a perceived threat, reactive fear constitutes a particular mode of engagement vis-à-vis such threatening agents. At this point, we should perhaps acknowledge the fact that our human vulnerability is not limited to the confines of interpersonal relationships—many different things can constitute a threat. But I want to argue that the kind of threat that a human agent can pose vis-à-vis another bears a special kind of interpersonal and ethical significance to us.

Consider again the schoolyard outcast—let's call him Orin—hiding in fear of Billy, the tormenting bully. I have already argued that we cannot reduce, or fully analyze, agent-directed fear in terms of some proposition concerning the feared agent. But the implication of this is not that whenever *A* reactively fears *B*, *A* cannot fear *that B* will act in ways that may cause harm to *A*. Orin might genuinely fear Billy who is out to get him, but that does not imply that Orin cannot also fear *that* he will be harassed and humiliated if Billy finds him. One might perhaps be inclined to say that cases like these involve two distinct but concurrent tokens of fear, each with its distinct intentional object. That, to me, seems both too simplistic and, more importantly, incorrect. What strikes me as more accurate is to say that while reactive fear initially focuses on the targeted agent, it may fleetingly draw the subject's attention toward potential events or state of affairs construed as *flowing from* the targeted agent. When Orin reactively fears Billy and fears that "Billy will perform some action φ," Orin will typically construe the possible event of Billy's performing some action φ as, in a crucial sense, *flowing from Billy*. Reactive fear is thus likely to give rise to a kind of "double vision," in which the subject's attention oscillates between the targeted agent and the imminent state of affairs. Orin's fear of Billy is likely to prompt images[17] of him being harassed and humiliated—images featuring Billy as *the acting agent* via whom the impending state of affairs is brought into the world.

The emphasis on the way in which Orin perceives and regards Billy is crucial and, to my mind, a distinctive feature of what it is like to reactively fear human agents. Orin's experience of fearing Billy is not simply an experience of a harmful event unfolding. Rather, his fear involves seeing and regarding Billy as a particular individual, someone with aims, intentions, desires, and personal projects. In the eyes of Orin, Billy is no sheer force of nature or a mere node in a causal network—he is a human agent with a particular evaluative orientation in life. And to the extent that Orin has any particular thoughts concerning potential ways in which Billy may act, he will see these potential actions as, in a critical sense, born out of Billy's character or practical identity (Watson 1996). He sees them as extensions of who Billy *is*. To reactively fear an agent *qua* agent thus involves relating to the agent from a distinctly non-detached human perspective, characterized by a thoroughgoing sensitivity to various aspects of who the feared agent is as a human agent.

Following Strawson (1962), one could perhaps say that reactive fear essentially involves, or is dependent on, one's taking a *participant stance*—as opposed to an *objective stance*—vis-à-vis the feared agent. The objective stance (or attitude) is depicted by Strawson as a mode of disengagement, when the object is seen as "an object of social policy," or treatment; as something to be "managed or handled or cured or trained; perhaps simply to be avoided" (1962, 5).[18] In that regard, the objective stance is—as Strawson points out—profoundly opposed to the participant stance, *viz.* a non-detached mode of engagement of which the reactive attitudes and feelings are an integral part, a cornerstone of our human way of life.[19] This kind of non-detached way of relating to other persons reflects "how much it matters to us, whether the actions of other people . . . reflect attitudes towards us of goodwill, affection, or esteem on the one hand or contempt, indifference, or malevolence on the other" (Strawson 1962, 3).

People's practical identities (or characters) matter to us a great deal and typically constitute the ground for modifying our relationships in various ways. Part of the explanation for this is simply that our human lives comprise things we care deeply about and need to nurture and protect, and we must thus know how to navigate the interpersonal space. We need to know who we can trust and rely on. We need to know who we can open ourselves up to and who to avoid for purposes of self-preservation. But a human life is also a life of friendships and other deep interpersonal bonds, and in order to cultivate those kinds of relationships one needs to have a sense of who a person is *qua* individual human being. Our individuality as persons and agents is largely constituted by the complex nexus of our cares, commitments, values, and *ground projects* (Williams 1981), and so on. Our sense of meaning, and our engagement with the world flows, in a profound sense, from these things and our practical identities are structured by them. And it is evident that a person's nexus of desires, projects, cares, and commitments, that is, her practical identity and evaluative orientation in life, can be structured in a way which poses a genuine threat to one's own evaluative orientation and practical identity. And I believe that we generally demand—implicitly at least—of other agents, or expect of them, that their evaluative orientations not be structured in such a way.

What it is for an agent's evaluative orientation to be genuinely threatening is a difficult question, and a thoroughgoing treatment of it will have to be provided elsewhere. Nevertheless, I contend that it would be bizarre to draw the conclusion that two people pose a threat to each other whenever there is conflict between their respective evaluative orientations. Conflict is inevitable, and perhaps even indispensable for having an evaluative orientation at all. It prompts negotiation, reconsideration, and reconstruction of our orientations. There is no denying that such processes can be intimidating and unsettling, but it would be a mistake to think that that constitutes a genuine threat—it's simply part of what it is to have an evaluative orientation. Rather, I think we should say something to the effect that an agent's evaluative orientation becomes genuinely threatening to someone else's orientation when the former starts to undermine the conditions for the sustainment of the latter.

To illustrate, let's revisit the case of Orin, the schoolyard outcast, and Billy, the bully. Orin's reactive fear of Billy is based on an awareness of Billy's practical identity or evaluative orientation as being structured in a particular way. For instance, Billy's practical identity may be structured in a manner which may give rise to certain malicious intentions to hurt or humiliate Orin. Such malicious intentions are fearsome and threatening because the hurtful actions to which they can give rise can have extremely detrimental effects on the offended person. Being subjected to harassment and humiliation—or being aware of the risk of being subjected to them—may have devastating effects on Orin. It can change his entire conception of himself, making him feel like a lesser human being or even worthless. It may impact his capacity to lead a life in accordance with his desires, values, and personal projects. It may impede his ability to express himself and engage with other people in various contexts, and it may even destroy his ability to see the value in things and in life in general. This is but one example of the ways in which an agent's evaluative orientation can be threatening to the practical identity of another.

To sum up, being human is to participate in interpersonal relationships, and that involves being sensitive to other people's practical identities and evaluative orientations, that is, their complex nexus of cares, commitments, values, and personal projects. With that comes a proneness to reactive fear, which, on the account I have been sketching, is to be understood as an affective mode of engagement vis-à-vis human agents *qua* agents. In reactive fear, the fearing subject's bodily comportment and entire being is structured and shaped around the feared agent, whose evaluative orientation is perceived as structured in a way that poses a threat to the fearing agent's practical identity. Reactive fear is thus a type of reactive attitude which involves a sensitivity and responsiveness to ethically significant features of agents as such. Of course, the arousal of reactive fear is surely dependent on a prior apprehension (either correct or incorrect) of some evidence of the threatening features of the agent in question, and it is a familiar fact that particular actions or pieces of behavior occasionally constitute such evidence. So, while the etiology of reactive fear may require a reference to some action or behavior of the targeted agent, the import of those actions or behaviors is primarily of an *epistemic* kind: they play an evidentiary role in suggesting the presence of a threatening practical identity or evaluative orientation. Last, as the kind of affective engagement that reactive fear is, it expresses an underlying concern of the fearing subject to protect and preserve her practical identity and reflects an expectation not to have her practical identity harmed by the feared agent.

Concluding Remarks: The Significance of Reactive Fear

There seems to be—among people in general—a widespread attitude of regarding fear as something to overcome. There is certainly no shortage of voices stressing the various psychological, social, and political problems associated with fear. I would thus like to end this chapter by reflecting a bit on the significance of reactive fear and its potentially positive function in our lives. While these remarks may be, to some extent, imprecise and tentative, I believe that the overall discussion serves the important purpose of drawing attention to issues which merit closer treatment than they generally receive.

Philosophers who work on moral responsibility seem to presuppose that all normal human adults have the requisite psychological and emotional capacity to engage in blaming practices and the ability to blame wrongdoers. To be sure, the issue of normative competence has received a great deal of attention in connection to moral responsibility. However, the issue is often framed in terms of whether normative competence is a necessary condition for *being* morally responsible, and consequently, whether normative *in*competence can exempt people from responsibility and blame altogether. Similarly, psychological disorders are often discussed as potential exempting conditions, as something that may render the subject as an unfitting *target* of blame (see Shoemaker 2015).

What is far less discussed is the matter of how, and to what extent, various psychological, cultural, or sociopolitical conditions might impede otherwise well-functioning agents' *ability to issue* blame. For example, it is a well-known fact that victims of systematized violence and oppression tend to suffer all kinds of psychological harms. As Cudd (2006) notes, members of oppressed groups are often made to feel humiliated or degraded, which can result in lowered self-esteem. These are powerful psychological mechanisms, and they can have an immense impact on the way in which marginalized individuals perceive themselves and make sense of their place in the world. Doubts about their abilities and a reduced sense of agency may influence their view of themselves as prospective blamers. In fact, to engage in blaming practices might not be a live option at all. The psychological capacity needed to respond with confrontational attitudes like anger, resentment, or indignation seems to be dependent on some sense of entitlement, as having a legitimate claim on others within the social and moral community. But if the community is structured by oppressive norms—norms which are internalized—then these marginalized individuals won't be in a position to distribute blame—they will lack *psychological standing to blame*.[20]

Victims of systematized violence and oppression are thus in a particularly vulnerable position to be stripped of their psychological power to express a demand for goodwill via paradigmatic blaming emotions. And it is here we can start to see the potential significance of reactive fear. As an affective mode of engagement vis-à-vis agents *qua* agents, reactive fear expresses a fundamental concern of the fearing subject to protect and preserve her practical identity and reflects an expectation not to have it harmed by others. Being prone to reactive fear is thus to be in touch with one's deepest commitments and cares, and its manifestation is an unmistakable affirmation of one's attachment to life. Reactive fear is a crucial expressive outlet of one's agency, and—as Williams (1973) probably would have wanted to emphasize—one's *integrity*. In that regard, reactive fear is a vital emotional resource.

Acknowledgments

I am indebted to Ami Harbin, Matthew Talbert, Alexander Velichkov, Anton Emilsson, Christine Tappolet, and Rodrigo Díaz for their insightful comments on earlier drafts of this chapter. I also want to thank Toni Rønnow-Rasmussen, Wlodek Rabinowicz, Fritz Gåvertsson, András Szigeti, Henrik Andersson, Marta Johansson Werkmäster, Jakob Werkmäster, Signe Savén, Jiwon Kim, Marianna Leventi, Daniel Telech, Anthony Öhnström, and Ingvar Johansson for their valuable feedback at the Higher Seminar in Practical Philosophy at Lund University.

Notes

1 For example, exciting essays have been written on *love* (Abramson and Leite 2011), *contempt* (Mason 2003), *hurt feelings* (Shoemaker 2019), and *disappointment* (Telech and Dahan Katz 2022), among others.

2 The connection between fear and threat/danger seems hard to dispute. Of course, philosophers and psychologists tend to have very divergent views about the precise nature of that connection. For example, some theorists have asserted that fear itself *represents* the feared object as dangerous—or as having the property of being dangerous (see e.g., Prinz 2004). Proponents of *perceptual theories* (e.g., Döring 2003; Roberts 2003; Rossi & Tappolet 2019) would likely claim that fear *is* a perceptual experience (or concern-based construal) of something as threatening. According to *evaluative judgment theories* (e.g., Nussbaum 2001, 2016), fear is seen as constituted by an evaluative judgment that the feared object is dangerous/threatening. Other theorists seem to account for the connection between fear and threat in terms of some putative (evolutionary) function of fear. For instance, Degerman, Flinders, and Johnson write that "Fear is the emotional response to perception of threat. It is a crucial motivating dynamic that enables humans, and other species, to survive" (2023, 791). Similarly, Jonathan Mitchell claims that the functional role of fear is "to *detect danger and avoid physical harm*" (2023, 82, italics in original). It has also been argued that fear involves various action tendencies and adaptive behaviors tailored to enable the organism to deal effectively with potential threats to its wellbeing (or other things that the organism values). Examples of such behaviors include freezing or tonic immobility (Hatzimoysis 2014), fleeing, and defensive attack (Adolphs 2013).

3 In the service of full transparency, I want to acknowledge that my general philosophical sympathies lie with attitudinalist theories of emotions, according to which emotions are sui generis evaluative reactions or attitudes (see e.g., Deonna and Teroni 2015, 2022; Müller 2017, 2018; Zamuner 2015). These sympathies

will occasionally shine through as the discussion will sometimes be couched in a parlance congenial to such a framework. However, readers with divergent theoretical persuasions should not be discouraged. Most of what I will say about reactive fear can be translated to fit with other approaches to the emotions.

4 Fear-related terms certainly admit of other linguistic applications as well. For example, "The train will be delayed, I'm *afraid*" is perfectly felicitous, although obviously a mere *façon de parler*.

5 *Believing* is standardly presented in the literature as *the* paradigm example of a propositional attitude, but *desiring*, *hoping*, and *fearing* are often treated as prototypical cases as well.

6 Grzankowski (2012) refers to them as *Propositionalism A* and *Propositionalism B*. I think that the labels *Strong* and *Weak* are somewhat more informative.

7 The other two kinds of fear he identifies are *propositional fear* and *experiential fear, viz.* the occurrent *state of fear* itself.

8 I think that Weak Propositionalism faces serious problems as well, but at least the view does not reject the claim that fearing relations can hold between subjects and individual agents. Hence, the view does not pose a problem for the aim of developing an account of fear as an agent-directed reactive attitude.

9 This example is my rendering of the persuasive arguments made by Forbes (2006, 66–67) and Grzankowski (2012, 382).

10 To the best of my knowledge, this particular problem has not been raised as an argument against propositionalism, but I might be wrong. At any rate, the argument builds directly on the displacement problem as presented by Forbes (2006) and Grzankowski (2012), so it is in large part due to them and their philosophical work that a potentially new argument against propositionalism has emerged.

11 By *normative reasons*, I simply mean considerations (of the right kind) that *count in favor* of having the relevant attitude. Of course, one can deny that there are normative *reasons* for affective attitudes (see, e.g., Maguire 2018), but the argument could still work provided that one accepts that affective attitudes can be normatively supported *in some way*, for example, by fit-making facts.

12 To be clear, these remarks do not show (nor has it been the aim to show) that there are *no* propositional attitudes. My only concern is to cast doubt on the idea that *every* mental attitude (or every fearing attitude) is a propositional attitude. I do believe that there are both propositional and non-propositional varieties of fear.

13 One might argue that these observations refer to things that can be translated into propositional terms, thus throwing us back to the original problem. Even if it is true that we *could*, in principle, always spell out what people care about in propositional terms (I am skeptical about this, though), it does not show that the fundamental object(s) of our cares always is some state of affairs. And even if it is true that the fundamental object(s) of our *cares* always is some state of affairs, that does not imply that the fundamental object(s) of our *fears* is always some state of affairs. Plausibly, caring about a state of affairs might evoke (and provide reasons for having) fearing attitudes vis-à-vis objects that are not state of affairs. Thanks to Christine Tappolet, Rodrigo Diaz, and Matthew Talbert for raising this issue.

14 Thanks to Matthew Talbert for urging me to address this question.

15 We can also note that it is not uncommon that people's "available answers" are *ex-post* rationalizations.

16 In the literature, this claim is standardly referred to as Strawson's *inescapability claim,* and it is commonly interpreted as a psychological claim (see e.g., Russell 1992). In contrast to the common interpretation, Emilsson (2024) has argued that the claim is a metaphysical one.

17 The term "images" is notoriously ambiguous. Theuse of it is intended as an illustrative placeholder for various kinds of mental (re-)presentations, such as *thoughts, beliefs, imaginations, visualizations,* and so on, that could occur in the mind of the fearing subject.

18 It is worthwhile to ask whether fears directed toward persons *can* involve the objective stance. For example, Harbin (2023) discusses a case of fear of a homeless person outside a condo building. The residents perceive the homeless person as a threat and try to manage it by removing him. In such a case—as well as in cases of, for example, fearing migrants—it seems that fearing another agent can involve the objective stance—treating the homeless person or the migrant(s) as an object to be managed. As I see it, the distinction between the participant stance and the objective stance should *not* be construed as strictly binary. Rather, we should see the two stances as opposite ends of a spectrum, and so agent-directed fear can indeed involve (elements of) the objective stance to a greater or lesser degree. However, I doubt that it is psychologically possible for humans to fear other agents in a wholly objective way, as one would fear physical objects, animals, or state of affairs. Thanks to Ami Harbin for urging me to address this question.

19 Interestingly, Strawson writes that the objective attitude "may be emotionally toned in many ways, but not in all ways: it may include repulsion or *fear*, it may include pity or even love, though not all kinds of love" (1962, 5 my italics). It seems evident to me that Strawson had garden-variety fear in mind—that is, the kind of fear we can feel toward objects, state of affairs, and events in general—and not the kind of fear I have been exploring here, namely *reactive fear.*

20 I develop this concept and ideas in more detail in my paper *Psychological Standing to Blame* (ms.).

Bibliography

Abramson, Kate, and Adam Leite. 2011. "Love as a reactive emotion." *The Philosophical Quarterly* 61(245): 673–699. https://doi.org/10.1111/j.1467-9213.2011.716.x.

Adolphs, Ralph. 2013. "The biology of fear." *Current Biology* 23(2): R79–R93.

Cudd, E. Ann. 2006. *Analyzing oppression.* New York: Oxford University Press.

Davis, A. Wayne. 1987. "The varieties of fear." *Philosophical Studies* 51: 287–310.

Degerman, Dan, Matthew Flinders, and Matthew Johnson. 2023. "In defence of fear: COVID-19, crises and democracy." *Critical Review of International Social and Political Philosophy* 26(6): 788-809. https://doi.org/10.1080/13698230.2020.1834744.

Deonna, Julien, and Fabrice Teroni. 2012. *The emotions: A philosophical introduction.* London: Routledge.

Deonna, Julien, and Fabrice Teroni. 2015. "Emotions as attitudes." *Dialectica* 69(3): 293–311.

Deonna, Julien, and Fabrice Teroni. 2022. "Emotions and their correctness conditions: A defense of attitudinalism." *Erkenntnis.* https://doi.org/10.1007/s10670-022-00522-0.

Döring, A. Sabine. 2003. "Explaining action by emotion." *The Philosophical Quarterly* 53(211): 214–230. https://doi.org/10.1111/1467-9213.00307.
Emilsson, Anton. 2024. *Minimal optimism: Reading P.F. Strawson on moral responsibility.* Doctoral dissertation. Media Tryck. Lund.
Forbes, Graeme. 2006. *Attitude problems: An essay on linguistic intensionality*. New York: Oxford University Press.
Gordon, M. Robert. 1980. "Fear." *The Philosophical Review*, 89(4), 560–578. https://doi.org/10.2307/2184736.
Grzankowski, Alex. 2012. "Not all attitudes are propositional." *European Journal of Philosophy* 23(3): 374–391. ISSN 0966-8373.
Grzankowski, Alex. 2013. "Non-propositional attitudes." *Philosophy Compass* 8/12: 1123–1137.
Grzankowski, Alex. 2018. "A relational theory of non-propositional attitudes." In *Non-propositional intentionality*, edited by Alex Grzankowski and Michelle Montague, 134–151. New York: Oxford University Press.
Harbin, Ami. 2023. *Fearing together: Ethics for insecurity*. New York: Oxford University Press.
Hatzimoysis, Anthony. 2014. "Passive fear." *Phenomenology and the Cognitive Sciences* 13: 613–623. https://doi.org/10.1007/s11097-014-9353-3.
Maguire, Barry. 2018. "There are no reasons for affective attitudes." *Mind* 127: 779–805.
Mason, Michelle. 2003. "Contempt as a moral attitude." *Ethics* 113(2): 234–272.
Massin, Olivier. 2021. "The reactive theory of emotions." *European Journal of Philosophy* 31(3): 785–802. https://doi.org/10.1111/ejop.12736.
Merricks, Trenton. 2009. "Propositional attitudes?" *Proceedings of the Aristotelian Society* 109: 207–232.
Mitchell, Jonathan. 2023. "Emotion and attention." *Philos Stud* 180: 73–99. https://doi.org/10.1007/s11098-022-01876-5.
Montague, Michelle. 2007. "Against propositionalism." *Noûs* 41(3): 503–518. http://www.jstor.org/stable/4494543.
Müller, Jean Moritz. 2017. "How (not) to think of emotions as evaluative attitudes." *Dialectica*, 71: 281–308. https://doi.org/ 10.1111/1746-8361.12192.
Müller, Jean Moritz. 2018. "Emotion as position-taking." *Philosophia* 46(3): 525–540.
Nussbaum, Martha. 2001. *Upheavals of thought: the intelligence of emotions*. Cambridge: Cambridge University Press.
Nussbaum, Martha. 2016. *Anger and forgiveness: Resentment, generosity, justice*. New York: Oxford University Press.
Pál-Wallin, Robert. (manuscript). "Psychological standing to blame."
Prinz, Jesse. 2004. *Gut reactions: A perceptual theory of emotion*. Oxford: Oxford University Press.
Roberts, Robert. 2003. *Emotions: An essay in aid of moral psychology*. Cambridge: Cambridge University Press.
Rossi, Mauro, and Tappolet, Christine. 2019. "What kind of evaluative states are emotions? The attitudinal theory vs. the perceptual theory of emotions." *Canadian Journal of Philosophy* 49(4): 544–563.
Russell, Paul. 1992. "Strawson's way of naturalizing responsibility." *Ethics* 102(2): 287–302.
Scarantino, Andrea, and De Sousa, Ronald. 2021. "Emotion." In *The Stanford Encyclopedia of Philosophy*, edited by Edward N. Zalta. https://plato.stanford.edu/archives/sum2021/entries/emotion/.

Searle, John. 1983. *Intentionality: An essay in the philosophy of mind*. New York: Cambridge University Press.
Shoemaker, David. 2015. *Responsibility from the margins*. Oxford: Oxford University Press.
Shoemaker, David. 2019. "Hurt feelings." *The Journal of Philosophy* 116(3): 125–148.
Strawson, Peter. 1962. "Freedom and resentment." *Proceedings of the British Academy* 48: 1–25
Telech, Daniel, and Katz, Leora. 2022. "Condemnatory disappointment." *Ethics* 132(4): 851–880.
Teroni, Fabrice. 2007. "Emotions and formal objects." *dialectica*, 61(3): 395–415.
Watson, Gary. 1996. "Two faces of responsibility." *Philosophical Topics* 24(2): 227–248.
Williams, Bernard. 1973. "A critique of utilitarianism." In *Utilitarianism for and against*, edited by J. J. C. Smart and Bernard Williams, 77–150. Cambridge: Cambridge University Press.
Williams, Bernard. 1981. "Persons, character and morality." In *Moral Luck*, edited by Bernard Williams, 1–19. Cambridge: Cambridge University Press.
Zamuner, Edoardo. 2015. "Emotions as psychological reactions." *Mind & Language* 30(1): 22–43.

Part II

Interdisciplinary Insights on Fear

8

Reasons for Fear

Against the Reactive Theory of Emotion

Rodrigo Díaz and Christine Tappolet

Fear is sometimes irrational. It can be triggered by harmless things, such as innocuous spiders, and make us waste mental and physical resources in situations that do not merit them. Because of this, it is tempting to consider that fear has little value. Against this negative view of fear, philosophers have argued that fear has an important epistemic function. When things go well, fear would allow us to be aware of dangers and act accordingly, either because fear itself is a representation of danger and/or because it leads us to generate beliefs about danger. Given this, fear would have an important epistemic value in spite of the fact that it sometimes misleads us into believing that something harmless is dangerous. This view finds support in perceptual theories of emotion (e.g., Prinz, 2004; Tappolet, 2016), as well as empirical studies on the relation between emotion and evaluative judgment (e.g., Díaz & Prinz, 2023).

The view that fear has an epistemic value which has been questioned recently. Advocates of the so-called reactive theory (Mulligan 2010; Müller 2019, 2022; Massin 2023) have argued that emotional episodes depend on prior non-emotional grasps of values. Because of this, emotions would depend on the awareness of value instead of making us aware of value. What is crucial is that on such an account, the prior grasps of value provide agents with motivating reasons for their emotion. Thus, when you feel fear, what happens is that you respond to (a prior grasp of) danger, which is the reason in light of which you feel fear.

If reactive theorists are right, fear is irrelevant to our knowledge of danger. We could be devoid of fear and be as capable of grasping danger, because that grasp is not made nor facilitated by fear itself but by a previous non-emotional state. In the reactivist picture, fear could still be valuable in prompting behaviors that help us avoid danger, but it would not contribute to our knowledge of danger. In other words, fear could have practical value but not epistemological value concerning danger. This goes against perceptual views of emotion and, more broadly, epistemic sentimentalism about values, that is, the claim that emotions contribute to our knowledge of danger and other ways in which things can be (morally) good or bad.

In this chapter, we raise a number of difficulties for the reactive theory of fear. In the second section, we present the reactive theory. Afterward, we consider the main arguments in support of a reactive theory of fear. We separate those into two sections. The third section considers arguments for the claim that fear is a response. We cast doubt on these arguments while stressing that, even if fear is a response, it can have epistemological value in making us aware of danger, as it needn't be a response to danger. The fourth section considers arguments for the claim that fear is a response to danger. We argue that the linguistic considerations adduced by reactive theorists to support this claim actually support the opposite conclusion; namely, that there are non-evaluative reasons for fear. Overall, our arguments speak against the reactive theory of fear and in favor of fear's epistemological significance.

Our discussion focuses on the emotion of fear. What justifies this choice is that fear is not only a paradigmatic emotion that has been extensively studied, but it is it one that has figured prominently in recent debates for and against the reactive theory. Furthermore, while the examples used in these debates make it clear that fear is associated with danger, it is not so clear what values are associated with other emotions. But even though we focus on fear, we see no reason why our conclusions could not be extended to other kinds of emotions.

The Reactive Theory

The central idea shared by advocates of the reactive theory is that emotions are reactions or responses that depend on non-emotional awareness or apparent awareness of value. Kevin Mulligan writes that emotions "are reactions to the grasp or apparent grasp of value" (2010, 485). Similarly, Jean Moritz Müller holds that "(. . .) emotions are consequent upon an apprehension as of value" (2019, 73). In Olivier Massin's terms, "emotions toward some objects are sui generis attitudes which arise in reaction to this object being presented as valuable" (2023, 792). Grasps, apprehensions, and presentations as of value are naturally taken to be states with evaluative content and can therefore be characterized as representations. Thus, reactive theories agree that emotions are dependent on prior non-emotional representations of values.

However, there are different views as to what these representations of values consist in. Mulligan (2010) follows Max Scheler (1973) and Dietrich von Hildebrand (1916) in holding that these prior states are feelings of value. The problem with this account is that it appears to leave one with a dilemma. Either feelings of values are nothing but emotional experiences or they are mysterious sui generis kind of states (Deonna & Teroni, 2012; Mitchell, 2019, 2021; Müller, 2019; but see Naar, 2023). Because of this, Müller rejects the idea that emotions depend on feelings of values and argues that emotions are based on concern-based evaluative construals. Note that this is surprising, since as Müller himself notices, concern-based evaluative construals are nothing but emotions according to Robert Roberts (2003). For his part, Massin advocates a pluralist conception. Emotions can be responses to nonconceptual perceptions of values, but also evaluative beliefs or judgments, intellectual evaluative intuitions, evaluative rememberings, evaluative imaginations, and suppositions, among others.

Reactive theorists further hold that the values (and disvalues) at stake are what are often called the "formal objects" of emotions, that is, the evaluative features by which emotions can be assessed as correct or incorrect.[1] In the case of fear, the formal object is generally considered to be dangerousness (or else being threatening, harmful, or fearsome—for the sake of simplicity, we will mostly talk about dangerousness, but see the fourth section). Fear can be assessed as correct or incorrect depending on whether what we are afraid of is dangerous or not. The reactive theorist's claim is that we need to represent something as dangerous in order to be afraid of that thing. Suppose your fear is based on seeing a tiger leaping at you, its sharp teeth ready to tear you apart. According to the reactive theory of fear, you first see the tiger and non-emotionally represent it as dangerous, and then you respond with fear to this apparent danger. Importantly, this is not merely a claim about what sometimes or even typically happens in fear. Reactive theorists posit that a state could not be fear if it were not for the prior non-emotional representation of danger. After all, there would be nothing to respond to otherwise.

What is crucial to understand is that this dependence claim is paired with a claim about reasons. The representation of something as dangerous is not only what your fear depends on, it also provides you with a reason to experience fear. Accordingly, in the context of the reactive theory, the terms "reaction" or "response" are not understood in a merely causal sense. Saying that emotions are reactions does not mean that emotions are *caused* by something, but that emotions are experienced *in light of* something. In other words, the claim is that representations of value provide motivating reasons for emotions, that is, reasons *for which* or *in light of which* we experience an emotion. Thus, Massin holds that "(t)o react to an object being apparently valuable (. . .) is, furthermore, to adopt an emotional attitude towards that object *for that very reason*. To fear the tiger in reaction to its being apparently dangerous is to adopt that attitude *for that very reason*" (2021, 9, italics in the original). In the same way, Müller (2019) claims that "the reason for which we have an emotional feeling always include an apparent exemplification of the corresponding formal object by its target" (2019, 69). Again, the claim is not merely that emotions can sometimes be responses that we have in light of motivating reasons of the kind postulated. To be an emotion of fear, a response has to be adopted for the reason that something is apparently dangerous.

In sum, the reactive theory as applied to fear can be captured by the two following claims:

(RT1) Fear of x necessarily depends on a prior non-emotional representation of x as dangerous.

(RT2) Fear of x is a response for which x being apparently dangerous is necessarily the motivating reason.

We disagree with both claims, not because we think that fear cannot depend on prior non-emotional representation of danger or cannot be motivated by (apparent) danger but because we believe that this is not always the case. We agree that fear occasionally depends on non-emotional representations of danger. Fear can depend on a belief concerning danger, such as when you feel fear because you believe that you are about to be attacked by a dangerous tiger. But we disagree that there needs to be a prior non-emotional grasp of danger in each case of fear. Fear, we hold, can depend on non-evaluative representations. For example, the belief that a tiger is about to attack you. Concerning the second claim, we contend that, if the concept of motivating reasons can be applied to emotions, the reason for which we fear something can be that this thing is apparently dangerous. However, we disagree with the claim that motivating reasons for emotions need to be evaluative. For example, the belief that a tiger is about to attack you can be a sufficient reason for fear.

Let us start by considering the arguments in favor of the thesis that fear is a response.

Is Fear a Response?

Reactive theorists hold that their account captures the relation between emotions and their objects better than perceptual theories. One of the main problems with perceptual theories, according to Müller (2019, chap. 3, pp. 58–62), is that emotions involve a movement from the individual who feels the emotions toward their objects, while the movement that characterizes perceptions has the opposite direction. Emotions are responsive, but perceptions are receptive. This, Müller argues, is suggested by a number of linguistic and phenomenological observations.

Let us start with arguments that appeal to linguistic observations. Müller claims that how we ordinarily talk about the objects of emotion is different from how we talk about the objects of perception, and this reveals a crucial difference between emotions and perceptions. We say that emotions are *directed toward* or *aimed at* things, while it sounds odd to say that perceptions are *directed toward* or *aimed at* things. Similarly, we say that we feel emotions *about* something ("you feel sad about something"), *at* something ("you feel anger at someone"), or *over* something ("you feel enthusiastic over something"). By contrast, the preposition that we use for perception is "of," such as when we say that we have a vivid perception *of* the landscape, and it is claimed that "rather than conveying a direction towards an object, 'of' here specifies what is registered" (Müller, 2019, 62).

A first problem with this argument is that it fails to fit fear. The most natural way to attribute an emotion of fear involving a tiger is to say, "you fear the tiger" or "you are afraid of the tiger." The point to stress is that this is exactly the kind of locution we use to report perception, as Müller himself notes. We say that we see the tiger, or that we are (visually) aware of the tiger.

In response to this observation, Müller argues that there is nonetheless a difference in meaning, something he claims is shown by the fact that we can replace "of" with "directed towards" or "aimed at," while this is not possible in the case of perception. If taken as a normative claim about how we should talk, claiming that we cannot say that perception is "directed towards" or "aimed at" simply begs the question against the perceptual theory. If taken as a descriptive claim, it seems true for "aimed at,"[2] but false regarding "directed towards." Indeed, Google searches[3] reveal that "directed towards" is sometimes used to specify the intentional object of perception (e.g., "*perception directed towards* the external world," "*perception is directed towards* relationships or patterns, not isolated elements" or "he then sat cross-legged as his *perception was directed towards* the Heavenly Path in the firmament"), and we have no independent reason to believe those are incorrect uses of the locution.

Now, one might worry that expressions such as "perception (is/was) directed towards" are technical expressions mostly found in academic texts. But the same seems true for expressions like "fear (is/was) directed towards," and "fear (is/was) aimed at." Google searches[4] for these expressions suggest that they are mostly found in academic philosophy and psychology sources.[5] Thus, when we say "your fear is directed towards the tiger" or "your fear is aimed at the tiger," not only are we saying something quite unusual, but in fact, we might be communicating something different from simply attributing an emotion of fear involving a tiger. In particular, we might be specifying that fear is like an arrow in that it is directed or aimed at something. It remains to be shown that these locutions are not simply technical ways to say that emotions, like perceptions and beliefs, are intentional states. What seems clear is that these expressions are not common in ordinary language.

A second problem is that even if we have to take these linguistic differences to indicate that emotions differ from perceptions in that they are, in some way or other, responses, it does not follow that emotions depend on evaluative representations. We can indeed say "you feel fear *towards* something," where this might be taken to mark a difference with attributions of perceptions. It could be argued that this marks the fact that in order to be afraid of something, we need a prior grasp, such as a perception or a belief, of that thing. But this grasp needn't be evaluative. You need to see or hear the tiger in order to experience fear of the tiger, but you could well have no evaluative awareness of it. We will consider this issue at length in the next section.

Let us turn to the phenomenological arguments in favor of the reactive theory. Again, Müller (2019, 59 sqq.) holds that emotions are felt as if residing in us and targeted at their objects. This "phenomenology of response," as Müller calls it, is seen as involving the taking of a position toward an object. In feeling fear, you are not simply registering the danger; you are taking a negative stance toward that object.

A first point is that this conception would seem to make emotions too active. When experiencing fear, it is not as if we adopt a position. It is rather that, given what we are or seem to be aware of, we are struck with fear. We find ourselves experiencing fear, rather than doing something like taking a stance. Given that fear at least typically comes with a motivation for safety, we will be motivated to do a number of things aiming at safety. Thus, we are likely to run away, hide, fight back, and so on, depending on the circumstances. But as such, fear does not seem to be something we actively undertake (but see Müller, 2021, for a discussion).

However, what should be stressed is that, once again, the opponent of the reactive theory could accept that emotions are responses that are, in some sense active and directed at objects without being dependent on evaluations of these objects. The thought that emotions are responses is not incompatible with the claim that emotions register values. As Jonathan Mitchell (2019, 2021) argues, one can hold that the emotional response is that through which one represents evaluative properties. Thus, the reaction of fear would not depend on a prior representation of danger. Rather, the response would be that through which one first represents the danger. In Mitchell's terms, "Fear, for example, is not a response to an evaluation, but a self-standing affective evaluation" (2019, 719).

In sum, the arguments for the claim that fear is a response are not conclusive, and even if one accepts that fear is a response, it can still be claimed that being a response does not exclude it from being a representation of danger.

Is Fear a Response to Apparent Danger?

The reactive theory opposes perceptual accounts of emotion, but also the epistemological value of emotion more generally, including fear's epistemological value in making us aware of danger. And to challenge the latter, one needs to show not only that fear is a response (rather than a perception) but also that fear is a response *to real or apparent danger*. In this section, we will assess extant arguments for this claim. For ease of exposition, we will sometimes talk about fear being a response to danger instead of it being a response to *real or apparent* danger, but note that the latter is what we have in mind.

The idea that fear lacks epistemological value is sometimes taken to derive from the very idea that fear is a response, but the argument requires additional premises. Two of them are particularly important. First, we are told that responses are made *in light of* something, that is, responses have motivating reasons. Second, it is assumed that we respond with fear *in light of danger*, that is, motivating reasons for fear are necessarily evaluative. Thus, we need to be aware of danger before being afraid, and fear cannot make us aware of danger. This argument can be reconstructed as follows:

1. Fear is a response.
2. Responses have motivating reasons.
3. (by 1 and 2) Fear has motivating reasons.
4. Motivating reasons for fear are necessarily evaluative (about danger).
5. In order for something to be a motivating reason, the subject has to be aware of it.
6. (by 4 and 5) In order to be afraid, the fearer has to be aware of the danger.
7. If someone is already aware of danger, they cannot be made aware of it.
8. (by 5 and 6) Fear does not make us aware of danger.

In this section, we will assess premise (4) in this argument (but note that one might also want to question premises (1), (2), and (5)). Proponents of the reactive theory have pushed two main arguments for premise (4), both linguistic. In this section, we will argue that the linguistic considerations adduced to support the idea that only danger provides reasons for fear actually support the opposite conclusion. Namely, that fear can be experienced for non-evaluative reasons.

Are Explanations of Fear in Terms of Danger Common?

The first linguistic observation in favor of fear being a response to danger is that we often mention danger when we explain or report the reasons for our fear. More specifically, we commonly use expressions of the form "afraid of [object] because [object] is dangerous." Note that "because" is sometimes used to report the cause of the fear. For example, if I say "I was afraid of my neighbors' dog because I forgot to take my anxiolytic medication," I am reporting the cause of my fear. But in other instances, the expression is supposed to report motivating reasons for fear. For example, when I say that "I am afraid of my neighbors' dog because that dog is dangerous," I would be reporting the reasons in light of which I experience fear. One might object that this claim reports the cause of my fear, not a motivating reason. But let us grant, for the sake of the argument, that statements like these concern motivating reasons and thus support the claim that fear is a response to apparent danger.

Several authors have appealed to the putative prevalence of certain ways to explain our reasons for fear to support the reactive theory. Müller claims that "we commonly explain emotions along the following lines: [. . .] Peter is afraid that he will lose his job because this likely prospect constitutes a threat for him. If we take such explanations at face value, we thereby recognize the respective pre-emotional construal as affording awareness of value" (Müller, 2017, 290). Similarly, Mulligan says that "(a)scriptions of emotions and of their formal objects are typically of the form: x emotes y because of the (dis)value of z [. . .] In this respect, reasons to feel (emote) behave just like reasons to desire, to act, and to believe. In the most basic cases, emotions neither present nor represent value. Rather, they are reactions to a grasp or apparent grasp of value" (Mulligan, 2010, 485).

The problem with this argument is that explanations of the form "afraid of [object] because it is dangerous" are not prevalent, and non-evaluative explanations for fear seem just as common. To defend this, we will present the results of a series of linguistic queries in the Contemporary Corpus of American English (COCA), a corpus that contains more than one billion words of text from spoken language, fiction, popular magazines, newspapers, academic texts, TV and movie subtitles, blogs, and other web pages from 1990 to 2019. The corpus is openly available at https://www.english-corpora.org/coca/, and thus anyone can replicate the results we report here (see footnotes for details about our corpus queries).

Looking at COCA's full collection of texts, do we find that people mention danger when explaining their reasons for being afraid? COCA contains 175 instances of "afraid because,"[6] which arguably report reasons for fear. However, among those 175 instances, only 3 are followed by "danger," similar terms like "threat," "risk," or "harm," or their derivatives (e.g., "dangerous," "threatening," "risky," or "harmful").[7] These are the three instances we found:

> I can't imagine that this will be the last time I'm *afraid because* of some *danger* my children face.
>
> My wife is *afraid because* she knows that—that it's *dangerous.*
>
> *She was deathly *afraid because* I guess he apparently *threatened* to go to my parents' house.

One might argue that the last sentence does not show that fear is experienced in light of danger/threat/risk. But even if it does, what we find is that only 1.7 percent (3 out of 175) instances of "afraid because" in COCA were followed by "danger" and related terms. Crucially, other instances of "afraid because" seem to be specifying non-evaluative reasons for fear. Consider, just as an example, the following three instances:

> But I was afraid of him, really *afraid because* he was roaring at me, he was yelling at me.
>
> People were very *afraid because* these shootings were happening on suburban highways during rush hour.
>
> And he was afraid of the place. *Afraid* because he knew it too well; knew how things could turn on you in a heartbeat.

These results suggest that reasons for fear needn't be evaluative. However, one could argue that the searches we performed were inadequate. The ordinary language expressions that Müller and Mulligan mention in their arguments first specify the object of danger (with the expression "afraid of"), and then explain why the subject is afraid of that object (using the "because" connector). Searching for "afraid because" would not allow us to find expressions of this kind. To address this issue, we performed further searches in COCA.

In follow-up searches, we tried to find expressions of the form "afraid of [object] because [object] is dangerous." The results show that, among the 630 instances of "afraid of [. . .] because" in COCA,[8] only twelve are followed by "danger," "threat," "risk," "harm," or their derivates.[9] Below is the full list, with instances that are arguably irrelevant marked with a star.

> If you're *afraid* of getting a real tan *because* of the *dangerous* rays, well, a fake tan never hurt anyone.

> *It's irrational to be *afraid of* tarantulas *because* they aren't actually *dangerous.*
>
> *I don't understand . . . people who are *afraid of* sex. *Because* sex is not *dangerous.*
>
> People were *afraid of* kusiga because of the *danger* of being killed by the king.
>
> *The idea of counterphobia fascinates me. That you could climb mountains because you are *afraid of* heights. Seek out dangers *because* the *danger* holds such fear for you.
>
> *Americans needn't be *afraid of* foreign terrorists, *because* the biggest *threat* to us is our own gubment [government] and their agencies.
>
> *Workers were *afraid of* voicing their complaints both *because* they faced *threats* of violence and because they were afraid of deportation.
>
> These ineffectual people are *afraid of* atheism+, exactly *because* it *threatens* their pretend privileged status on the atheism debate.
>
> In one of these books, Mary Magdalene says to Jesus that "I'm *afraid of* Peter *because* he *threatens* me" "and hates all my sex."
>
> We Americans are *afraid of* militant Islam *because* it *threatens* our safety and freedom.
>
> Tito is *afraid of* this vitality *because* it *threatens* his ability to control her.
>
> Many people are *afraid of* nuclear power *because* of the *risks* caused by severe accidents.

Once again, even if we count all our results, we find that only 1.9 percent (12 out of 630) instances of "afraid of [. . .] because" in COCA are followed by "danger," "threat," "risk," "harm" or their derivatives. In other words, among all texts putatively explaining why someone is afraid of something, only 1.9 percent mention evaluative reasons. Importantly, other corpus matches for "afraid of [. . .] because" mentioned non-evaluative reasons. For example:

> You can either be *afraid of* it *because* it's so powerful and strong, or you can go stand.
>
> And people who were *afraid of* fire *because* it can kill you.
>
> People were *afraid of* us *because* we were always in numbers and uniforms and marching.

Against reactive theorists' claims, the way we ordinarily explain and express reasons for fear suggests that reasons for fear needn't be evaluative. In response, one could argue that the few fear explanations followed by "danger" we found in COCA support the idea that fear is a response to real or apparent danger. But remember that the reactive theory does not claim that fear is *sometimes* a response to danger. Instead, it posits that fear is *necessarily* a response to danger. For example, Müller claims that "the object of the feeling could not properly fulfill its role as a motivating reason unless it was apprehended by the subject in suitable evaluative terms" (Müller, 2022, 4). Ordinary explanations of fear in terms of danger are not prevalent enough to support this view.

Our systematic linguistic observations suggest fear responses are often explained in non-evaluative terms. These, in turn, suggest that fear is intelligible as a response to non-evaluative reasons, pace Müller. However, proponents of the reactive theory claim that we accept non-evaluative reasons for fear *just because* they imply or presuppose that what they invoke is considered dangerous. In the next section, we will consider their main argument for this claim.

Do Non-Evaluative Reasons of Fear Presuppose Danger?

According to the argument we considered in the previous section, the fact that we explain fear reactions by appealing to danger (using expressions like "she is afraid of it because it is dangerous") supports the idea that fear is a response to danger. Against this, we found that these explanations are not prevalent. Indeed, many ordinary explanations of fear appeal to non-evaluative aspects.

However, reactive theorists claim that non-evaluative explanations of fear imply or presuppose danger assessments, and such explanations succeed in making fear intelligible just because of this. Along these lines, Müller states that "explanations such as 'Maria feels glad because of the landscape she is watching' or 'James is afraid because of the approaching dog' do not make the respective feeling intelligible if we suppose that it is felt in light of the scene or the dog simpliciter. We fail to comprehend how these objects could make their subjects feel the way they do unless we suppose that they are in one way or another apprehended by them as good or dangerous, respectively" (Müller, 2022, 4).

This reasoning flags the relationship between intelligibility and reasons. Actions or attitudes are intelligible if they can be explained or justified by reasons, and conversely, reasons make actions and attitudes intelligible. Given this link, when reactive theorists say that non-evaluative facts do not make fear intelligible, they are committed to saying that non-evaluative facts do not constitute reasons for fear. In other words, there are no non-evaluative reasons for fear; reasons for fear are necessarily evaluative.

If non-evaluative explanations of fear imply or presuppose danger assessments, the non-evaluative reason explanations we found in COCA would not directly threaten the reactive theory. The relative absence of evaluative explanations would still defuse reactive theorists' first argument *for* the claim that fear is a response to danger (see the beginning of the fourth section), but the presence of non-evaluative explanations would not necessarily speak *against* this claim. Indeed, proponents of the reactive theory would reply that those non-evaluative explanations imply danger assessments. But why should we believe that this is the case? What is the argument for the claim that non-evaluative reason explanations of fear imply danger assessments?

According to reactive theorists, we can tell that non-evaluative reason explanations of fear imply danger assessments because it sounds odd to say that one is afraid of something because of its non-evaluative properties and then deny that those properties are danger-making. Consider the following examples:

> I'm afraid of the dog because it has big sharp teeth, which does not make him dangerous in the least. (Massin, 2023, p. 799)
>
> I'm afraid of eating street food because it can cause food poisoning, but food poisoning is not dangerous.
>
> I'm afraid of the cliff edge because it is high and slippery, but being high and slippery doesn't mean dangerous.

Müller (2019, 69–70) and Massin (2023, 799) claim that these sentences sound odd because the first part ("afraid of [object] because of [object's property]") implies or implicates that the specified property is dangerous, and the second part explicitly denies it. When I say "I'm afraid of eating street food because it can cause food poisoning," hearers assume that I consider what causes food poisoning dangerous, and that's why it sounds odd to follow with "but food poisoning is not dangerous." However, this is not the only possible explanation for why this and similar expressions sound odd.

Another explanation for why the target expressions sound odd is that it is difficult to make sense of someone being afraid of something that they *consider not dangerous*. Note that this is not the same as saying that it is difficult to make sense of someone being afraid of something that they *do not consider dangerous*. Representing something as not dangerous is different from not representing it as dangerous. We believe that reactive theorists' argument trades on conflating these two. The oddness of sentences with the form "afraid of [object] because of [object's property] but [object's property] is not dangerous" shows that it is difficult to make sense of fear directed toward something that is represented as not dangerous, but it doesn't show that it is difficult to make sense of fear directed toward something that is not represented as dangerous.

To recap, reactive theorists have argued that the oddness of expressions like "afraid of [object] because [object's feature], but [object's feature] is not dangerous" shows that non-evaluative explanations of fear imply danger assessments and, in turn, support the idea that fear is only intelligible as a response to danger. But the oddness of such expressions can be explained in at least two different ways. The expressions might sound odd because:

(a) explanations of fear in non-evaluative terms imply or presuppose that those features are considered dangerous (and the second part of the expression denies it), or because
(b) it is difficult to make sense of fear directed towards something that is considered not dangerous (as the second part of the expression states).[10]

Only (a) supports the reactive theory of fear. However, (b) is as valid as an explanation for why the expressions sound odd. Thus, we need additional evidence to favor (a) over (b). In the following, we propose a direct way to test (a), one that doesn't depend on the oddness of certain expressions.

Proponents of the reactive theory claim that explanations in terms of non-evaluative properties like "it can cause food poisoning" explain fear toward the property bearers *just because* they imply or presuppose a danger assessment (e.g., "what can cause food poisoning is dangerous"). If this is the case, people accept that non-evaluative properties provide reasons for fear *just because* they assume that those properties are considered dangerous-making. We tested this prediction in a short survey study.

Participants in the study[11] were presented with two of the three following statements (in random order):

(Animal) The fact that an animal has big sharp teeth and is rapidly approaching gives reasons to[12] be afraid of it.

(Food) The fact that unhygienic street food can cause food poisoning gives reasons to be afraid of it.

(Cliff) The fact that a cliff edge is high and slippery gives reasons to be afraid of it.

Participants were asked to rate their agreement with each statement using a scale from 1 ("strongly disagree") to 7 ("strongly agree"). After each rating, they were asked to justify their answer (they were asked "Why? Please briefly justify your answer").

If people accept non-evaluative properties (e.g., having big sharp teeth) as reasons for fear *just because* they suppose those properties are dangerous-making, participants who agree with the statements in our study should mention "danger" or similar evaluative terms when asked why they agree that non-evaluative properties provide reasons for fear. But this prediction was not borne out.

Results show that most participants agree with our statements (see table 8.1). That is, most participants agree that non-evaluative properties (e.g., having big sharp teeth) give reasons to be afraid of their property bearers (e.g., an animal). However, when participants were asked to explain why they agreed, only a relatively small percentage of them (25 out of 87) mentioned evaluative terms such as "danger," "risk," "threat," "harm," and their derivates (see table 8.1). Results (including participants' explanations for their responses) are openly available at https://osf.io/sy3cf/?view_only=5aa3d1a2157643188f0072632ef36023.

Most of the participants who accepted non-evaluative reasons for fear did *not* do so because of evaluative considerations. These results suggest that, pace reactive theorists' claims, it is not the case that we accept non-evaluative reasons for fear just because we assume danger assessments. Once again, our systematic linguistic observations both

Table 8.1 Results of Our Survey Study

Statement	Mean Agreement	Participants Who Agreed / Gave Ratings > 4	Danger* Mentions	Threat* Mentions	Risk* Mentions	Harm* Mentions	Total Evaluative Mentions
Animal	6.03	31 / 33	1	2	0	5	8 / 31
Food	5.30	28 / 37	0	1	3	1	5 / 28
Cliff	5.84	28 / 32	8	1	3	0	12 / 28
Total	5.71	87/102	9	4	6	6	25 / 87

Asterisks following our target evaluative terms (Danger*, Threat*, Risk*, Harm*) mean that results include derivate terms such as "dangerous," "threatening," "risky," or "harmful." The Total evaluative mentions column shows the results for participants who agreed with the corresponding statement, i.e., participants who gave agreement ratings higher than four.

Figure 8.1 Most common words in participants' justifications for their agreement with the three statements in our study. Stopwords (e.g., "a," "the," etc.) and words contained in the statements (e.g., "animal" or "sharp," plus also "fear," "animals," and "cliffs") are filtered out. The size of the word in the image indicates its frequency. *Source*: Image created by Rodrigo Díaz and Christine Tappolet.

defuse the main premise of reactive theorists' argument and provide support for the opposite claim. Most of the words that participants used when justifying why they agreed with the statements in our study were non-evaluative, such as "attack," "sick," or "fall" (see figure 8.1). This suggests that fear is perfectly intelligible as a response to non-evaluative properties of its object or, in other words, that there are non-evaluative reasons for fear.

Before closing, we would like to consider a few possible responses to our results. One possible response is that the non-evaluative terms that participants used in their justifications ("attack," "sick," "fall," etc.) presuppose negative evaluations. But this response does not vindicate reactive theorists' claims. Rather than a linguistic argument for the reactive theory, this is a way to make the theory unfalsifiable by linguistic evidence. Indeed, if one can always reply that non-evaluative terms presuppose evaluations, there is no way of providing evidence against the idea that reasons for fear are necessarily evaluative.

One might have complaints about the design of our study. For example, instead of asking participants why they accept non-evaluative reasons for fear and see whether they use evaluative terms in their explanations, one might have wanted us to ask participants whether they agree or disagree with a statement like "[non-evaluative properties] make [property bearer] dangerous." But this would not tell us whether participants accept non-evaluative reasons for fear just because they assume danger assessments. Indeed, participants might agree with a given danger assessment that they were not supposing and that wasn't the reason why they accepted non-evaluative reasons for fear.

Finally, note that the fact that some participants used evaluative terms in their explanations seems to rule out the possibility that evaluative suppositions are too hard to articulate or, to the contrary, too obvious to be worth stating.

Conclusion

We believe our investigations leave the reactive theory unsupported at best, refuted at worst. We have argued that linguistic and phenomenological arguments for the claim that fear is a response are unconvincing, at least in any sense that would exclude fear from being a representation of danger, as perceptual theories posit. We also assessed arguments for the claim that fear responds to real or apparent danger and found that their premises do not hold. Evaluative reason explanations for fear are not common, and non-evaluative reason explanations for fear do not seem to imply or presuppose danger assessments. Thus, there seems to be little reason to claim that when we fear something, we necessarily respond to that thing being dangerous. Indeed, against Reactive Theories' core tenets, we have given reason to believe that the awareness (or seeming awareness) of non-evaluative properties can well provide you with reasons for fear. This is good news for rival theories, such as, foremost, perceptual theories, which hold that emotions have evaluative representational content. More generally, it is good news for the view that emotions have epistemic value in contributing to knowledge of evaluative properties such as danger. The fear you experience at the sight of the tiger, albeit motivated by the tiger's looks, can well be crucial in your grasp of the dangerousness of the tiger.

Acknowledgments

We are grateful to Ami Harbin, Charlie Kurth, Olivier Massin, Moritz Müller, and Mauro Rossi for comments and discussions.

Notes

1 But see Massin (2023) for a different definition, according to which the formal object is what the intentional object of an emotion must purportedly exemplify for being an emotion of that kind. Mulligan (2010) is an exception here, for he accepts that a feeling of generosity can be the prior grasp for admiration.

2 Searches conducted on April 20, 2024, for "perception aimed at," and "perception is aimed at" (using scare quotes to get exact matches). Looking at the results, we could not find cases in which "aimed at" was followed by the intentional object of perception. Instead, the locution "aimed at" seems to be mostly used to specify the function of perception (e.g., "Perception *is aimed at* recognizing the cognitive features of the perceived object").

3 Searches conducted on April 20, 2024, for "perception directed towards," "perception is directed towards," and "perception was directed towards" (using scare quotes to get exact matches).

4 Searches conducted on May 1, 2024, for "fear directed towards," "fear is directed towards," "fear was directed towards," "fear aimed at," and "fear is aimed at," "fear was aimed at" (using scare quotes to get exact matches). Note that results suggest that the locution "aimed at" is mostly used to specify the function of fear (e.g., "Fear *is aimed at* self-preservation"), but also sometimes to specify the intentional object of fear (e.g., "*fear aimed at* a minority").

5 The same seems to be the case for "fear (is/was) directed at" (searches conducted on May 1, 2024, for "fear directed at," "fear is directed at," "fear was directed at" using scare quotes to get exact matches). Furthermore, we could not find a single instance of "fear (is/was) directed towards," "fear (is/was) aimed at," or "fear (is/was) directed at" in the online Corpus of Contemporary American English, which contains more than one billion words of text.

6 This result was obtained through a simple list search for "afraid because."

7 These results were obtained through four collocates searches introducing "afraid because" as the target word/phrase, and "danger*," "threat*," "risk*," or "harm" as the collocates (adding a star allows to search for derivate terms such as "dangerous," "threatening," "risky," or "harmful") among the nine words to the right of the target phrase. Using "fearsome" as the collocate yielded no results.

8 This result was obtained through a collocates search with "afraid of" as the target word/phrase and "because" as the collocates, restricted to the nine words to the right of the target phrase.

9 These results were obtained by performing four further collocates searches with "afraid of" as the target word/phrase and "danger*," "threat*," "risk*," or "harm*" as the collocates (adding a star allows to search for derivate terms such as "dangerous" or "threatening"). The search was restricted to the nine words to the right of the target phrase, and manually selecting instances that contained the word "because" between "afraid of" and "danger*," "threat*," "risk*," or "harm*." We found no results for the same search using "fearsome" as the target word.

10 There are several possible explanations for why it might be difficult to make sense of fear directed toward something that is represented as not dangerous. It could be that fear itself is understood as a representation of danger, or just that we

are commonly afraid of dangerous things. What seems hard to deny is that the ordinary understanding of fear is tightly connected to representations of danger (Díaz 2022).

11 Totally, 51 participants (26 female, 1 non-binary, mean age = 41.82, SD = 14.16, age range 21–77) were recruited through Prolific and completed the survey for a monetary payment.

12 One could argue that the wording we used in our statements ("reasons to") refers to normative reasons, and reactive theorists' claims here refer to motivating reasons. But even if this is true, reactive theorists agree that there is a tight relation between normative and motivating reasons for fear and that both must invoke danger (Müller, n.d.).

Bibliography

Deonna, Julien, and Fabrice Teroni. 2012. *The Emotions: A Philosophical Introduction*. New York: Routledge. https://doi.org/10.1016/B978-0-12-415956-3.000014.

Díaz, Rodrigo. 2022. "What Do People Think Is an Emotion?" *Affective Science* 3 (2): 438–50. https://doi.org/10.1007/s42761-022-00113-w.

Díaz, Rodrigo, and Jesse Prinz. 2023. "The Role of Emotional Awareness in Evaluative Judgment: Evidence from Alexithymia." *Scientific Reports* (0123456789): 1–8. https://doi.org/10.1038/s41598-023-32242-y.

Hildebrand, Dietrich von. 1916. "Die Idee Der Sittlichen Handlung." *Jahrbuch Für Philosophie Und Phänomenologische Forschung* (3): 126–251.

Massin, Olivier. 2023. "The Reactive Theory of Emotions." *European Journal of Philosophy* 31 (3): 785–802. https://doi.org/10.1111/ejop.12736.

Mitchell, Jonathan. 2019. "Pre-Emotional Awareness and the Content-Priority View." *Philosophical Quarterly* 69 (277): 771–94. https://doi.org/10.1093/pq/pqz018.

Mitchell, Jonathan. 2021. *Emotion as Feeling Towards Value. Emotion as Feeling Towards Value*. https://doi.org/10.1093/oso/9780192846013.001.0001.

Müller, Jean Moritz. 2019. *The World-Directedness of Emotional Feeling: On Affect and Intentionality*. Vol. 75. Palgrave MacMillan. https://doi.org/10.1353/rvm.2021.0052.

Müller, Jean Moritz. 2021. "The Spontaneity of Emotion." *European Journal of Philosophy* 29 (4): 1060–78. https://doi.org/10.1111/ejop.12625.

Müller, Jean Moritz. 2022. "The World-Directedness of Emotional Feeling: Affective Intentionality and Position-Taking." *Emotion Review* 14 (4). https://doi.org/10.1177/17540739221085573.

Müller, Jean Moritz. n.d. "In Defence of the Content-Priority View of Emotion." *Dialectica*: 1–26.

Mulligan, Kevin. 2010. "Emotions and Values." *The Oxford Handbook of Philosophy of Emotion* (June 2018): 1–29. https://doi.org/10.1093/oxfordhb/9780199235018.003.0022.

Naar, Hichem. 2023. "Value Feelings: A Defense." *Philosophies* 8 (4). https://doi.org/10.3390/philosophies8040069.

Prinz, Jesse. 2004. *Gut Reactions: A Perceptual Theory of Emotion*. New York: Oxford University Press.

Roberts, Robert C. 2003. *Emotions: An Essay in Aid of Moral Psychology*. Cambridge: Cambridge University Press.
Scheler, Max. 1973. *Formalism in Ethics and Non-Formal Ethics of Value*. Evanston: Northwestern University Press.
Tappolet, Christine. 2016. *Emotions, Values, and Agency*. New York: Oxford University Press. https://doi.org/10.1093/acprof:oso/9780199696512.001.0001.

9

Fear as Preventer

Timothy R. Kearl and Robert H. Wallace

Within human ethical life broadly construed, fear often prevents us from acting as we want to or should. Our goal in this chapter is to explore, clarify, and defend fear's role as a preventer. We will offer answers to the following two questions: (1) How exactly does fear prevent us from doing as we want or should? and (2) What (dis)value, if any, is there to fear playing this preventative role? Our answers turn on taking fear's role in shaping our agency seriously.

Our answer to the first question draws on recent ideas in action theory and the metaphysics of abilities. We suggest that fear often functions as a *robust preventer* or *obstacle*, which renders agents unable to act in certain ways (compare Lewis 2020). We work through one way that fear might be such that the function of fear might be realized; the way that fear construes or represents a situation as dangerous or threatening can robustly prevent the agent from availing herself of certain contextually salient options, not only causing her not to act on those options (*preventing*), but being such that it would cause her not to act on them even if things were just a bit different than they actually are (*robustly* preventing).

This conception of fear-as-preventer explains why certain instances of inner conflict, ones in which an agent acts out of fear and against her better judgment (what we might call cases of "fear-driven *akrasia*"), are used to exemplify a kind of irrationality via compulsion. The view also explains how fear can be a source of self-alienation and of wider disvalue. Viewing fear as a preventer (often an obstacle) vindicates not only an intimate connection between an agent's emotional profile and her abilities but also her self-conception and even the moral worth of her actions.

Nevertheless, one important consequence of our conception of fear is that it works against the somewhat pessimistic view that fear is somehow inherently vicious or otherwise disvaluable, something we should strive to minimize, perhaps even something that ideal or ideally virtuous agents would lack altogether.[1] We offer, against these pessimists, a principled reason to think that overtly negative conceptions of fear are wrongheaded; while fear is often stylized as an emotion that, in its function as a preventer, directs agents away from what is choiceworthy or ultimately good, it also, by those very same mechanisms, sometimes compels agents to act well, or to avoid acting poorly, directly out of a concern for what ultimately matters. And this allows us to appreciate why, for instance, fearlessness is a specious virtue.

We conclude with a plea on behalf of fear's rightful place in our ethical lives. Indeed, by considering fear from this perspective, broadly in terms of its function with respect to agents' abilities, we can better appreciate the ways it relates to our other mental states, like hope, and also how it relates to our evaluative perspective in general, in particular, to the ways in which we show due regard (Strawson 1962; Frankfurt 1971; Arpaly 2002). If different—perhaps in certain ways better—beings than us could cope without fear, we should not strive to be them.

Fear and Inhibition

Both in the science of emotion and in ordinary thinking, we tend to conceive of emotions, at least in part, as motivators. Anger drives us to strike out; disgust to push something away. Indeed, there is some consensus in the psychological literature that emotions involve three components, which any theory of emotions must account for: "appraising a stimulus a particular way, feeling a particular way, and being motivated to act a particular way" (Scarantino 2014, 156; cf. Deonna and Troni 2015). This consensus has seen some uptake in conceptual moral psychology. In his work on anger, for instance, David Shoemaker (2021) calls these three components an emotion's characteristic "syndrome."

Moral anger, for instance, appraises a situation as one in which an injustice has occurred. It feels bad, perhaps even overwhelming, but also energizing. Your focus narrows. Your body engages in a "fight-or-flight" response. A motivation to correct some perceived wrong is within or manifests moral anger's characteristic syndrome. You then act on the basis of your anger. You might, for instance, express blame or righteous indignation.

It is natural to think that many cases of fear fit this paradigm (e.g., Tappolet 2009, 326). Fear involves an appraisal of a situation as involving a threat, real or perceived. It also involves a "fight-or-flight" response. Nevertheless, we confess to finding something odd about how fear fits into this template as stated when it comes to being motivated to act in a particular way; at least, the fit is odd if we are anchored around thinking about the ways in which anger or disgust motivate. Consider the following paradigmatic case of fear:

> *Snake: Diane is hiking along a desert trail in Tucson, Arizona. While placidly admiring the Saguaro cacti, she spots something out of the corner of her eye by her feet. It seems to be a rattlesnake! Diane becomes so frightened that she cannot move.*

Diane's emotional response and attendant phenomenology are not accompanied by some obvious characteristic motivation (her fear does not, for instance, prompt her to flee). Rather, in some natural and intuitive sense, Diane is *paralyzed* by fear; she's scared stiff. Moreover, we can stipulate that Diane would be condemned to similar inaction even if, say, she were in a bit of a hurry to make it back to the trailhead to pick her daughter up from piano practice, or if she were especially thirsty, or if the (apparent) snake were just a bit to the right of where it appears to be, and so on. Thus, there is something strikingly different about at least some instances of fear in comparison with, say, anger. While both emotions have various normal or paradigmatic expressions in an agent's behavior, fear does not (or, more cautiously: need not) motivate in the way anger does. Granted, there is a way of talking about Diane's inaction—her being scared stiff—in terms of being motivated to act in a particular, *omissive* or *non-doing* way. But this feels unnatural, or at least unwieldy. Rather than think that Diane is motivated to act, perhaps by omission, we think that she has been rendered, in her fear, *unable to act*; Diane cannot but remain frozen.[2]

To be clear, our aim is not to say that the syndrome view is false, let alone that its falsity is demonstrated by quick reflection on cases like *Snake*. If anything, we are inclined to think that it is part of fear's syndrome that fear prevents action, sometimes robustly so. It can, but not always, do this in a kind of inhibitive way, as in *Snake*, where the protagonist is prevented from doing anything, or perhaps anything but omitting to act. Indeed, fear has a wide variety of actional and non-actional manifestations, attending to which should prompt more careful consideration of fear's syndrome.

By way of comparison, consider that Christine Tappolet (2009) has commented on the fact that fear often results in freezing or tonic immobility responses, although it can also lead to fleeing and even sometimes fighting. In particular, she has argued that some fears lack any motivational import at all (2009, 338–339). She cites a famous passage from Kendall Walton (1978, 5):

> Charles is watching a horror movie about a terrible green slime. He cringes in his seat as the slime oozes slowly but relentlessly over the earth, destroying everything in its path. [. . .] The slime, picking up speed, oozes on a new course straight towards the viewers. Charles emits a shriek and clutches desperately at this chair.

Tappolet (2009, 338) thinks, as does Walton, that "Charles . . . appears to have no motivation resulting from this intense fear." But whereas Walton implausibly concludes that Charles is not *really* afraid of the slime since he does not, for instance, run out of the theater, Tappolet suggests that Charles's fear is purely contemplative. Like Tappolet, we want to push back against a rather narrow conception of fear's syndrome.

This much exposition is meant only to get the reader thinking about fear's *preventative function*. Inhibition of the sort Diane feels is one natural way to see this function realized. In the next section, we will articulate our position in greater detail, and we will address a wider range of cases, ones in which notions like "inhibition" or "freezing" play no special role. Our aim will be to explain even this wider range of expressions of fear in terms of prevention, notably in cases of "recalcitrance," but also even in cases of putative "direct motivation," ones which better fit the letter of the orthodox view about syndromes. To do this, we will first need to think more carefully about how fear prevents us from taking certain courses of action, whether through inhibition (*Snake*) or something resembling direct motivation.

Fear as Preventer

In this section, we explain and apply the preventer model of fear. In particular, we argue that cases like *Snake*, which are ostensibly ones of inhibition or "freezing," and even some cases where fear ostensibly motivates action, can be seen as expressions of a unified underlying phenomenon, *that of modifying and diminishing an agent's abilities*. We then explain how various conceptions of fear might interface with our thesis about fear's preventative function.

We will defend the rather strong thesis that *part of what makes fear what it is* is that it has this preventative function. But it is worth noting that, in motivating the strong thesis, we thereby motivate a weaker one, namely that many paradigmatic instances of fear can be illuminated by thinking in terms of prevention. This weaker thesis will not be our emphasis, although we will note a few points at which a reader might wish to keep it in mind. Let us put forward, in a bit more detail, the fear-as-preventer view. Recall that, in *Snake*, Diane's situation seems more naturally explained in terms of inhibition than motivation; she is *frozen* in fear. And to be inhibited is to be prevented in some way. This connection reveals a path forward. David Lewis's notes for an unpublished manuscript titled "Nihil Obstat: A Compatibilist Analysis of Abilities" (2020) develop what we can call the "Obstacle Free Analysis" of abilities, or OFA:

You're able to X iff, for some basic action A:

(1) Doing it would be Xing, and
(2) There is no obstacle to doing A,

> where something is an obstacle to Xing iff it would prevent you from Xing even if things were just a little different (that is, you would be caused not to X in relatively similar counterfactual scenarios).

Lewis relies on the technical notion of a *preventer*, which he suggests is something that "would cause you not to do something" (2020, 243). In a word: preventers prevent. Our use of "preventer" follows Lewis's. He also relies on the notion of a *basic action*, those things we do without doing anything else—perhaps *wiggling one's ears*, *clenching one's fist*, *deciding on a course of action*, or, in general, *trying to do something* (where this is different from doing it, or even beginning to do it). These are basic, but the content of the list of basic actions is not particularly important for our discussion. We note this technical point to set it aside, noting only that, as a matter of bookkeeping, whenever fear (or anything else, for that matter) prevents, it does so, in the first place, by preventing the performance of some basic action.

With that said, let us expand on a crucial part of the OFA, namely that not all preventers prevent equally. Some may stop you from acting but not render you unable;

sometimes we just get unlucky, or we can't be bothered. Other times, we are prevented in a more thoroughgoing way: we lack the strength, the money, or the tools, and still other times we are depressed, deranged, or detained (Lewis 2020, 23). In the face of these more robust preventers or *obstacles,* it would take more than a slight change to how things actually are for you to succeed in acting. The basic idea enshrined in the OFA is that, while preventers cause you not to do something, only suitably modally robust preventers render you unable to do it.

Rather than take the OFA as an *analysis* in the strict sense of offering a reductive set of necessary and sufficient conditions for ability-attributions, or even taking the OFA on as a comprehensive conception of the nature of agential abilities, let's just say that it articulates something important about an agent's abilities.[3] What an agent is able to do is, in an important sense, *constrained* by her obstacles, those things that robustly prevent her from acting.

Our suggestion can now be stated flat-footedly. Fear is such that it can and often does cause us not to do something. That is, fear is a preventer. But more than that, fear is such that, in cases where it causes us not to do something, it is often true that *it would cause us not to do that thing even if circumstances were different.* Fear is often a *robust* preventer, an obstacle.[4]

We think that part of what makes something *fear* (as opposed to some other emotion, or some other type of attitude entirely) is that, at a very high level of generality, fear has a certain preventative function in response to threat or danger, real or perceived. Thus, the relationship between fear and our agentive abilities is roughly functionalist in shape. Fear is a preventer, often a robust one, of the performance of some (basic) actions, and thus literally changes what an agent is able to do in a particular situation.[5] In *Snake*, fear robustly prevents Diane from doing anything (or, if you like: anything but freeze). She is, intuitively, rendered unable to act. That prevention—in response to a real or perceived threat—is part of what makes her attitude *fear* rather than something else, like curiosity, doubt, surprise, anger, or belief. The fear-as-preventer view captures this central feature of the case, which concerns a familiar but inchoate connection between an agent's fears and abilities.

Recall now our first question: how exactly does fear prevent us from doing as we want or should? We answer: fear often literally renders us unable to act as we want or should; it causes us not to perform certain (basic) actions, and would likewise cause us not to act if things were just a bit different. (We comment more on preventing valuable actions in the next section.) Before exploring how the fear-as-preventer view could be realized in different ways, we want to work through two things that the view gets right: wider expressions of fear that do not seem to be matters of freezing or inhibition, as *Snake* is, and cases of "recalcitrant" fear.

Let us present the former idea in the form of an objection. An imagined objector might offer the following remarks: if fear functions so as to prevent action (in the face of real or perceived danger), then it seems that fear never motivates "directly" in the way that other emotions characteristically do. They might offer a case like the following to illustrate such "direct motivation":

> *Avalanche: Huey is hiking along a snowy trail around Mt. Baker. While huffing and puffing along, a strong wind picks up and he hears an ominous cracking sound under his feet. It seems to be an avalanche! Huey, fearing for his life and without a second thought, makes a sideways break for safety.*

Let us grant to the imagined objector that it seems strange to think about Huey's making a break for it in terms of action *inhibition*. His response to (real!) danger more closely resembles answering a call to action. He runs, and rightly so; anything else seems to lead to disaster.

But recall that the fear-as-preventer view suggests that fear *prevents* the performance of certain actions. It doesn't say that fear necessarily *prevents by inhibition*. The point about inhibition was simply to make salient an underappreciated connection between fear and prevention, inhibition being a fairly straightforward and intuitive way to bring that connection into view. We think that Huey's fear (of the avalanche) actually constrains what he can do in this case; in particular, he is such that *he cannot but make a break sideways*.[6] And that is because, we might imagine, his fear renders him such that no matter what he tries to do, he makes a break sideways.

We think it is fair to imagine *Avalanche* as a case in which Huey's fear prevents him from trying, considering whether to, or deciding to do anything other than break sideways. More than that, his fear would prevent him from doing those things even if, say, he had yet to keep his promise to his mother to take photos from the hike, or if he hadn't yet finished packing up his campsite (he lives by the motto: *leave no trace*), or even if the weather were just so lovely that day that, moments earlier, he couldn't imagine being anywhere else. In actual, flesh-and-blood situations, it would be difficult, or perhaps impossible, to get information about how his fear interacts with his ability to perform such mental actions. Nevertheless, that it is even possible to understand *Avalanche* in this way highlights our point. Even in cases that ostensibly reveal fear's capacity for "direct motivation," this is explicable in terms of prevention. In particular, when fear directly motivates, we think that it does so by rendering all other options unactionable because unthinkable, so to speak. For fear to perform its preventative function, it need not be the case that it must always resemble a paradigmatic case of "freezing" or inhibition, only that it interfaces with an agent's abilities in accordance with the OFA.

Let's now turn to another issue where we think the fear-as-preventer model gets things right. You might think that when fear brings about the kind of inaction that it does in *Snake*, this is because the agent fully believes that the fear is accurately appraising the situation or that, more generally, something about the fear is right (is apt or fitting). Indeed, Walton (1978, 6–7) asserts that "it seems a principle of common sense, one which ought not to be abandoned if there is any reasonable alternative, that fear must be accompanied by, or must involve, a belief that one is in danger." He suggests that, at least with respect to being afraid of a horror movie, we experience at best a kind of make-believe "quasi-fear," an attitude like fear in many respects except it is not accompanied by a belief that one is (really) in danger. But hard cases make bad law. Consider one way that *Snake* could continue:

Upon a closer look, the rattlesnake is just a funny-shaped root sticking out of the ground. But Diane can't shake her fright.

That Diane can't shake her fright is compatible with Diane disbelieving that there is a snake, and with Diane disbelieving that she is in danger. She might even avow that she is embarrassed for being saddled with such an overwhelming feeling. Diane's fear is *recalcitrant* in this case (D'arms and Jacobsen 2003, 129); it persists despite her better judgment that she is not in danger (cf. Paytas 2021, 3–5). Perhaps this is a case where the cause of Diane's fear (the root) is different from the object of her fear (snakes) (Harbin 2023). But it is clearly a case in which fear comes apart from beliefs about danger. Whether Diane's attitude is somehow deviant, nonstandard, misplaced, or otherwise defective in virtue of this fact, it is fear. The fear-as-preventer view both vindicates this idea and can explain it in a principled way that does not route through Diane's "better judgment."

There is a great deal of attention paid to Diane's practical (ir)rationality in these sorts of situations. For instance, Bennett Helm (2001) diagnoses these as cases of irrationally conflicting practical import—Diane judges that the root is not worthy of attention and action and yet *feels* that it is so worthy (2015, 430–431). Sabine Döring (2014) argues that in cases like this, the agent is not irrational; she really is in a situation that is parallel to a visual illusion (cf. D'arms and Jacobsen 2003, 141). In the same way that an agent need not *assent* to the visual illusion—the stick is not really bent even though it seems to be—an agent need not assent to the construal of a recalcitrant emotion (2014, 134–135). She suggests that Helm wrongly assumes that agents must always passively assent to their emotions, and such assent then conflicts with their judgments. What would be irrational, Döring suggests, is *acting* on that perception-like illusion; recalcitrant emotions "interfere with the reasoned pursuit of [an agent's] goals by moving them so as to act against those goals" (2014, 135).

We think the conflict between Diane's judgment and her fear need not be understood in terms of a putatively distinct kind of irrationality. She may indeed be irrational. It's just that, if we only focus on this particular normative quality of her predicament, we risk overlooking a deeper explanation of what is troubling about recalcitrance, which is that it can engender a distinctive sort of persistent inability, one which can interfere with an agent's pursuits.

The view that fear is a preventer is thus in good standing with respect to the recalcitrance to fear. Fear is often recalcitrant, and that is central to the kind of case where we find that fear conflicts with what we judge to be choiceworthy. So much so, in fact, that Taylor Paytas (2021, 5) defines fear in terms of recalcitrant desires to avoid perceived danger. As Paytas notes, a recalcitrant fear need not conflict with an agent's evaluative judgments; it's just that the fear *wouldn't* go away in light of conflicting judgments. So, our view agrees with Paytas's "recalcitrant desire avoidance model" of fear, at least to the extent that both think of fear in modal terms. But rather than explicitly define fear in terms of its connection to recalcitrance, or to certain sorts of desires, or even of judgments about fearworthiness, the fear-as-preventer view sees the recalcitrance of fear as part of the same unified and general phenomenon as exhibited in *Snake* and *Avalanche*, namely, (sometimes robust) prevention. When the fear is strong enough, it would cause you not to act even if things were different. Indeed, in both cases, fear becomes an obstacle, rendering agents unable to act in certain ways.

Notably, the fear-as-preventer view is neutral with respect to substantive theories of emotion, that is, theories that could offer explanations of what the state that realizes the function of fear is like. We think this even with respect to theories that put a high premium on motivational states like desires (Tappolet 2016, Paytas 2021), which can obviously and robustly prevent.[7] To advertise this neutrality, we'll discuss an alternative to the action–motivation paradigm in order to explore how fear prevents in more detail.

Consider the idea that emotions are like sensory perceptions. One common form of this view suggests that they are a kind of evaluative perception, a way of "seeing" an emotion's formal object (e.g., Tappolet 2016, Roberts 2013, 2003). This is only sometimes metaphorical; Peter Goldie (2007) suggests that we can sometimes know what the thing to do is because we can *literally see* the relevant normative properties. We take no stand on the plausibility of this idea, but we want to explain how our fear-as-preventer model could likewise be slotted into it. Robert C. Roberts (2013, 2003) suggests that emotions are *quasi-perceptual* "concerned construals," ways that things appear to the subject of the emotion that are derived from their desires (2003, 23). Fear, he says, construes the world as containing a threat (Roberts 2013, 47; 117–118). In a similar vein, Bronwyn Finnigan's (2023) Buddhist analysis of fear suggests that "to fear some object is to construe it as dangerous, and to construe something as dangerous is to anticipate it will cause suffering or other unwanted effects such as the loss or harm to an object of value or concern" (2023, 137). Drawing on an analogy to predictive processing accounts of perception, she suggests that this anticipation has a counterfactual element. We fear that the object would cause unwanted effects if we were to act in certain ways (2023, sec. 4.1).

The idea that fear is a concerned—perhaps also anticipatory—construal fits nicely with our suggestion that fear is importantly connected to an agent's abilities. Supposing, for the sake of argument, that fear's construal gives us the impression that if we were to move in certain ways, for instance, then we would have to face the threat or the danger, then it's plausible to think that such construals could cause one not to move in certain ways, perhaps in light of the anticipation of unwanted negative effects on the objects of one's concern. Indeed, we think that if an agent has a quasi-perceptual impression that if she were to act in certain ways, bad things would occur, it would be *unsurprising* for this impression to be an obstacle to her acting in those ways. In *Snake*, the fearful construal of the snake as an anticipated danger causes Diane to freeze up. She's unable to do anything but stand still. In *Avalanche,* the fearful construal of the ominous cracking sounds as anticipating a dangerous avalanche renders Huey unable to do anything but make a break for it. In this case, Huey is prevented, perhaps, by the overwhelming choiceworthiness of getting out of there (given how he construes his situation), from doing anything else.

Let us end this section by giving due to one final skeptical concern regarding fear's putative distinctive phenomenological feel. So far, we have been silent on the details of fear's phenomenology. Doesn't it make sense to think that fear's *felt scariness*, or some other putative property of the feeling of fear, maybe that it involves felt desires to avoid danger and threat, constitutes the core or nature of fear itself? What of fear's feeling, of fright?[8]

We have, to be sure, omitted extended discussion of *what it is like* to feel fear, and a certain sort of philosopher thinks that fear's qualitative feeling is what is most interesting about it. But we think that the apparent force of this objection stems from a mistake. We have tried to explain fear in terms of its characteristic preventative function: that of diminishing or otherwise rearranging an agent's abilities. To pay no heed to what fear feels like would render our discussion incomplete, but we insist that, contrary to appearances, we have paid heed to it, albeit indirectly. A theory of what fear is, in particular a theory of what fear is that is concerned with fear's distinctive functions, is eo ipso a theory of what it is like to be in that state.[9]

The Good of Prevention by Fear

To sum up the preventer view of fear: fear prevents, sometimes robustly enough to change what the fearing agent is able to do. One of the chief virtues of the preventer view of fear is that it enables us to see a level of complexity in *how* fear prevents that is absent or underexplored in other ways of thinking about fear. The complexity consists in, for instance, sometimes preventing by construing some options as more choiceworthy and, alternatively, other times preventing by inhibiting agents from acting so as to bring about the options they recognize to be choiceworthy. This section moves from a theory of fear and fear's function to a discussion of the purported disvalue of fear, the purported virtue of fearlessness, and a more general point about stereotypically negatively valenced emotions.

Fear is often an antagonist in discussions of ideal practical agency; weak-willed or akratic agents fail to do (or to be motivated to do) that which they deem choiceworthy, or that which comports with their "better judgment," sometimes because they are too afraid to take up the relevant means to some righteous end. As Paytas (2021) argues, building on the Stoic tradition, fear can hinder acting well. That's both because it can be psychologically disunifying and express biased or otherwise corrupt values. For instance, insofar as fear is often recalcitrant, it pushes against one's own evaluative perspective. And fear often involves a vicious concern for one's own safety and well-being (Paytas 2021, 8).[10]

We will argue against the position that an ideally practical or fully virtuous agent would feel no fear, or at least have no use for it. In fact, our argument for the good of fear suggests that, in fact, the virtuous agent might feel afraid (whether or not they, for instance, feel fear in quite the same way we do). In particular, what seems to drive these arguments against fear as a part of ideal agency is the dogma that what fear prevents is valuable action. Let us return to (practical)[11] akrasia, which again is the phenomenon whereby an agent acts in a way that is discordant with her better judgment. Alan

Gibbard's psychological-normative explanation of akrasia sees it as a picture of "motivational systems in conflict," according to which our acceptance of certain *norms* applies one sort of relatively compartmentalized motivational pressure, one which sometimes competes with, and then sometimes fails to override, an "animal" system, one we share with creatures not sophisticated enough for normative acceptance.[12] In another vein, Alfred Mele (1995, 74) argues that akratic action can be understood as a conflict between one's practical commitments and competing motivations.[13] When an agent is weak-willed, the opposing motivation trumps their practical commitment. Mele consistently appeals to fears, for instance when it expresses a failure of nerve, to illustrate akratic action.[14]

Setting aside the differences between these various conceptions of akrasia, we can observe that akrasia is supposed to be bad, other things equal. And it is no wonder; akratic actions are borne of a kind of motivational incoherence, and the cases that capture our attention are typically, at least, ones in which that incoherence has certain deleterious effects. The akratic agent is stylized as one who succumbs to vice or baser sentiments and, with appetite steering reason, places bad bets, all within a story the lesson of which is the value of a certain sort of coherence. One would be forgiven for wanting to cast to the flames the salient baser sentiments that enter into conflict with reason and render agents thus conflicted selfish, irrational, self-undermining, pitiable, reprehensible, or otherwise non-ideal, fear chief among them.

And yet, we think that the received wisdom about the badness of fear has much to do with what makes for a compelling example, and very little to do with fear per se, or even fear that moves the agent against her better judgment. The vilification of fear is nothing but good marketing. We note that, for instance, Mele's own vignettes sometimes concern agents whose fear prevents them from doing a *bad* thing. He offers an example concerning Bruce the Cub Scout, who agrees to break into a neighbor's house along with some wayward scouts; at the last minute, he "chickens out," as the other scouts would derisively put it (2010, 393–394, see also 1995, 60).[15] Overcoming fear per se does not render any agent rational, laudatory, or otherwise ideal; the crook overcoming his fear of being caught red-handed has nothing going for it. This, we hope, will not strike anyone as particularly controversial. Even so, it is worth pausing to consider other cases of action borne of fear and incoherence, ones that cast fear in a different light within our ethical lives.

For the sake of exposition, this is as simple as imagining cases of *inverse akrasia* (cf. Arpaly and Schroeder 2013, 1999) in which the protagonist, exhibiting the same structural inner conflict as more familiar cases of akrasia, *acts well*, going against her "better" judgment, where the quotations indicate that the judgment in some respects is grossly mistaken.[16] Here, we imagine one such case in which the agent acts well in virtue of being afraid:

> *Secret Police*: *Alice is on the precipice of a morally compromising choice: turn her friend Bob over to the Secret Police or lie about his whereabouts. And Alice has been raised to feel, by and large, that the Secret Police were keeping the peace, their sometimes grisly means a tithe to the greater good. And part of Alice—the purely*

> *self-interested part—does dwell on her own safety, as anyone would; she thinks to herself that she ought to turn Bob (or anyone else!) in, for her sake and for the sake of that abovementioned greater good. But what Alice, friend that she is, fears most is that Bob might be captured by nefarious forces, subject to unthinkable tortures, and shipped off to rot in some distant gulag. And she is ultimately compelled to lie to the Secret Police at the door.*

Alice's fear expresses a concern for her friend Bob's well-being. And this fear grips her so vividly as to compel her to lie—at risk to herself—to the Secret Police at the door. We think Alice's behavior is, perhaps with certain details filled in, supererogatory, a real act of courage driven, perhaps ironically, *by fear*. That is, if Alice's fear is strong enough, she cannot but lie to the Secret Police, and it is precisely because her fear, attuned as it is to the very real threat to the well-being of someone she cares about, is an obstacle to her doing anything but lying (that is, her fear does and would prevent her from turning over Bob, even if things were just a bit different) that her care is deep and courageous.[17]

In sum, what seems to drive these arguments against fear as a part of ideal agency, or as having any central role in a theory thereof, is a dogma that what fear prevents is *acting well*. But this conclusion loses its appeal when we consider cases in which an agent does the right thing for the right reasons *because they are afraid*, perhaps even while thinking the reasons for which they act are bad reasons. If fear plays an important role—when it does—in explaining why akratic agents fail to act well, fear likewise plays an important role—when it does—in explaining why inverse akratic agents act well.

Moreover, let us confess that, when we look out into the world, what we see is that the ways in which fear is positively valenced are legion. Imagine the fear of losing a loved one during a pandemic or the fear one feels for the safety of a parent, a spouse, or a child. Imagine the fear of being caught lying to protect a friend in need or helping members of the resistance in times of oppression. Think of the fear of disappointment, perhaps of disappointing those whose opinions matter most to you. These are instances in which fear expresses concern, care, or other forms of regard, much as anger and grief can express love.[18] It is not always vicious to be afraid, even if we have a tendency to think and talk about cases in which it is.[19]

Thus, we hope to have motivated not only that fear's connection to the purportedly disvaluable incoherence of akrasia is contingent, but also that fears can—sometimes through mechanisms generating a similar sort of incoherence—express concern for what matters, an attunement to the right and the good. This sort of incoherence obviously has something going for it, even if it nevertheless falls short of some rational ideal. It is hard to imagine how our way of living together, variously participating in or escaping the strains of involvement, would be changed were we to lose the capacities for care paradigmatically expressed through fear, just as it would be hard to imagine life without hope, love, grief, or anger.[20] Each of these can be misplaced or misproportioned, but serve, collectively, as interfaces for navigating and coping with life together, and often the means by which we express what we ultimately care about.[21] And in this respect, fear is not special; it is just one among many obstacles from within the agent herself, sometimes but not always resembling chains, sometimes but not always expressing due regard.

Nevertheless, the fear-as-preventer view can explain why the would-be fearless are getting something right. Fear plays a certain functional role in our moral psychology, say by construing certain options as less choiceworthy so as to prevent—sometimes robustly—the agent from acting on them, thereby rendering her unable to act. The would-be fearless correctly see that this is sometimes a bad thing. But it is not *always* a bad thing, perhaps not even *often*, and that is their mistake.

Fear and Hope

In the previous section, we offered some reasons in favor of the idea that ideally practical or fully virtuous agents might still feel fear. Fear prevents us from acting, but sometimes this has positive value. In this section, we consider a connection between fear and hope, the latter of which has sometimes been understood as the "positive mirror image of fear," for fear concerns what is possible and threatening, whereas hope concerns what is possible and attractive (Roberts 2003, 281). Seneca even suggests that in order to cease being afraid, one should cease to hope (Letters 5).

By centering on how fear's preventative function relates to hope, we consider a novel way to explain the close relationship between fear and hope. While fear plays a preventative role in our psychology, hope may play an *enabling* one. Some of us fear *badly* (Harbin 2023), by taking harmful actions against perceived but non-actual threats. Hope might provide a counterbalance to fear by enabling alternative modes of engagement with objects of perceived danger. Conversely, fearing *well* might place a constraint on our poorly conceived hopes.

We cannot offer an account of hope in this space, but we can end by sketching out its enabling role. As Adrienne Martin (2014, 34–35) suggests, hope involves a "licensing stance" toward the objects of one's hopes; the probability and felt attraction of the desired outcome justify certain modes of action and planning. And as Cheshire Calhoun suggests, hope involves acting under a "phenomenological idea of the determinate future whose content includes success" (Calhoun 2018, 86), which is to say, hoping involves a kind of judgment-insensitive positive anticipation. Put in our preferred terminology: hope enables a person to act, that is, it puts them in a position to do things, perhaps because it provides a causally efficacious positive construal of the situation under which those actions make sense to the agent, given their goals and aims. This positive construal sometimes has modally robust causal force; it "opens up" courses of action that the agent might otherwise be (robustly) prevented from taking up.[22] When an agent is hopeful, other things being equal, they would not be prevented from acting thus-and-so, at least not to the same degree, even when things were different.

Hope is often understood to be uniformly positive. We think this largely follows from the fact that hope often expresses positive moral concern, care, or otherwise reflects what is good in our evaluative perspective concerning the future. But just as we see fear as bad because of a particularly narrow diet of examples, our view of hope is inversely skewed. Imagine:

> Seaworthy: *Clifford has an extremely hopeful disposition. Instead of focusing on the very real possibility that his ship is not seaworthy, Clifford hopes that it will safely make the voyage. Indeed, his hope is recalcitrant with respect to his better judgment about the state of the ship; he just can't shake the feeling that things are going to turn out fine. And so, Clifford sets his plans into motion, and the ship sinks.*

In this case, hope was not a good thing. It was recalcitrant, psychologically disunifying, and a corruptive influence on Clifford's practical agency.

What would have helped Clifford avoid his mistake? Perhaps among other things, Clifford could use a good dose of fear (the fear of litigation, at least). As McGeer (2004, 123) has pointed out, *hoping well* involves more than just aiming at good things; it involves not relying too much on other people but also recognizing that what you hope for is not entirely in your control. We might add this idea that one's hopes need to be tempered; there are some things one ought not to hope for. Fear is one avenue by which hope might be tempered, by rendering us less able to take certain courses of action pursuant to our hopes.

Given the broadly functionalist suggestion of our thesis about fear and ability, it isn't surprising that fear and hope are related in this way. Functionalism about mental states does, to the chagrin of some, imply holism about mental states (Lewis 1972). We would be inclined to say that emotions are, among other things, ways in which our abilities to act are constrained or set free by our own psychological makeup. Given this, it is not surprising that fear and hope interact by preventing and enabling, seeing as both are responses to perceptions about the future. Indeed, one might think that holism itself undermines the motivation for trying to rid ourselves of particular emotions, like fear, if our emotional capacities come as something of a package deal. If fear and hope can each in their own way express care or concern or manifest corruptive influence, and if the two can help keep one another in check, allowing one to hope and fear better, why not imagine an ideal agent whose fears and hopes are not ideally fitting and so ideally *balanced*?

In sum, there can be corruptive hopes—for political domination, say—that might enable people to act poorly. And there can be fears that express deep moral concern—fear of catastrophic climate change—which might also render agents *unable* to act poorly. Nevertheless, it is clear that both fear, and relatedly, hope, have reputations at odds with their function in our agential psychology. This is, perhaps, the lesson to be learned by looking, clear-eyed, at fear. Ideals should not be overly fetishized. We are emotional beings, and as we aim for virtue, we have to work with and through the tools that we've got.

Conclusion

Fear is a preventer, sometimes an obstacle diminishing an agent's abilities. In the limiting case, the agent cannot help but orient herself along fear's vector. This preventative function can as much reflect the agent's deep-seated concerns as other, more stereotypically positively valenced attitudes do. Indeed, whatever was left of Jekyll's humanity found expression in his fear of becoming Hyde.

Acknowledgments

Our thanks to Ami Harbin, Guy M. Crain, and Gwen Cuccia for their helpful feedback on this chapter.

Notes

1 As two recent articles note, the Stoic tradition (Paytas 2021) and the Buddhist tradition (Finnigan 2021) each counsel the elimination of fear on these grounds.
2 We offer *Snake* as a central case of fear inhibiting action, preventing one from acting in any way but freezing up. "Freezing" is, of course, only sometimes an omission; other times, it is a deliberate and self-conscious positive action (think about playing a game of freeze tag). This case is not meant to be about freezing per se, nor about the distinction between actions and omissions. Instead, it is just to make salient how fear characteristically diminishes or changes one's abilities, sometimes rendering one unable to do otherwise than one does. Thanks to Guy Crain for prompting this clarification.
3 See Kearl and Wallace (2024) for an argument that it cannot succeed as a strict analysis.
4 All kinds of emotions can be preventers, sometimes robust ones; fear need not be special in this way, even if it is especially suited to reveal something more general about the connection between emotions and abilities to act. We will comment on this idea toward the end of this chapter.
5 See Laoiza (2024) for the case that a functionalist account of emotions can integrate into scientific practice *despite* criticisms (e.g., Scarantino 2018 and Barrett 2016). As Laoiza suggests, we understand functions in a causal-dispositional sense (c.f. Lewis 1980).
6 Compulsion modals are duals of ability modals. An ability modal is a claim in natural language that expresses that an agent is able to x. Compulsion modals are the duals of ability modals in the logical sense (for any operator O, a dual of O is ~ O ~): an agent is not able to not x. As Mandelkern, Schutlies, and Boylan (2017: 302) put it in their explication of compulsion modals: "When someone says, 'I cannot but eat another cookie', she is saying that refraining from eating another cookie is not an option for her."
7 Consider my overwhelming desire to keep my life when presented with the choice: your money or your life.

8 See Deonna and Teroni (2015) for a discussion of qualia and the phenomenology of emotions.
9 Compare Lewis (1980) on pain.
10 Paytas uses the term "fear" to refer to a construct that is helpful for thinking about virtue theory rather than trying to capture the full breadth of the folk-psychological notion. Hence, he wants to set aside many of the cases which, in our view, fall directly under the folk-psychological concept.
11 We set aside cases of epistemic akrasia. Cf. Horowitz (2013), Greco (2014), Kearl (2020).
12 Gibbard (1990), see especially pp. 56–7.
13 Indeed, we might view this picture as one in which the agent is causally compelled to act against her best judgment. See Nie (forthcoming) for related discussion.
14 Compare Davidson's (1973) use of fear to illustrate how actions might be unintentional because they are deviantly caused.
15 In a variant of Mele's case where the agent succeeds in overcoming his fear through strength of will, this overcoming might still be inconsistent with his better judgment (Mele 2010, 393–394). The idea that fear is always or even typically an antagonist to reflectively endorsed courses of action is a nonstarter.
16 Compare Arpaly's (2003) discussion of Huck Finn.
17 To the objector who complains that Alice is not moved by fear but *despite* fear, we register the following. Perhaps Alice's fear for her own well-being is "warm," and in that it is accompanied by feelings of panic, avoidance urges, and trembling; her heart races, and her breathing is elevated. Others, the "cold" ones, don't. But it is no part of our view that only warm fears prevent, or even that the warmer ones tend to triumph over colder. Although it's natural to think that fear always involves the "warm" feelings of an intense "fight-or-flight" activation, we think a broader construction of the term "fear" is better. It captures, for instance, certain cases of dread experienced in a calm hour. Compare Lewis (1988, 323).
18 See Kaupinnen (2018) for a defense of the value of anger in expressing concern, and Goldie (2016) for an extended discussion of the value of grief.
19 Some, like Martha Nussbaum (2018), have suggested that fear is a source of political value-corruption (compare Stockdale 2021).
20 Cf. Strawson (1962).
21 This fits nicely with so-called "real self views" of morally worthy action, but we do not commit to such views here. Compare Arpaly (2002), Frankfurt (1971), or Sripada (2015).
22 Michele Moody-Adams (2022) suggests that hope plays a central role in our political lives and the success of social movements.

Bibliography

Arpaly, Nomy. 2002. *Unprincipled Virtue: An Inquiry into Moral Agency*. Oxford: Oxford University Press.

Arpaly, Nomy, and Timothy Schroeder. 1999. "Praise, Blame and the Whole Self." *Philosophical Studies* 93 (2): 161–88.

Arpaly, Nomy, and Timothy Schroeder. 2013. *In Praise of Desire*. New York: Oxford University Press.

Barrett, Lisa. F. 2016. "Functionalism Cannot Save the Classical View of Emotion." *Social Cognitive and Affective Neuroscience* 12: 34–36.
Calhoun, Cheshire 2018. *Doing Valuable Time: The Present, the Future, and Meaningful Living*. New York: Oxford University Press.
D'Arms, Justin, and Daniel Jacobson. 2003. "The Significance of Recalcitrant Emotion (or, Anti-quasijudgmentalism)." *Royal Institute of Philosophy Supplement* 52: 127–45.
Davidson, Donald. 1973. "Freedom to Act." In *Essays on Freedom of Action*, edited by T. Honderich, 137–56. London: Routledge.
Deonna, Julien A., and Fabrice Teroni. 2015. "Emotions as Attitudes." *Dialectica* 69 (3): 293–311.
Döring, Sabine A. 2014. "Why Recalcitrant Emotions Are Not Irrational." In *Emotion and Value*, edited by Sabine Roeser and Cain Samuel Todd, 124–136. Oxford: Oxford University Press UK.
Finnigan, Bronwyn. 2021. "The Paradox of Fear in Classical Indian Buddhism." *Journal of Indian Philosophy* 49: 913–29.
Finnigan, Bronwyn. 2023. "Fear Is Anticipatory: A Buddhist Analysis." *Journal of Consciousness Studies* 30 (7): 112–38.
Frankfurt, Harry G. 1971. "Freedom of The Will and The Concept of a Person." *Journal of Philosophy* 68 (1): 5–20.
Gibbard, Allan. 1990. *Wise Choices, Apt Feelings: A Theory of Normative Judgment.* Cambridge, MA: Harvard University Press.
Goldie, Peter. 2007. "Seeing What Is the Kind Thing to Do: Perception and Emotion in Morality." *Dialectica* 61 (3): 347–61.
Goldie, Peter. 2012. *The Mess Inside: Narrative, Emotion, and the Mind*. Oxford: Oxford University Press.
Greco, Daniel. 2014. "A Puzzle about Epistemic Akrasia." *Philosophical Studies* 167 (2): 201–19.
Harbin, Ami. 2023. *Fearing Together: Ethics for Insecurity*. New York, US: Oxford University Press
Helm, Bennett W. 2001. *Emotional Reason: Deliberation, Motivation, and the Nature of Value.* Cambridge: Cambridge University Press.
Helm, Bennett W. 2015. "Emotions and Recalcitrance: Reevaluating the Perceptual Model." *Dialectica* 69 (3): 417–33.
Horowitz, Sophie. 2013. "Epistemic Akrasia." *Noûs* 48 (4): 718–44.
Kauppinen, Antti. 2018. "Valuing Anger." In *The Moral Psychology of Anger*, edited by Myisha Cherry and Owen Flanagan, 31–48. Rowman & Littlefield.
Kearl, Timothy. 2019. "Epistemic Akrasia and Higher-Order Beliefs." *Philosophical Studies* 177 (9): 2501–15.
Kearl, Timothy, and Robert H. Wallace. 2024. "Agentive Modals and Agentive Modality: A Cautionary Tale." *American Philosophical Quarterly* 61 (2): 139–155.
Lewis, David. 2020. "Outline of Nihil Obstat: A Compatibilist Analysis of Abilities." *The Monist* 103 (3): 241–44.
Lewis, David K. 1972. "Psychophysical and Theoretical Identifications." *Australasian Journal of Philosophy* 50 (3): 249–58.
Lewis, David K. 1980. "Mad Pain and Martian Pain." In *Readings in the Philosophy of Psychology*, edited by Ned Block, 216–22. Harvard University Press.
Lewis, David K. 1988. "Desire as Belief." *Mind* 97 (418): 323–32.

Lewis, David K. 2020. Nihil Obstat: A Compatiblist Analysis of Abilities. *The Monist* 103 (3): 241–244.
Mandelkern, Matthew, Ginger Schultheis, and David Boylan. 2017. "Agentive Modals." *Philosophical Review* 126 (3): 301–43.
Martin, Adrienne. (2014). *How We Hope: A Moral Psychology*. Princeton: Princeton University Press.
Mele, Alfred. 1995. *Autonomous Agents: From Self Control to Autonomy*. New York, US: Oxford University Press.
Mele, Alfred. 2010. "Weakness of Will and Akrasia." *Philosophical Studies* 150: 391–404. https://doi.org/10.1007/s11098-009-9418-2.
McGeer, Victoria. 2004. "The Art of Good Hope." *Annals of the American Academy of Political and Social Science* 1: 100–27.
Moody-Adams, Michele. 2022. *Making Space for Justice: Social Movements, Collective Imagination, and Political Hope*. New York: Columbia University Press.
Nussbaum, Martha C. 2018. *The Monarchy of Fear: A Philosopher Looks at Our Political Crisis*. Oxford: Oxford University Press.
Paytas, Tyler. 2021. "Be Not Afraid: The Virtue of Fearlessness." *Philosophers' Imprint* 21 (23): 1–13.
Roberts, Robert C. 2003. *Emotions: An Essay in Aid of Moral Psychology*. New York: Cambridge University Press. https://doi.org/10.1017/CBO9780511610202.
Roberts, Robert C. 2013. *Emotions in the Moral Life*. New York: Cambridge University Press.
Scarantino, Andrea. 2014. "The Motivational Theory of Emotions," In *Moral Psychology and Human Agency*, edited by Justin D'Arms and Daniel Jacobson, 156–185. Oxford: Oxford University Press. https://doi.org/10.1093/acprof:oso/9780198717812.003.0008.
Scarantino, Andrea. 2018. "Comment: Two Challenges for Adolphs and Andler's Functionalist Theory of Emotions." *Emotion Review* 10: 202–3.
Seneca, Lucius Annaeus. 1969. *Letters from a Stoic*. Edited by Robin Campbell. Harmondsworth: Penguin Books.
Shoemaker, David. 2018. "Defending Angry Blame." In *The Moral Psychology of Anger*, edited by Myisha Cherry and Owen Flanagan, 67–88. Rowman & Littlefield.
Sripada, Chandra. 2016. "Self-Expression: A Deep Self Theory of Moral Responsibility." *Philosophical Studies* 173 (5): 1203–32.
Stockdale, Katie. 2021. *Hope Under Oppression*. New York: Oxford University Press.
Strawson, Peter F. 1962. Freedom and Resentment. *Proceedings of the British Academy* 48: 187–211.
Tappolet, Christine. 2009. "Emotions and Motivation: The Case of Fear." In *The Oxford Handbook of Philosophy of Emotion*, edited by Peter Goldie, 325–48. Oxford University Press.

10

Art-Horror, Social Anxiety, and the Moral Imagination

Saraliza Anzaldúa

Modern media has proliferated the availability of a good scare for audiences. From horror novels, horror films, horror TV shows, and dark tourism to Halloween haunted houses, urban legends, horror conventions, and online horror channels—it seems that audiences looking to be terrified have no shortage of options to pursue.

Yet despite this cultural prominence, the role of fear in art-horror (fictional narratives in the horror genre across media) has only been recently examined in philosophical circles. In particular, contemporary philosophy has tried to answer the question: "Why would we want to be scared if fear by definition is an unpleasant experience?"

This question, dubbed the "paradox of horror," has been answered in various ways (Carroll 1990, 159–160). Some have claimed that there are other overriding emotions besides fear that attract audiences or that what audiences really experience isn't fear at all. Others claim that fear can be a pleasurable experience depending on the context. However, little attention has been given to the role that art-horror plays in our moral imagination and the use of fear to give audiences a phenomenological exercise in ways of moral inquiry.

In this chapter, I lay out the most popular positions concerning art-horror and show why we need an understanding of moral imagination if we are to answer the question of why audiences like being scared. In my view, the real appeal of art-horror is the processing of social anxiety. Furthermore, I claim that such experiences make use of our moral intuitions.

Discourse on Art-Horror

Philosophical treatment of art-horror has been a fairly recent discussion beginning with Noël Carroll's *The Philosophy of Horror, or Paradoxes of the Heart* (1990). While there were earlier discussions about fear in general, and even the attraction of fear such as in Edmund Burke's *A Philosophical Enquiry into the Origin of Our Ideas of the Sublime and Beautiful* (1757), philosophers didn't seem concerned with the nature of narrative horror or its particular experience of fear. Carroll kicked off that discussion, so I'll provide a brief overview of his position and then discuss alternative positions that arose through that discourse.

Carroll thinks that what is particular to art-horror is the monster, which is stipulated as an impossible entity that defies contemporary science.[1] That impossibility is characterized by the crossing of distinct boundaries, which makes the monster an impure entity that blurs what we normally take to be pure (Carroll 1990, 32–33). For example, vampires are both dead and alive—a state that violates known biological categories because an entity that is alive can't also be dead. The vampire is impossible, that is, shouldn't exist, because principles of contemporary science say it shouldn't occupy both states simultaneously. While Carroll acknowledges that there are examples of art-horror that don't have a monster, he thinks these are outliers and not characteristic of the genre.[2]

When we are confronted by the art-horror monster, the particular kind of fear we feel is characterized by a reaction to the threat and impurity monsters embody as impossible entities. That is, we are both horrified by the danger to ourselves and disgusted by the contaminated nature of the monster, which is abhorrent to our contemporary scientific worldview.

What attracts us to art-horror, despite this unpleasant experience, is our curiosity about the monster. If it is impossible, how did it come to be?[3] In search of those answers, we are willing to endure jump-scares, gore, and any number of aesthetic devices artists throw at us. Thus, Carroll's position is dubbed the "curiosity paradigm" and he notes how a significant portion of art-horror narrative arcs are preoccupied with the drama of proof: discovering the monster, finding explanations for its existence, proving the monster exists to other people and authorities, and so on (1990, 183).

In opposition to the curiosity paradigm, Berys Gaut theorizes an enjoyment paradigm: "the simplest, most straightforward explanation of the phenomenon of horror is that sometimes people *enjoy* being scared" (1993, 337).[4] Audiences of art-horror are willing to be scared because they enjoy the thrill of the experience. This position has intuitive appeal, especially when considering the work of sociologist Margee Kerr, who examines why people enjoy visiting haunted houses and seek out terrifying experiences in real life. In a discussion with neuroscientist Greg Siegle, she writes:

> [O]ne of the biggest mistakes we make when thinking about fear is trying to separate it from other high arousal states like pain, or being really excited, or laughing, or being sexually aroused. A lot of the same brain mechanisms are present in all these states, and it's up to us to give them meaning, as when I switched from fear to anger during the street fight outside my house. Our sympathetic nervous system becomes aroused, and then we interpret the arousal with cognitive manipulation and coordination between the limbic system and prefrontal cortex. This is why I switched from fear to anger so quickly during the street fight, and why people scream and then laugh at scary things when they know they're safe, and why makeup sex has a reputation for being especially hot. (2015, 212–213)

According to this account of fear, there is no mutual exclusion between enjoyment and horror as Carroll assumes. An individual can experience a similar "high" of arousal from fear just as with sexual activity or an intensive workout. While fear may have particular cognitive features, such as beliefs regarding a monster, because of its resemblance to other high arousal states (due to using the same neural systems), there is no reason why individuals can't derive pleasure from fear. It all depends on how individuals interpret the situation.

Carroll disagrees with Gaut regarding the mutual exclusion between horror and enjoyment, and their disagreement plays out through a mountaineering case. Does a mountain climber, undergoing a dangerous and potentially life-threatening event, feel fear throughout the experience, a mixture of fear and joy, or only enjoyment? Gaut answers that the joy arises from the experience of fear and the thrill of the adventure; thus, there is no intrinsic relation between horror and displeasure. Carroll, on the other hand, answers that fear is pushed to the side in order to concentrate on the task at hand: staying alive. So the adventure is not a constant state of fear, and the lack of fear allows for the experience of joy. Therefore, such a case would not be relevant to the paradox of horror question because it is not a true representative of the art-horror experience (Carroll 1995, 70). Gaut notes, however, that Carroll has failed to demonstrate that fear distracts one from the task at hand. In fact, fear can motivate concentration all the more on a task, particularly if it is fear connected to one's survival (Gaut 1995, 287).

These two positions, the curiosity and enjoyment paradigms, fall into the larger camps of non-integrationist and integrationist. The curiosity paradigm believes fear and enjoyment to be mutually exclusive, and thus they may exist within the same experience but never simultaneously. Furthermore, in a fearful experience, all other emotions are incidental and not characteristic of the experience. On the other hand, the enjoyment paradigm believes fear and enjoyment can exist simultaneously as an integrated event. To focus only on one emotion or to prioritize one emotion over another would be to reduce and misunderstand the overall experience.

This disagreement between integrationist and non-integrationist accounts is further illustrated in the discussion between Carroll and Susan Feagin. Feagin's position is the affect paradigm. While the discussion about the distinction between emotion and affect is still ongoing, in general, affect is understood to be the underlying mood of an experience, while emotion is the more acute mental state produced by cognitive functions. In the case of art-horror, audiences are drawn to the media because it gives them a particular affective experience of fear (which includes other affective sensations as well) and not because they have specific cognitive beliefs about the monster which elicit fear (Feagin 1992, 80). She notes that Carroll's "account is *not* intended to be one which captures the structure of *all* affective or feeling responses to fiction, such as those which might arise from sensory non-propositional thoughts, visual or auditory imaginings, or sensory experiences" (1992, 76). Rather, Carroll's account relies on a narrow interpretation of the art-horror experience which prioritizes singular mental states of fear that are cognitively interpreted (our reaction to the monster). Another way to put this dispute would be to say that Feagin takes a holistic view of the entire art-horror experience, whereas Carroll is only focusing on a slice of that experience under the microscope.

Carroll disagrees with this interpretation and, in a response, reaffirms his non-integrationist position through a roller coaster case: "She says that roller-coaster enthusiasts, among whom I include myself, must enjoy such things as the queasiness they feel as they plummet through space and take nearly upside-down turns. But queasiness is not what I enjoy when I ride a roller-coaster. What I enjoy is the novel way of moving through space at all those unusual angles and orientations at such palpable high speed" (1992, 87). Whereas Feagin sees queasiness as a characteristic part of riding a roller coaster (along with all the other sensations), an integrationist account, Carroll views queasiness as only a part of the experience and not characteristic of it, a non-integration account. Again, Carroll responds that such an experience is not representative of art-horror.

Last, there is the social anxiety paradigm, which situates art-horror in its context as a psychological means to connect audiences to their historical experience.[5] For example, Adam Lowenstein examines Romero zombie films and connects them to histories of U.S. racism, the Vietnam War, and the Iraq invasion. The films serve as allegorical moments that connect the audience to pasts saturated with traumatic memory (2012, 167). That traumatic memory can only become "fully comprehensible as traumatic through their deferred distribution across several different temporalities" (2012, 157). Through art-horror, audiences are encouraged to come to terms with histories that have been denied, minimized, or misremembered by re-remembering them in the present experiences of horror films.

Carroll is skeptical about psychological answers to the paradox of horror that don't rely on cognitive features, and in particular about psychoanalytic explanations. While he admits that some narratives can be read in terms of Freudian repression and sexual wish fulfillment, the pattern doesn't always work, and "it is far more difficult to see the way in which humans trampled by big gorillas or emulsified by Godzilla's death-dealing halitosis can gratify a *sexual* wish" (1990, 171). As we will see later, this understanding of psychology is very narrow and assumes that anxiety must be bound up with sexual repression. With that assumption, Carroll also assumes that Godzilla has nothing to do with anxieties about the atomic bomb, the destruction of life itself, and the retaliation of nature.

What's Missing from the Conversation

A serious problem with the discourse of art-horror so far is that there are actually two questions being asked but treated as one. This obscures the conversation because scholars are talking past each other, with each party thinking they are discussing one issue while the other party thinks they are discussing another. Furthermore, because two questions are under discussion, an answer posed for one may be applied to an entirely different question than intended. If the conversation regarding art-horror is to be productive, clarification on this point is necessary.

There is the question of attraction: Why are audiences drawn to art-horror in the first place? A separate question is the endurance question: Why are art-horror audiences willing to tolerate an unpleasant experience over time? While these questions are related, if what I expect of art-horror is what draws me to art-horror, then I must be willing to endure a harrowing experience in order to fulfill my expectations, by conflating them we miss nuances of art-horror that have significant implications.

For example, the curiosity paradigm relies on plot devices and the drama of proof as evidence to explain why we endure the horrific experience of art-horror: the film we are watching engages our curiosity about the impossible monster, and so we tolerate the fear/disgust in order to satisfy our curiosity. This seems like a plausible answer to the endurance question, but a weak one to the attraction question even though Carroll states his purpose is to answer the latter. Presumably, as a potential audience member familiar with the genre, I know the usual explanations of the monster: a mutation caused by a virus or radiation, an unhinged scientist stitching together various organisms, a supernatural entity summoned from another dimension, an alien entity visiting from the darkest regions of space, and so on. While Carroll might reply that I don't know which of these answers the director has in mind or how a particular scenario will play out, it doesn't seem like a strong enough incentive for me to sit through two hours of nausea, cold sweat, and trembling. Truly novel origins of the monster are rare and not characteristic of the art-horror genre.[6] Given that, as an audience member, I'm not expecting to be surprised about the origins of a monster and have my curiosity satisfied about its impossibility because I already have my answers. In fact, it seems like part of the experience of art-horror is that I know what to expect if we take the repeated use of certain art-horror tropes and narratives as any indication of their ubiquity. Furthermore, with early marketing media like posters, movie trailers, director interviews, and so on, audience members know going into the experience what to expect of the monster—whether it be of mad scientist or supernatural origin. So we are still without an answer to the attraction question: What draws us to art-horror to begin with?

The second problem with the current discourse of art-horror is that the role of imagination has for the most part been overlooked. This is strange, considering the large function that the imagination of both the artist and the audience plays in the dialectic of art-horror. As we saw in the conversations between Carroll, Gaut, and Feagin, their disagreement was not about the role of the imagination in determining whether climbing a mountain or not climbing a mountain/riding a roller coaster is like art-horror, but about how large a role fear played in those cases and its relation to the overall affect. In trying to answer the paradox of horror, many scholars take a universalist approach (all instances of art-horror can be treated the same, and there is a single answer that can be applied to all cases) and often use an atomized conception of fear. From this position, the fear I experience when I see a spider on my ceiling is equivalent to my fear for the art-horror protagonist as they run from a horde of zombies. This overlooks not only the significance of the media itself as a creative art form which utilizes the imagination and how it may distinctly influence the audience's emotions/affect, but also any implications of that media which might suggest answers to the paradox of horror. Thus, any robust explanation of art-horror will give consideration to the function of the imagination in that media and its role to both attract audiences and encourage them to endure a terrifying experience.

Solving the Paradox of Horror

Despite problems with the curiosity paradigm of horror, Carroll does inadvertently provide an answer to the attraction question, which in turn provides a better answer to the endurance question:

> It is frequently remarked that horror cycles emerge in times of social stress, and that the genre is a means through which the anxieties of an era can be expressed. That the horror genre should be serviceable in this regard comes as no surprise, since its specialty is fear and anxiety. What presumably happens in certain historical circumstances is that the horror genre is capable of incorporating or assimilating general social anxieties into its iconography of fear and distress. Film history provides several well-known examples of this. The horror films in the style of what is called German Expressionism were produced in the crisis milieu of the Weimar Republic; the Universal cycle of horror classics, in the United States, occurred during the Great Depression; the early science fiction/horror cycle of the early fifties, in America, corresponds to the early phase of the Cold War. Moreover, these different cycles tended to use their horrific imagery to express certain anxieties that correlate with the uneasy temper of their times. (1990, 207–208)

Carroll notes that each era of art-horror is concerned with a particular theme that speaks to the social anxiety of the period, and this provides a better answer about why would we seek out horror media in the first place: we are already in a state of anxiety, and horror media, through the catharsis of art-horror, provides us with a way to ease that anxiety. This, in turn, gives us a better answer to the endurance question that doesn't rely on assumptions about genre standards: we sit through an unpleasant experience in hopes of processing our anxieties through a specific fear. The monster focuses my nebulous worry about existing in the world into a specific emotion (fear) toward a particular object related to that worry. Like a reverse prism that unites fractured light rather than disperses it, art-horror is the medium by which our generalized anxiety becomes focused through a specific entity to fear. For example, while my anxiety about the government manipulating my behavior for military and capitalistic purposes may be a generalized sense of worry, my fear of the tethered clone in Jordan Peele's *US* (2019) is toward the specific entity (the monstrous government-made clone of the protagonist/me) that distills the heart of my anxiety into fear that I can confront through the protagonist and perhaps process.

If the monster represents our social anxiety, then through the protagonist, we come to terms with it. How this may happen depends on the interaction between the characters and the monster, as well as the final outcome. If the monster is destroyed, we may feel better because the object that triggered our anxiety is gone. If the monster isn't destroyed because the relationship between it and the protagonist has changed, then perhaps our relationship with the origin of our anxiety will shift too. We might see our "monster" in a different way and thereby ease our anxiety by learning to live with the monster/anxiety. Last, it's possible that the monster wins in the end, and we the audience must face the possibility that the source of our anxiety might also overcome us. This sub-genre is sometimes called "dread horror," in which there is no coming to terms or happy ending. Instead, the audience is left with an overwhelming feeling of dread and hopelessness that they must learn to live with.

One may object that there is no guarantee that our social anxieties will be alleviated. If the purpose of art-horror is to trigger our social anxiety so that we may come to terms with it, then wouldn't art-horror be a failure if we were left with our anxiety at the end of watching a horror film? I don't think so because the three outcomes of horror media outlined above suggest that there are different ways of confronting our anxieties rather than a single method for curing them. Furthermore, the differing sub-genres as well as the varied creativity of the artists provide the audience with a wide range of experiences in relation to their monster/anxiety. There is no one size fits all, as with anything to do with mental health. Art-horror is a way to confront social anxiety, and possibly even ease it, by facing our anxiety through horror media rather than reality.

It is true that the audience won't know what the outcome will be, whether the anxiety as monster will prevail, but the experience still provides a way to confront anxiety, and by confronting that anxiety in the relatively safe world of art, the experience provides a way to come to terms with it. As Katerina Bantinaki notes: "Through our encounter with horror fiction we are given a chance to confront or learn to cope with fear in a safe environment: we learn to control our fear feelings and display mastery over our reactions to frightening stimuli; to direct our thoughts—often aided by the narrative" (2012, 390). The horror genre offers an arena by which the audience navigates and negotiates their anxiety (and response) in relative safety through a fear surrogate that represents the true source of their anxieties. The outcome of that battle will depend on the narrative and the individual. Inevitably, horror fans, depending on their particular needs/preferences, will gravitate to certain narratives and sub-genres of horror. Some may be attracted to happy endings that depict the protagonists vanquishing the monster and find catharsis through those hopeful art-horror narratives. Other audiences will prefer world-ending conclusions where the monster triumphs and there is no hope. Sometimes we prefer our nihilistic misery, and it might be the case that self-punishment is its own kind of catharsis. These two opposite ends of the art-horror experience are on a spectrum with countless experiences in between—a choose-your-own-adventure to confront your anxiety by turning it into a specific entity to fear. Whether or not you prefer to overcome it, and how you confront it via the range of protagonists offered by the genre is a personal preference. What influences these preferences is a question beyond the scope of this chapter to answer.

An example of the social anxiety paradigm can be found in the period of "torture porn" horror fiction which gained prominence roughly around the Bush administration (2000–2010). The two franchises of *Saw* and *Hostel* are characteristic of this period, and the plots center around mostly white middle-class victims being tortured in gruesome ways. Art-horror scholars theorize that audiences dealing with anxieties surrounding their guilt about complicity in torture by the U.S. government used the films as a means of catharsis. Specifically, white middle-class audiences dealing with the cognitive dissonance of upholding values of freedom and democracy while simultaneously advocating for torture alleviated their guilt by being tortured themselves through art-horror proxy.[7] By appealing to social anxiety as an explanation, a more satisfying answer is given to the attraction question because it tells us why audiences seek out art-horror despite the unpleasantness of the genre while also taking into account the variety the genre offers as well as the context of particular socio-historical circumstances. This sub-genre of art-horror is an example of the extreme end of narratives where the monster triumphs and there is no hope for a happy ending. Audiences looking to process social anxiety might be willing to sit through hours of fear/disgust because the discomfort of self-punishment provides a cathartic way to process feelings of complicity in government-sanctioned torture. This is not to say that everyone with such feelings will seek out art-horror or that everyone seeking out art-horror is looking to process those feelings. Many others chose to confront those feelings with protests and political action, and there were more sub-genres of art-horror during this period than torture porn. Rather, the social anxiety paradigm gives us a nuanced insight into the myriad possibilities of art-horror and the audiences it attracts.

The above answer to the attraction question also provides a better answer to the endurance question: monsters hold our attention despite the unpleasant emotions we experience in art-horror consumption because it is through the monster-as-anxiety that we confront our anxiety outside horror media. The monster embodies our anxiety, which already holds our attention outside the movie theater or the book in our hands. Through the monster, we get to examine our anxiety more closely as a specific fear-object via the protagonist's need to survive, which is a manifestation of our desire to overcome our anxiety.

Furthermore, we are able to do so in a safe manner because the monster provides distance from the actual reality of our anxieties. As Marcia Eaton notes in "A Strange Kind of Sadness":

> In controlled surroundings, tragedy permits us to purge ourselves of bottled-up feelings. Indeed we seek out tragedies (and other art works) in the belief that a controlled experience will excite, enrich, purge, and/or sensitize us in certain ways. (1982, 60)

The safety of the movie theater helps us navigate anxieties by giving us a measure of control over our experience. Through that control, the monster-as-anxiety threatens us in a less direct way than what is truly threatening us. Using the example above, it takes much less cognitive work to despise the torturer-as-monster than it does to despise a corrupt government that tortures people and in which I might be implicated through my support of that system. Of the two options, the former is a much safer alternative for the status quo of daily living.

Answering Questions

Some scholars object to the social anxiety paradigm based on its popularity or lack thereof. Gaut thinks that if this answer were plausible, more people would engage in this kind of art as a way to process anxiety, and yet it seems to be the least attractive way to engage with one's fear. Gaut notes, "one needs to be in a fairly robust psychological state in order to enjoy these fictions at all" (1993, 336). However, it's not clear why the horror genre must have broad appeal in order to be attractive as an engagement with social anxiety or even how popular it would need to be. Few, if any scholars would claim that the mystery genre needs to be generally popular in order for audiences to feel attracted to the art medium because it engaged their affect in a particular way through solving a mystery. One can still enjoy solving puzzles or playing escape rooms without being attracted to mystery films or novels. Nor would the affective experience of the mystery genre need to be redefined because only a small portion of the population engaged. Different populations and individuals will gravitate toward various genres of art and that in no way diminishes the power of those art forms. Why specific individuals/communities engage with particular kinds of art is a question beyond our current concern. Gaut even admits that this problem is to be left to "empirical, psychological investigation" (1993, 344). We only need to answer that art-horror gives a particular experience not that everyone should want to consume it for the sake of that particular experience.

Another challenge to the social anxiety paradigm is that it sidesteps the integration vs. non-integration discussion. What scholars concerned with this debate seem to disagree over is how much fear has to be involved in order for it to be relevant to the art-horror case, how much the emotion characterizes the experience, and whether other sensations contribute to that experience. What they miss, however, is the role of imagination in distinguishing these cases. As John Morreall notes, one of the key features of art-horror is that "we can 'enter into' the characters, we can vicariously feel their pleasure" (1985, 102). When I ride a roller coaster or climb a mountain, imagination plays little if any role because I am embodied in the current experience. I may suddenly imagine falling to my death or the car falling off the track, but this fleeting image pales in comparison to the hour or so I'm involving my imagination in the terrifying trials of the art-horror protagonist. The social anxiety paradigm brings out the distinctiveness of art-horror as a specific kind of fear experience under particular controlled circumstances that engage the imagination and avoids these kinds of questions. Roller coaster rides and mountain climbs have nothing to do with social anxiety or the imagination. Therefore, they involve a different kind of emotional experience than that provided by art-horror. The latter experience is characterized by what Andrea

Sauchelli calls "H-mood" (horror mood), stylistic art devices that intentionally evoke a dark atmosphere through "a morbid attention toward (principally) death, murder, and evil" (2014, 43). Examples include lighting, music, camera angles, certain forms of prose, and so on; all of which are intended to build a specific environment conducive to elicit the audience's imagination for the purposes of art-horror. Such an artistic mood is absent from the roller coaster and mountain climbing cases and doesn't entice the imagination. While questions about whether fear is mutually exclusive to enjoyment, and how much it characterizes the art-horror experience may be interesting avenues of investigation, by reducing art-horror to those questions scholars have overlooked the artistic use of audience imagination in art-horror. This has also meant that the implications for our moral imagination have likewise been overlooked in answers to the paradox of horror.

Art-Horror and the Moral Imagination

Philosophy has long used the imagination, in particular the moral imagination, as a tool to work out moral problems and sharpen our moral intuitions. From Zhuangzi's swimmer to Philippa Foot's trolley problem, we imagine cases that test our intuitions in order to illuminate the nuances that may inform our moral understanding, decisions, and actions. In particular, extreme cases like Kant's murderer at the door put us in positions of fear with high stakes so that we may unpack our moral assumptions.

However, there are limits to such thought experiments. First, even when facts about a case are stipulated, people tend to think about them in different ways. One way is how we imagine probabilities to play out in scenarios. I might think that a certain outcome is intuitively unlikely and therefore not worth the moral risk, whereas someone else might have a different intuition. For example, a moral agent might be willing to pull the lever diverting a train to another track in order to save five people if they think that the one person on the other track whom the train hits might survive. In "Intuitive Probabilities and the Limitation of Moral Imagination" (2018), cognitive science researcher Arseny Ryazanov and colleagues demonstrate that moral imaginations resist stipulations (imagining alternatives like in the trolley example above), impose their own probabilities, and understand scenarios in creative ways; all of which poses challenges to moral psychology and philosophy.

Another limit of the moral imagination is that my own embodied experience restricts my ability to consider important phenomenological concerns outside that direct experience. Catriona Mackenzie and Jackie Leach Scully consider such limits regarding disability and the moral imagination. They reason that since there is no mental activity without a body, our embodied mind has "constraints on our capacities to both imagine ourselves otherwise and to imaginatively put ourselves in the place of others" (2007, 342). In the case of disability, trying to determine the quality of life and make subsequent decisions for others with non-normative bodies is limited by the imagination of normative bodies and the biases/assumptions therein. Given the high stakes of making sometimes life-and-death decisions for other people, this is especially problematic, when considering that some non-normative bodies don't consider themselves disabled or their quality of life diminished as others would imagine them to be. For example, caregivers considering whether or not to subject their dependents to potentially life-threatening surgeries because they think that without such interventions the life of their loved ones will be severely diminished and, in extreme cases, unlivable. Knowing the limits of their moral imagination to imagine that life from the position of their own embodiment, and trusting those living with such disabilities about their own life assessments might assist caregivers in making a more informed decision.

Given these two limitations, art-horror is uniquely situated to help us overcome these challenges to the moral imagination and allows us an intuitive way into philosophical questions. The horror genre plays out scenarios in graphic detail and triggers my body into coming along for the ride. While seated at my desk, I may think that it's a sound idea to sacrifice my loved one for the good of the world if they are patient zero for the zombie apocalypse. But watching a protagonist struggle with that actual choice in a film might push me to reconsider when I start to sweat and shake alongside them; and then see the scenario play out in full over the course of the film. Art-horror can invoke our deepest fears and make us experience phenomenologically in ways that traditional thought experiments can't. As Stephen Asma notes, monsters can be a powerful philosophical tool made up of social context and moral questions that test our intuitions through imagination:

> Monsters can stand as symbols of human vulnerability and crisis, and as such they play imaginative foils for thinking about our own responses to menace . . . In a significant sense, monsters are a part of our attempts to imagine the good life or at least the *secure* life. Our ethical convictions do not spring fully grown from our heads, but must be developed in the context of real and virtual challenges. In order to discover our real values, we have to face trials and tribulation, and monsters help us imaginatively rehearse. Imagining how we will face an unstoppable, powerful, and in-human threat is an illuminating exercise in hypothetical *reasoning* and hypothetical *feeling*. (2017, 154)

Herein lies an important implication that art-horror has for our moral imagination that has been mostly overlooked in discussions of the paradox of horror, while providing answers to both the attraction and endurance questions. We come to art-horror to address our anxieties and sit through an agonizing experience in order to address those anxieties.[8] In working out those anxieties, we utilize our moral imagination through a phenomenological experience that gets our blood pumping, our palms sweaty, and our heart racing in a way that discussing a thought experiment lacks. Through the protagonist, we are faced with extreme challenges and often heart-breaking choices. But rather than thinking through these moral questions in a low arousal state, such as when I'm in a classroom or at my desk, art-horror embodies me in a high arousal state in which these questions occur, thereby helping me to bypass the problems of the moral imagination by making the stakes/possibilities of the situation clear/non-negotiable, and illuminating assumptions/biases I might have when I use my imagination to mentally construct a situation from past embodied experiences in a low arousal state. I'm attracted to art-horror as a unique method to engage my social anxiety and endure the high arousal state, which involves my moral imagination so that I can come to terms with that anxiety.

This is not to say that all art-horror succeeds as a means of moral imagination or that it gives us a perfect way into certain experiences. It's not clear what intuitions films like *Leprechaun* (1993) are testing, and there are plenty of horror films that engage social anxiety but make little use of the moral imagination; instead, they prefer to give simple, safe narratives that don't challenge audience assumptions.[9] There is also the danger of taking one's experience of art-horror as true, such as in the case of the genre's problematic use of non-Christian religions as a source of evil entities and curses. Furthermore, the trajectory of certain art-horror narratives might lead us to questionable moral conclusions. For example, it might suggest that it's morally permissible to indiscriminately kill people who have been infected with a virus, as in the case of many zombie horror films.

Still, even with its problems, art-horror is a fertile ground for testing our moral imaginations. For example, one of the common questions played out is, "How far are you willing to go to protect yourself?" In order to engage this question, the film *The Invitation* (2022) pushes the protagonist Evie with extreme circumstances like being held captive by one's family and forced to marry Dracula. As the film progresses, the options become limited for Evie, who tries escaping, finding help, and defending herself to no avail. Left with no other options, she submits to becoming a vampire in hopes of killing Dracula. The narrative of captivity and forced marriage mirrors a colonial subtext, and the audience is confronted with a moral quandary reminiscent of Audre Lorde: "When all other options have been exhausted, can you tear down the master with his own tools?"[10] Social anxiety regarding our existence in a colonial-capitalistic world is triggered through both Evie's loneliness and lack of community/family, as well as the Euro-aristocratic characters in the film who hold racist values. That anxiety is crystallized into a specific object of fear by the monster Dracula who stands on top of a multifamily conglomerate that has exploited the world for centuries in order to build their wealth. Through Evie, the audience is put into a high arousal state where the question of survival is put into increasingly higher stakes that are non-negotiable: "Would you work in a dehumanizing job?" "Would you kill another person?" "Would you submit and live an enslaved life?" and "Would you risk assimilation and death for the chance of freedom?" These are questions that have been and continue to be played out in a world marked by colonialism, slavery, and exploitation. Through the safe media of art-horror, the audience tests their intuitions on these questions by engaging their moral imaginations while having a phenomenological experience that is triggered by the film. In this example, we see how art-horror puts the audience in a specific position (captivity and enslavement) with high arousal (fighting for one's life against a vampire) so that anxiety about an exploitative world can be worked through in a relatively safe embodied state. Whether or not the audience agrees with the conclusions implied by particular instances of art-horror, or if they continue to think about those moral questions afterward is beyond the capacity of philosophers to answer.

In trying to understand why audiences are compelled to undergo terrifying experiences and why art-horror continues to be a popular media form, we can't overlook the significance of the moral imagination and its phenomenological features. As Asma notes, life is "messy, always changing, open-ended, and relentlessly coming at you in high speed" (2017, 270). We are not always given the luxury of working out our decisions calmly on paper or during a three-hour philosophy seminar. Sometimes we are confronted with epidemics, car crashes, and war; given only seconds to make a decision while fear overcomes us, our hands shake, and our vision is blurred by tears. Even given its imperfections, art-horror is one of the ways people attempt to work through the existential terrors and conundrums. Art-horror is not just a way to satisfy our curiosity or have a good scare, though it can do both. Rather, it's a way to confront our anxious selves and test out our intuitions about the kind of people we think we are.

Acknowledgments

Thank you, Pamela Hieronymi, Zara Zimbardo, Ami Harbin, and Parker Haratine, for your feedback.

Notes

1 Carroll stipulates that supposed monsters in fantasy narratives do not qualify on this definition because they are not impossible. Rather, their existence is built into the narrative and their existence is unsurprising: "In fairy tales . . . monsters are part of the everyday furniture of the universe" (1990, 16).

2 By using the impossible monster as the foundation of his answer to the paradox of horror, Carroll brushes aside many sub-genres of horror which have no monster and overlooks other means by which art-horror evokes audience fears. For example, the film *Scream* (1996) is considered a horror classic and has spawned a whole franchise without using a monster. Instead, the protagonists are hunted by an unknown but very much human killer. However, the narrative and film aesthetics are distinctly horror rather than thriller or mystery. As we'll see, not all philosophers of horror (myself included) are so narrow in focus as Carroll but rather make room for monsters, the monstrous, and the non-monster alike.

3 The question of existential impossibility, how something exists in spite of known scientific laws, differs from other seemingly impossible questions of art-horror, such as how parents can harm their children (*The Monster*, dir. Bryan Bertino, 2016) or the rich exterminate the poor (*Purge* franchise). The latter questions are not particular to art-horror and can be found in other media genres such as drama, sci-fi, and so on.

4 Sometimes referred to as the pleasure paradigm.

5 Also called the expressionist or catharsis paradigm.

6 There is also the issue of whether the drama of proof is industry standard. Carroll only gives a few examples, and we could name just as many or more art-horror examples that are epitomes of the genre but lack the drama of proof narrative, such as *The Thing* (1982) and *Ginger Snaps* (2000). Both films have protagonists that are more concerned with surviving than satisfying their curiosity and lack the search for origins or proof of existence that the curiosity paradigm relies on for evidence. Given the vastness of art-horror, it seems that the drama of proof may exist in some examples and be non-existent in others without being a necessary feature or industry standard.

7 Examples include "Torture Porn: 21st Century Horror" (2014) by Isabel Pinedo and "Carnographic Culture: America and the Rise of the Torture Porn Film" (2010) by Beth A. Kattelman.

8 Though it's an interesting question to think about whether or not audience members are consciously aware of why they come to and endure art-horror, it is beyond the scope of this chapter to answer. Given the variety of groups/personalities attracted to art-horror, it's not beyond reason to assume that some engage with art-horror consciously while others engage in a more subconscious manner. This question would need more socio-psychological research to address.

9 Though it's beyond the scope of this chapter to properly address, I don't think it's possible to engage social anxiety through art-horror without also engaging the moral imagination. Even in cases with reductive narratives that aim to provide happy endings for audiences, the media taps into their imagination regarding what's expected and morally permissible. Rather than challenge the moral imagination, such sub-genres might make use of a habituated imagination to engage social anxiety.

10 Audre Lorde's famous phrase "The master's tools will never dismantle the master's house" comes from a talk given at the Second Sex Conference in 1979 and an essay later published in the anthology *This Bridge Called My Back* (1981) edited by Cherríe Moraga and Gloria Anzaldúa.

Bibliography

Asma, Stephen. 2017. *Evolution of the Imagination*. Chicago: University of Chicago Press.

Bantinaki, Katerina. 2012. "The Paradox of Horror: Fear as a Positive Emotion," *The Journal of Aesthetics and Art Criticism* 70, no. 4: 383–392.

Carroll, Noël. 1990. *The Philosophy of Horror; Or Paradoxes of the Heart*. New York: Routledge.

Carroll, Noël. 1992. "Disgust or Fascination: A Response to Susan Feagin," *Philosophical Studies: An International Journal for Philosophy in the Analytic Tradition* 65, no. 1/2: 85–90.

Carroll, Noël. 1995. "Enjoying Horror Fictions: A Reply to Gaut," *British Journal of Aesthetics* 35, no. 1: 67–72.

Eaton, Marcia M. 1982. "A Strange Kind of Sadness," *The Journal of Aesthetics and Art Criticism* 41, no. 1: 51–63.

Feagin, Susan. 1992. "Monsters, Disgust and Fascination," *Philosophical Studies: An International Journal for Philosophy in the Analytic Tradition* 65, no. 1: 75–84.

Gaut, Berys. 1993. "The Paradox of Horror," *British Journal of Aesthetics* 33, no. 4: 333–345.
Gaut, Berys. 1995. "The Enjoyment Theory of Horror: A Response to Carroll," *British Journal of Aesthetics* 35, no. 3: 284–289.
Lowenstein, Adam. 2012. "Living Dead: Fearful Attractions of Film." In *Fear: Across the Disciplines*, edited by Jan Plamper and Benjamin Lazier, 148–169. Pittsburgh: University of Pittsburgh Press.
Mackenzie, Catriona and Jackie Leach Scully. 2007. "Moral Imagination, Disability and Embodiment," *Journal of Applied Philosophy* 24, no. 4: 335–351.
Morreall, John. 1985. "Enjoying Negative Emotions in Fiction," *Philosophy and Literature* 9, no. 1: 95–103.
Ryazanov, Arseny A., Jonathan Knutzen, Samuel C. Rickless, Nicholas J. S. Christenfeld, and Dana Kay Nelkin. 2018. "Intuitive Probabilities and the Limitation of Moral Imagination," *Cognitive Science* 42: 38–68.
Sauchelli, Andrea. 2014. "Horror and Mood," *American Philosophical Quarterly* 51, no. 1: 39–50.

11

Fear and Motivated Reasoning

Lessons from the Satanic Panic

Guy Crain

The Satanic Panic (circa 1980–1992) was a moral panic that included various alleged but ultimately baseless threats posed by Satanists primarily to children. Some philosophers characterize fear as predominantly epistemically compromising—that is, it skews reliable perception, judgment, and belief formation (de Sousa 2009). Philosophers with such a view of fear would likely point to a broad fear-driven social phenomenon like the Satanic Panic as a prime example of fear's deleterious epistemic effects. But that characterization oversimplifies and over-villainizes the role of fear in the Satanic Panic. I will argue that the Satanic Panic illustrates fear performing its proper epistemic functions, and the "blame" lies rather in the way those functions can be unwittingly misdirected by people's motivations.

In this chapter, I present an overview of the Satanic Panic. Next, I present what psychologists call *motivated reasoning*—briefly, it occurs when an agent's reasoning is unwittingly guided by motivations other than accuracy. Then, I consider the panic through the lens of motivated reasoning by first exploring the epistemic effect people's fears had on their reasoning and then proposing explanations for why people were motivated to prefer frightening but ultimately implausible conclusions.

Overview of the Satanic Panic

The Satanic Panic consisted of at least five "interrelated and mutually reinforcing expressions" (Poole 2010, 169).

Recovered-Memory Expression

Allegations of what was called Satanic ritual abuse (SRA) arose in the context of recovered-memory therapy (Bottoms and Davis 1997). Many scholars agree the catalyst for SRA allegations was the 1980 publication of the book *Michelle Remembers*

(Richardson, Best, and Bromley 1991, 11). Co-written by psychiatrist Lawrence Pazder and his patient-turned-spouse Michelle Smith, the book purported to be a true account of Smith's memories recovered during therapy of her suffering SRA in childhood (Smith and Pazder 1980). The popular book inspired professional conferences where therapists were warned that SRA might underlie their patients' comparatively milder problems (Robbins 2002, 98–99). Therapists were encouraged to use recovered-memory therapy, as Pazder had with Smith, to detect SRA in patients' pasts. Recovered-memory therapy consists of guided-imagery exercises, asking closed-eyed patients to imagine how events that *might* have taken place in their past *would* have taken place (Loftus 1993). After numerous sessions, many patients come to experience these imaginings as genuine memories. During the panic, therapists pressed patients to explore via guided imagery how present symptoms of mere anxiety or depression could be manifestations of repressed SRA memories. Like Smith, many patients came to believe they were childhood victims of SRA with some even naming their abusers, some of whom were convicted based solely on the evidence of these alleged memories (Flahive 2023). Suspiciously similar to Smith's, these alleged recovered memories included elements like abduction by Satanists, elaborate rituals performed in secret, and female children used as "breeders" for babies that were sacrificially murdered or eaten. *Michelle Remembers* was thoroughly discredited immediately following its release (Grescoe 1980). Nevertheless, the book was widely influential; the authors promoted their story in interviews and at conferences. The recovered-memory techniques were also empirically discredited at the time (Loftus 2004), yet their use persisted widely among clinicians.

Law Enforcement Expression

The Satanic Panic overlapped with the "Stranger Danger" panic, in which child disappearance statistics were misleadingly presented or exaggerated (Best 1990; Glassner 1999). Satanic Panic proponents were quick to piggyback on these numbers, claiming that many of those abductions must be occult-related (Best 1991, 97). This, along with the recovered-memory therapy patients, led to the emergence of "occult cops," alleged experts in dealing with Satanic crime (Poole 2010, 173). Law enforcement personnel underwent SRA trainings, warning them about crimes perpetrated by networks of Satanists. Cops were trained to decipher alleged encrypted communiques between Satanists in everything from music to graffiti (Leon 2020). Such cops were also featured presenters at conferences for educators, social workers, victim advocates, and clergy (Robbins 2002, 95). The buzz in the air led police to investigate some crimes on the presumption they must have been committed by Satanists (Wade 1999).

Daycare Scandal Expression

There were allegations of SRA taking place at daycare centers (deYoung 1997). Scholars agree the flashpoint of this expression was the McMartin preschool case in California (Jenkins and Maier-Katkin 1991). The McMartin scandal began with a dubious allegation of abuse reported to police. Police then warned other parents whose children attended the daycare. Parents frantically questioned their children, all of whom denied experiencing any abuse (including the child in the initial report). Parents shared their fears with one another. Sharing became rumors of suspected SRA (Nathan 1991, 82). Charges were filed against the daycare workers. Abuse experts—ears probably ringing with SRA-themed conference presentations—interviewed the children repeatedly. After repeated denials of any abuse, the children eventually said what they suspected interviewers wanted to hear; the children were clearly right because interviewers rewarded the children's increasingly bizarre claims with praise. The claims included that abusers wore black robes and inverted crosses, made children drink blood from sacrificed animals, took children to cemeteries and forced them to dig up corpses that were then mutilated, flushed children down toilets to secret sewer rooms to be abused, flew through the air, and magically turned some children into mice (Beck 2015). The case attracted attention from SRA experts, including Pazder and Smith, who traveled to California to consult with parents and investigators. The daycare owners were charged and tried based solely on the children's testimony gleaned from deeply flawed interviewing techniques (Garven, Wood, and Shaw 1998). The McMartin trial remains the most expensive in U.S. history, lasting seven years and costing California $15 million to prosecute yet produced no convictions (Hixon 2018). By the time the trial ended, there were approximately one hundred other daycare cases across the United States similar in origins, accusations, interviewing techniques, bizarre testimony, and glaring lack of corroborating evidence. While some cases ended in charges being dismissed for lack of evidence, others resulted in the incarceration of innocent people who spent decades in prison before being exonerated (deYoung 2007; Rabinowitz 1995).

Pop Culture Expression

Satanic influence allegedly permeated pop culture. Rock bands were accused of promoting Satanism—an accusation some bands selling an image of rebellion were happy to cash in on (Headley 2020). They purportedly did so by way of lyrical themes promoting drug use and other immoral acts (Brackett 2018) or by backward masking (Aranza 1983). There were also suspicions about games, toys, and cartoons. Some teen suicides were blamed on the role-playing game Dungeons & Dragons (Martin and Fine 1991). A TV movie depicting the game's sinister influence gave credibility to the panic (Lazarus and Jaffe 1982). Authors and speakers claimed that toys like He-Man and cartoons like The Smurfs were Satanic (Phillips 1986). Further, rumors about a shampoo company's 150-year-old logo being Satanic spread so widely the company decided to change it (Poole 2010, 178).

Conspiracy Expression

Allegedly, there was a powerful, virtually impossible-to-detect cabal of Satanists spread across the United States, orchestrating many events in the previous expressions

(Victor 1998, 3). The cabal's existence was touted at workshops for police and social workers (Bromley 1991). The idea was mainstreamed by congressional testimony given by a social worker who explained the McMartin preschool events as the work of an "organized operation of child predators" that "serves as a ruse for a larger, unthinkable network of crimes against children" that has "greater financial, legal, and community resources than any of the agencies trying to uncover it" (deYoung 1997, 22–23). The cabal was invoked to explain strange events ranging from cemetery vandalism to teen suicide (Victor 1991). By the late 1980s, rumor panics about cabals being responsible for such events had occurred in most states in the United States (Victor 1990).

Motivated Reasoning

Motivated reasoning occurs when people unwittingly employ standards or methods in reasoning tasks not for their accuracy but for their likelihood of supporting preference-consistent conclusions. Motivated reasoning is *reasoning*. It is neither mere wishful thinking nor blatant partiality. Motivated reasoners operate under a *reasons-sensitivity constraint*. They do not bring themselves to believe something merely because they want to. There must be prima facie evidence for the preferred conclusion. In many reasoning tasks, there is what Christopher Hsee (1996) calls "elasticity" among "justifiable factors"—that is, it is not straightforward how relevant pieces of evidence should be weighted or compared. For example, imagine judging a piano performance competition. One contestant plays a difficult piece, making minor mistakes. The other plays an easy piece, making no mistakes. Music difficulty and mistake frequency are justifiable factors to consider, but how they should be comparatively weighted is elastic. *Unjustifiable* factors a reasoner has motive to consider might affect how elasticity is handled—for example, whether one contestant studied at your alma mater.

The reasons-sensitivity constraint sounds as though motivated reasoning is more limiting than mere partiality or wishful thinking, but Hsee found evidence to the contrary. Hsee tasked study participants with appraising a condo for sale. Some were presented with justifiable factors, including differences between the condo and another condo previously appraised at $100,000, but the differences allowed for elasticity. The unjustifiable factor Hsee introduced was whether the buyer or the seller was purported to be the participants' fiancé. Other participants were not presented with differences between the condos but only with information about their fiancé's role in the sale. Hsee found that both groups appraised the condo above $100,000 when their fiancé was the seller and below $100,000 when their fiancé was the buyer. However, the elastic justifiable factors group's appraisals were significantly farther away from $100,000 than appraisals of the group provided only with incentive for partiality. Thus, while motivated reasoners operate under a reasons-sensitivity constraint, this very feature results in a *reasons-sensitivity-granted permissiveness*—that is, if there appears to be evidence for a desirable conclusion, this functions as permission to draw more extreme conclusions in a direction favorable to the reasoners' motivations than mere partiality would allow.

Motivated reasoning is *motivated* in the sense that accuracy is not the primary factor determining reasoning methods or evidential standards; these are determined by their likelihood to result in preference-consistent conclusions. Motivated reasoners can reason for straightforwardly desirable conclusions—for example, whether people with personalities similar to their own are likely to have successful relationships or succeed academically or whether their assessment of a medical test's reliability allows them to maintain belief in their own good health (Kunda 1987; Ditto and Lopez 1992). Motivated reasoners, though, can reason toward conclusions the preferability of which seems counterintuitive. A 2015 study found that how people process scientific information about the risks of climate change can depend on how they are primed to relate that information to their identities (Kahan et al. 2015). One group of participants read an article about geoengineering—technologies developed by private corporations to solve climate change-related problems faster than the current scientific consensus predicts. Next, they read a science article about climate change and were asked to rate its credibility. Conservatives in this group gave the climate change article a higher credibility rating than conservatives in a control group who did not read about geoengineering. While one might expect conservatives to tend to discredit information about climate change, the geoengineering article served as a sort of buffer, making the information about climate change more identity-palatable. Thus, whether people credit or discredit information regarding complex issues might not reflect the quality of that information but rather whether it has been "suffused with meanings that threaten their cultural outlooks" (Kahan et al. 2015, 205–206). While people may genuinely take themselves to be evaluating complex information in hopes of accurately assessing the external world, they might be engaging in activities that are, in fact, identity performative.

Further, motivated reasoning is not sophistry or guile. As Kahan (2016, 2) notes, motivated reasoners "unwittingly conform their assessment of information to some goal collateral to determining its truth." Geoffrey Cohen's study (2003) featured two fabricated welfare policies—one generous and the other stringent. Participants had previously indicated being either liberal and in favor of welfare or conservative and opposed. Participants read an article detailing one of the two policies where the party supporting the policy was manipulated—participants read either a version that included quotes expressing support from their own political party or a version with support expressed by the opposing party. Participants rated the degree to which they agreed with the policy and the degree to which various factors had contributed to their agreement/disagreement with the policy. Most participants claimed the policy content and their own philosophy of government were the greatest contributors and all participants rated in-party support as contributing least. Yet, Cohen found that whether the policy was generous or stringent, the strongest predictor of participants rating the policy favorably was whether the article expressed in-party support. Despite participants' self-reported reasons, policy content demonstrably had no effect. Participants were genuinely unaware of the degree to which their reasoning was motivated.

The Satanic Panic as Motivated *Reasoning*

The Satanic Panic was not a product of the poor reasoning or malice of one individual or a clearly delineated set of individuals. It was a complicated phenomenon, one that included both good-faith and bad-faith actors navigating an epistemic environment with structural elements like media, law enforcement, religion, and the healthcare profession. Consequently, I will not focus on the reasoning of any individual; thankfully, though, motivated reasoning can shed light on the Satanic Panic as the broad social phenomenon it was.

The term "moral panic" can be too easily used dismissively when, normally, the spread of moral panics requires a "core of plausibility" (Buckingham and Jensen 2012). Similarly, as implausible as the Satanic Panic might seem now, it was not fabricated whole-cloth. SRA allegations came at a time when the health profession had only begun to confront the nature and scope of child abuse (Boyer and Kirk 1998). While physical abuse had been medically acknowledged in the 1960s (Crane 2015), broad acknowledgment of sexual abuse came later (Olafson, Corwin, and Summit 1993). The year 1979 marked America's first national conference devoted to the theme of child sexual abuse, and attention ballooned from there (Jenkins 1993). Given that so many Americans were reporting being subjected to abusive sexual contact in their youth, the new and growing concern for child safety was not as groundless.

Further, the early 1980s saw a rise in efforts to locate missing children. Despite most cases involving non-custodial parents, public emphasis was squarely on abduction by strangers. The made-for-television movie *Adam*, based on the true story of the abduction and murder of six-year-old Adam Walsh, aired in 1983 with a viewership of thirty-eight million; it aired twice more in as many years, ending with on-screen pictures of missing children (Divoky 1986). By 1985, half of America's dairies were printing pictures of missing children on milk cartons (Palmer 2012). Critics pointed out that advocates misrepresented the proportion of stranger abductions in missing children cases, but the size and influence of advocates' platforms far surpassed that of their critics.

There were self-professed Satanists operating openly. Anton LaVey's Church of Satan had existed since the 1960s (Boulware 1998). While the admittedly atheistic, materialist organization attracted only a tiny number of adherents, LaVey was quite the theatrical public relations agent and, as such, served as a handy kernel of truth for Satanic Panic peddlers. There were also well-publicized crimes with Satanic themes. Richard Ramirez drew pentagrams at murder scenes and forced his victims to "swear to Satan" (Thompson and Deutsch 2013). Sean Sellers, a juvenile who killed his parents and a convenience store clerk, claimed to be a demon-possessed Satanist (Clay and Thornton 1999). Tommy Sullivan Jr. killed his mother and then himself—an event, the press eagerly noted, that happened after Sullivan wrote a school essay about Satanism (Card 2022). Scam artists pretended to be former members of Satanic cults. Mike Warnke gained significant and lucrative popularity, especially among evangelicals, by claiming to be a former Satanic priest (Ross 2000). Lauren Stratford garnered attention by claiming to have been raised as a "breeder" for a Satanic cult (Sidey 1990). Ironically, both their stories were debunked in a Christian magazine (Trott and Hertenstein 1992; Passantino, Passantino, and Trott 1989).

Sadly, the readership of the magazine was only a fraction of the readership of Warnke's and Stratford's books, let alone the viewership of media specials that featured them as guests, presenting their stories as incontrovertible fact (Shewan 2017). ABC's 20/20 aired an episode titled "The Devil Worshippers" in 1985 that featured Pazder (Downs 1985). In 1988, Geraldo Rivera hosted "Devil Worship: Exploring Satan's Underground"—the highest-rated television documentary at the time (Romano 2021). In 1989, Sally Jesse Raphael and Oprah Winfrey devoted episodes of their talk shows to SRA (Sipchen 1993). To most at the time, these shows occupied a liminal space between journalism and entertainment—"infotainment" that packaged conservative-defined threats as news (Hughes 2015, iv). This is unsurprising given that the period marked the cultural and political ascendancy of the religious right. Thus, the panic was not a historical rupture; rather, the panic's expressions reflected Christian fundamentalists' concerns at the time, such as sex, drugs, and the dissolution of "traditional" gender roles (Hanna 2017, 29–31; Glassner 1999). The language the religious right used to express these concerns had broad cultural cachet.

There was, then, prima facie evidence in support of the panic. But when examined carefully, the evidence was, as experts noted at the time, seriously flawed (Bromley 1991). As I noted before, Smith's, Warnke's, and Stratford's stories were all discredited. There was no corroborating evidence in the daycare scandals. FBI investigators concluded that none of the daycare SRA allegations were credible (Lanning 1989). There was no corroborating evidence to support SRA allegations made by recovered-memory therapy patients nor any organizational records linking anyone to a network of Satanists. There was no evidence that any of the self-styled Satanist criminals belonged to a larger group. And there was no evidence of any cabal breeding or killing children despite monumental efforts by law enforcement to produce such.

How, then, were people reasoning their way into accepting a conspiracy of this magnitude? Two epistemic effects of fear offer answers. A study by Parker and Isbell (2010) found that fearful epistemic agents tend to spend more time with information presented to them. This may sound as though fear causes epistemic agents to draw conclusions more carefully. However, fear affects the way people assess information about risk. According to several studies (Lerner and Keltner 2001; Lench and Levine 2005; Garrett et al. 2018; Butler and Matthews 1987), fearful people think negative events are more likely to occur than non-fearful people, and as fear increases, so does the likelihood people assign to negative events. I will refer to this as *fear-induced pessimism*. Some studies (Lerner et al. 2003; Scherer 1984) have found that fear is often accompanied by a sense of loss of control. A sense of control loss can affect reasoning by increasing the sense of perceiving patterns. Other studies (Whitson and Galinsky

2008; Simonov et al. 1977), for example, found that participants primed to feel a sense of control loss were more likely to perceive images in random assortments of dots and were more likely to perceive causal connections between unrelated events (such as knocking on wood and subsequently experiencing career success) than participants not primed to experience loss of control. I will refer to this as *fear-induced pattern-seeking.*

These effects shed light on public credulity toward the Satanic Panic's expressions. Information sources were disproportionately tilted toward alarmists. To the degree that those claims were fear-inducing, they affected people's probability assessments for the alleged events and their risk of falling prey to similar events. As Phillips Stevens (1990) noted at the time, there were better-credentialed, better-reasoned voices calling for pause and calm, but they were not heard. However, even if people were exposed to such sources, given potential fear-induced pessimism, they would have failed to properly weigh the testimony of skeptics relative to alarmists. In effect, people navigating this environment would have occupied something between what C. Thi Nguyen (2020) calls an "epistemic bubble" and an "echo chamber." Some suffered the poor coverage reliability of the bubble; they were not even exposed to skeptical voices. Others suffered the trust disparity of a chamber; fear undermined their ability to accurately weigh the credibility of skeptical voices. Given the effects of fear in their epistemic environment, the scant evidence supporting the panic's expressions would have seemed like a far greater portion of the total evidence than it was.

Further, fearful people would have been more likely to see patterns and connections where there were none. This is especially likely when moral panics involve identifying new social deviants. As Victor (1998) observes, doing so often involves investigating newly perceived deviance by relying on diagnostic tests that are oversimplified and ambiguous. Thus, fearful people likely found dubious tests for threat detection all the more persuasive. Consequently, similarities between Satanic symbols and a company's logo did not seem like mere coincidence. Neither did the resemblance between the sound of backward-played music and sinister messages. Neither did the fact that both zombies and Smurfs have blue skin and black lips (Phillips 1986). Neither did the fact that some rock bands' names could be interpreted as acronyms for Satanic phrases (Simmons 2001, 68–69). Neither did the fact that a crime happened on or near calendar dates purportedly special to Satanists—some lists of which included over forty dates, making it nearly impossible to avoid suggesting some ritual significance to a routine crime (Jenkins and Maier-Katkin 1991, 61). Neither did the lack of corroborating evidence for SRA or the cabal—that lack of evidence, itself, seeming like evidence of a conspiracy.

There is an understandable temptation to criticize, as some did, panickers as having "abandoned" "rational thinking" (Stevens 1990, 31). But that is an oversimplification. Panickers were likely navigating what C. Thi Nguyen calls (2021, 230) "hostile epistemology"—environmental features subverting the efforts of well-meaning epistemic agents. More importantly, that oversimplified assessment suggests that fear is the culprit for Satanic panickers' epistemic failings. But that evaluation mischaracterizes the cognitive function of fear as well as humans as epistemic agents.

Flesh-and-blood humans are, as Nguyen describes, "cognitively finite beings" (2021, 231). We do not have the cognitive resources necessary for flawless accuracy in our beliefs and judgments. Moreover, our faculties are not necessarily built for accuracy but for the survival of ourselves and our progeny (Hoffman 2019). Given our limited resources, our faculties have to tolerate some error rate. Given our survival interests, the comparative cost of false positives versus false negatives is not fixed. In situations of threat, for example, the costs of false negatives will, on average, exceed the costs of false positives (Fessler, Pisor, and Navarrete 2014). Some apparent patterns could be mere coincidences; but reacting to a perceived rattlesnake that turns out to be a branch is better than ignoring a perceived branch that turns out to be a rattlesnake (Bader et al. 2020, 131). Fear, as a response to situations of threat, orients cognitive faculties toward higher sensitivity to threat detection—that is, toward more true positives and fewer false negatives; the trade-off is that tolerance for false positives is unmoved or increased.

Fear, then, is an adaptive coping strategy for cognitively finite beings bound to commit some errors who must navigate an environment with fluctuating survival costs. Even so, public credulity toward the Satanic Panic's expressions seems less excusable than mistaking branches for snakes. However, as I have argued, fear qua cognitive coping strategy was not the problem. Panickers did not accept implausible conclusions because the fear they experienced failed to produce its appropriate epistemic effects. Fear's epistemic effects are a survival strategy. Surely, it is in an epistemic agent's interest to survive. Epistemic effects geared toward an epistemic agent's own survival are, then, not an epistemic *malfunction* even if those effects can be more or less beneficial given that agent's environment and goals. The problem, rather, is that fear mediated between people's processing of the evidence and, as I will argue below, preference-consistent and preference-inconsistent conclusions. People operated under a reasons-sensitivity constraint, but this gave them reasons-sensitivity-granted permission; the epistemic effects of fear produced apparently legitimate lines of reasoning that functioned as permission to draw conclusions favorable to their motivations. The "blame," then, lies not with fear's epistemic effects, but rather with the way in which fear-induced epistemic states were hijacked by people's motivations.

The Satanic Panic as *Motivated* Reasoning

If motivated reasoning is a process by which reasoners unwittingly work their way toward preference-consistent conclusions, why think it explains public credulity toward the Satanic Panic's expressions? Was the belief that Satanists were harming children really a conclusion panickers found preferable? This very puzzle was posed in an interview with Ken Lanning. Lanning was an FBI agent specializing in the investigation of child sexual abuse. Lanning (1992) claimed the daycare scandal expression was groundless. The interviewer asked, "Why do so many people believe it then? . . . nobody wants to believe that little children are being tortured and killed" (Rundle 2020).

That no harm was befalling children is a straightforwardly desirable conclusion. So, why did motivated reasoners not reason their way toward that instead? The factors concerning whether there was abuse were inelastic. Denying the existence of harm was not a reason-sensitive option. The elasticity of factors concerning the primary source of harm—that is, where panickers' fear should be directed—was less clear. The medical and academic literature (Gebhard et al. 1965, 71) as well as federal law enforcement had concluded that the primary threat to children was and likely always had been family or trusted acquaintances—the threat was "internal": The person most likely to pose a threat to children is "one of us"—people like the panickers themselves; they likely to some degree genuinely share the panickers' beliefs, values, and way of life. The Satanic Panic's spotlight was squarely on an "external" threat: The people who threaten children are strangers who are "out there" and not "like us." Again, the case supporting the external-threat explanation was deeply flawed, but panickers navigating the epistemic landscape likely would not have experienced the comparative evidentiary weights so starkly.

Could unjustifiable factors have affected how panickers handled the perceived elasticity and thus explain why their reasoning was motivated toward the external-threat explanation? While the psychological payoffs of accepting the explanations are clearly unjustifiable factors, the payout of each was not the same. Lanning responded to the interviewer, saying, "This is exactly what people want to believe. What people don't want to believe is that mothers and fathers abuse their children." While someone accepting the internal-threat conclusion could enjoy the smugness of avoiding a witch hunt and feeling smarter than the masses, for many panickers, it would have had unattractive downsides. Believing the internal-threat conclusion complicates the problem; abusers are not easily identifiable and signs of the familiar are not marks of safety. Believing that "normal everyday church-going people" were capable of such things or that children were more likely to suffer harm within the home was "a step into the dark too far" (Cleary 2022, 176). Accepting the internal-threat conclusion and who it likely incriminated might have felt like an uncomfortable look in the mirror—like a threat to panickers' moral identities.

During the interview, Lanning continued his response, "What [people] want to believe is in stranger danger; they want to believe in evil monsters; they want to believe in good and evil, black and white." Lanning's response suggests two psychological payoffs of the external-threat explanation, both of which are best understood in terms of how a Satanic threat allowed people to engage in scapegoating to alleviate their social and identity-related anxieties.

First, experimental evidence (Rothschild et al. 2012) suggests that people experiencing a loss of control scapegoat as a means of regaining a sense of control. This explanation seems puzzling given that the scapegoat in the Satanic Panic was a powerful cabal. But experimental evidence (Sullivan, Landau, and Rothschild 2010) also suggests that people experiencing loss of control compensate by attributing significant influence and power to a scapegoat; the regained sense of control is thus epistemic rather than practical. The internal-threat explanation offered a complicated picture of the world. Child abuse is heinous and horrifying, but internal-threat abusers would not seem comparably heinous and horrifying; abusers were not members of a highly deviant powerful cabal of moustache-twirlingly evil conspirators, but rather flawed but otherwise comparatively mundane individuals. That discrepancy between perpetrator and crime would be psychologically hard to rectify. By contrast, the external-threat explanation offered simplicity—a sense of "black and white." It offered what Nguyen (2021) calls the "seduction of clarity." Clarity is seductive because it offers the pleasurable sense of understanding—of successfully having grasped parts of the world and their relationships. According to Joel Best, such explanations can both increase and decrease our fears: they frighten us by "characterizing the world as a most dangerous place, the scene of a titanic battle between the forces of good and a conspiracy of evil," but they also comfort us by "making sense of the world, explaining the inexplicable" (1999, 85).

But, second, that frightening "titanic battle" portrait of the world offered its own psychological payoff. Experimental evidence (Rothschild et al. 2012) also suggests people scapegoat to maintain a sense of the moral value of their own identity. According to the work of Benjamin Jones (2022, 111), stereotypes of "who we are" frame how a group comes to explain and respond to a crisis through attributing blame to a particular scapegoat. Satanists as a scapegoat were permeated with meanings that threatened people's cultural outlook. The external-threat explanation allowed panickers to engage in reasoning that was, at least in part, a performative expression of identity affirmation. Satanists embodied a stark contrast to, and thus posed a threat to, the norms, values, and beliefs that characterized the panickers. Granted, the external-threat explanation included a frightening "titanic battle" image of the world, but by affirming the evil image of enemy Satanists, panickers were by default on the "good" side and thereby confirmed the essential goodness of their social identities (Victor 1991, 233). By contrast, the internal-threat explanation offered no such scapegoat and instead invited penetrating criticism of that identity.

What was the appropriate object of fear about children's safety, and what was at stake? As I have argued, panickers had potential grounds for being motivated to accept the external-threat explanation rather than the internal-threat explanation. Those motivations, however unwittingly, likely directed panickers' fears toward detecting external threats. Fear did what fear was supposed to do, but it was ultimately misdirected toward the wrong object in an environment of hostile epistemology. Had panickers accepted the internal-threat explanation, they might have benefited from fear-induced pessimism and pattern-seeking—seriously considering the degree of risk potential internal threats posed to their children and being more sensitive to potential patterns (e.g., "why does this trusted adult seek so much time alone with that child?"). It would have been a difficult and complicated world to navigate—far more complicated than sorting branches from rattlesnakes; but fear directed toward potential internal threats would have been far more likely to generate true positives (detection of actual harms to children) than it was when directed toward "fiends who reside primarily in the imaginations of adults" (Glassner 1999, 24).

Conclusion

Human cognitive faculties include strategies for coping with potential cognitive errors in light of basic human needs like threat avoidance, the epistemic effects of fear, among them. Humans also have psychological needs like a sense of control and identity affirmation and are motivated to get those needs met. Those needs can become complexly enmeshed with how people reason and process information. Sometimes motivations to get psychological needs met parasitize vulnerabilities in cognitive coping strategies to maneuver cognition toward meeting those needs at the expense of accuracy.

The Satanic Panic offers a case study of not only the degree to which motivated reasoning can lead to wildly implausible beliefs seeming plausible but also the serious consequences this can have. As Nathan and Snedeker (2001) note, there is an ultimate irony here: many people sincerely trying to protect children from past or present harm were unwittingly maneuvered in their reasoning such that they themselves engaged in practices that were ultimately harmful to children—the more resources those trying to protect children gave to Satanism, the more they spread the panic and its harmful effects: the billions of wasted dollars in police investigations, trials, and imprisonments (Glassner 1999, 24), implanted rich false memories of abuse that were, despite being false, still traumatizing (Belluck 1997; Loftus 1997), the financial and social ruin of falsely accused childcare workers, the wrongful imprisonment of innocent people and, consequently, the developmental harm suffered by their child dependents, and, even more disturbing, the misdirected attention that likely allowed "internal," "like us" abusers to continue to operate without detection and, consequently, the harm suffered by their victims. As a case study, then, the Satanic Panic is a cautionary tale about the dangerous degree to which motivated reasoning can undermine the otherwise potentially beneficial epistemic effects of fear.

Acknowledgments

I am grateful to Stephen Ellis for encouraging me to make a submission to this anthology and for giving me feedback on a very early draft. I also want to thank Ami Harbin and Songyao Ren for some excellent review comments that resulted in a much stronger final draft.

Bibliography

Aranza, Jacob. 1983. *Backwards Masking Unmasked.* Shreveport: Huntington House.
Bader, Christopher D., Joseph O. Baker, L. Edward Day, and Ann Gordon. 2020. *Fear Itself.* New York: New York University Press.

Beck, Richard. 2015. *We Believe The Children: A Moral Panic in the 1980s*. New York: Public Affairs.
Belluck, Pam. 1997. "Memory Therapy Leads to a Lawsuit And Big Settlement." *New York Times*. November 6, 1997.
Best, Joel. 1990. *Threatened Children: Rhetoric and Concern about Child-Victims*. Chicago: University of Chicago Press.
Best, Joel. 1991. "Endangered Children in Antisatanist Rhetoric." In *The Satanism Scare*, edited by James T. Richardson and David G. Bromley, 95–106. Aldine de Gruyter.
Best, Joel. 1999. *Random Violence: How We Talk About New Crimes and New Victims*. Berkeley and Los Angeles: University of California Press.
Bottoms, Bette. L., and Suzanne L. Davis. 1997. "The Creation of Satanic Ritual Abuse." *Journal of Social and Clinical Psychology* 16, no. 2: 112–132.
Boulware, Jack. 1998. "A Devil of a Time." *The Washington Post*, August 30, 1998.
Boyer, Peter J., and Michael Kirk, writers. 1998. *Frontline*. Season 17, episode 7. "The Child Terror." Aired October 27, 1998. PBS.
Brackett, John. 2018. "Satan, Subliminal, and Suicide." *American Music* 36, no. 3: 271–302.
Bromley, David G. 1991. "Satanism: The New Cult Scare." In *The Satanism Scare*, edited by James T. Richardson and Joel Best, 49–74. New York: Aldine de Gruyter.
Buckingham, David and Helle Strandgaard Jensen. 2012. "Beyond 'Media Panics.'" *Journal of Children and Media* 6, no. 4: 413–429.
Butler, Gillian, and Andrew Mathews. 1987. "Anticipatory Anxiety and Risk Perception." *Cognitive Therapy and Research* 11: 551–565.
Card, Kirsty. 2022. "Satanic Boy Scout 'Obsessed with Death' Knifed Mum before Drawing Pentagram on the Floor. *Daily Star*, January 11, 2022.
Clay, Nolan, and Anthony Thornton. 1999. "Sellers Executed for 3 Murders." *The Oklahoman*, February 4, 1999.
Cleary, Sarah. 2022. "Better the Devil You Know." *Gothic Studies* 24, no. 2: 167–184.
Cohen, Geoffrey L. 2003. "Party Over Policy." *Journal of Personality and Social Psychology* 85, no. 5: 808–822.
Crane, Jennifer. 2015. "The Bones Tell a Story the Child is Too Young or Too Frightened to Tell." *Social History of Medicine* 28, no. 4: 767–788.
da Sousa, Ronald. 2009. "Epistemic feelings." *Mind and Matter* 7, no. 2: 139–161.
deYoung, Mary. 1997. "The Devil Goes to Daycare." *Journal of American Culture* 20, no. 1: 19–25.
deYoung, Mary. 2007. "Two Decades after McMartin." *The Journal of Sociology & Social Welfare* 34, no. 4: 9–33.
Ditto, Peter H., and David F. Lopez. 1992. "Motivated Skepticism." *Journal of Personality and Social Psychology* 63, no. 4: 568–584.
Divoky, Diane. 1986. "Missing Tot Estimates Exaggerated." *Lodi News-Sentinel*, February 18, 1986.
Downs, Hugh, host. 1985. *20/20*. Season 7, episode 6, "The Devil Worshipers." Aired May 16, 1985. ABC News.
Fessler, Daniel M.T., Anne C. Pisor, and Carlos David Navarrete. 2014. "Negatively-Biased Credulity and the Cultural Evolution of Beliefs." *PLoS One* 9, no. 4: e95167.
Flahive, Paul. 2023. "Texas Continues to Exonerate People Who Were Wrongly Convicted During 'Satanic Panic.'" *NPR: All Things Considered*, April 18, 2023.

Garrett, Neil, Ana Maria Gonzalez-Garzon, Lucy Foulkes, Liat Levita, and Tali Sharot. 2018. "Updating Beliefs under Perceived Threat." *The Journal of Neuroscience* 38, no. 36: 7901–7911.
Garven, Sena, James M. Wood, Roy S. Malpass, and John S. Shaw III. 1998. "More Than Suggestion." *Journal of Applied Psychology* 83, no. 3: 347–359.
Gebhard, Paul H., John H. Gagnon, Wardell B. Pomeroy, and Cornelia V. Christenson. 1965. *Sex Offenders: An Analysis of Types.* New York: Harper & Row.
Glassner, Barry. 1999. *The Culture of Fear*. New York: Basic Books.
Grescoe, Paul. 1980. "Things that go Bump in Victoria," *McClean's*, October 27, 1980. https://archive.macleans.ca/article/1980/10/27/things-that-go-bump-in-victoria.
Hanna, Joshua. 2017. "For Unlawful Carnal Knowledge: The Satanic Panic in the United States, 1968–2000." PhD diss., Oklahoma State University.
Headley, Janice. 2020. "The Dark Lord's Rise and Fall in 1980s Heavy Metal." *KEXP*, October 30, 2020. https://www.kexp.org/read/2020/10/30/dark-lords-rise-and-fall-1980s-heavy-metal/.
Hixon, Michael. 2018. "Book Gives Insider's View of the McMartin Preschool Case and One of the Most Expensive Trials in US History." *The Beach Reporter*, October 30, 2018. https://www.dailybreeze.com/2018/10/30/book-gives-insiders-view-of-the-mcmartin-preschool-case-and-one-of-the-most-expensive-trials-in-us-history/.
Hoffman, Donald. 2019. *The Case Against Reality: Why Evolution Hid the Truth from Our Eyes.* New York: WW Norton & Company.
Hsee, Christopher K. 1996. "Elastic Justification." *Organizational Health and Human Decision Processes* 66, no. 1: 122–129.
Hughes, Sarah. A. 2015. "American Monsters: Tabloid Media and The Satanic Panic, 1970–2000." PhD diss., Temple University.
Jenkins, Philip. 1993. *Moral Panic: Changing Concepts of the Child Molester in Modern America*. New Havin: Yale University Press.
Jenkins, Philip, and Daniel Maier-Katkin. 1991. "Occult Survivors: The Making of a Myth." In *The Satanism Scare,* edited by James T. Richardson, Joel Best, and David G. Bromley, 127–44. Aldine de Gruyter.
Jones, Benjamin M. 2022. "'Who We Are' and 'Who We Blame': A Social Identity Model of Scapegoating." PhD diss., Australian National University.
Kahan, Dan. 2016. "The Politically Motivated Reasoning Paradigm." *Emerging Trends in Social & Behavioral Sciences*: 1–24.
Kahan, Dan, Hank Jenkins-Smith, Tor Tarantola, Carol L. Silva, and Donald Braman. 2015. "Geoengineering and Climate Change Polarization." *The Annals of the American Academy of Political and Social Science* 658: 192–222.
Kunda, Ziva. 1987. "Motivated Inference: Self-serving Generation and Evaluation of Causal Theories." *Journal of Personality and Social Psychology* 53, no. 4: 636–647.
Lanning, Kenneth. 1989. "Satanic, Occult, Ritualist Crime: A Law Enforcement Perspective." *The Police Chief* 56, no. 10: 62–83.
Lanning, Kenneth. 1992. "Investigator's Guide to Allegations of 'Ritual' Child Abuse." Washington, DC: Federal Bureau of Investigation, Behavioral Sciences Unit.
Lazarus, Tom, and Rona Jaffe, writers. 1982. *Mazes and Monsters*. United States: McDermott Productions, Proctor & Gamble Productions, film.
Lench, Heather, C. and Linda Levine. 2005. "Effects of Fear on Risk and Control Judgments and Memory." *Cognition and Emotion* 19, no. 7: 1049–1069.

Leon, Harmon. 2020. "The Untold Inside Story of 'Law Enforcement Guide to Satanic Cults." *MEL,* May 3, 2020. https://melmagazine.com/en-us/story/the-untold-inside-story-of-law-enforcement-guide-to-satanic-cults-the-ultimate-satanic-panic-educational-video.
Lerner, Jennifer S., and Dacher Keltner. 2001. "Fear, Anger, and Risk." *Journal of Personality and Social Psychology* 81, no. 1: 146–159.
Lerner, Jennifer S., Roxana M. Gonzalez, Deborah A. Small, and Baruch Fischhoff. 2003. "Effects of Fear and Anger on Perceived Risks of Terrorism." *Psychological Science* 14, no. 2: 144–150.
Loftus, Elizabeth. 1993. "The Reality of Repressed Memory." *American Psychologist* 48, no. 5: 518–537.
Loftus, Elizabeth. 1997. "Creating False Memories." *Scientific American* 277, no. 3: 70–75.
Loftus, Elizabeth. 2004. "Dispatch from the (un)civil Memory Wars." *The Lancet* 362: 20–21.
Martin, Daniel, and Gary Alan Fine. 1991. "Satanic Cults, Satanic Play." In *The Satanism Scare*, edited by James T. Richardson, Joel Best, and David G. Bromley, 107–26. Aldine de Gruyter.
Nathan, Debbie. 1991. "Satanism and Child Molestation." In *The Satanism Scare*, edited by James T. Richardson, Joel Best, and David G. Bromley, 75–94. Aldine de Gruyter.
Nathan, Debbie, and Michael Snedeker. 2001. *Satan's Silence*. Lincoln, NE: Authors Choice Press.
Nguyen, C. Thi. 2020. "Echo Chambers and Epistemic Bubbles." *Episteme* 17, no. 2: 141–161.
Nguyen, C. Thi. 2021. "The Seductions of Clarity." *Royal Institute of Philosophy Supplement* 89: 227–255.
Olafson, Erna, David L. Corwin, and Roland C. Summit. 1993. "Modern History of Child Sexual Abuse Awareness." *Child Abuse & Neglect* 17, no. 1: 7–24.
Palmer, Brian. 2012. "Why Did Missing Children Start Showing Up On Milk Cartons?" *Slate,* April 20, 2012.
Parker, Michael T., and Linda M. Isbell. 2010. "How I Vote Depends on How I Feel." *Psychological Science* 21, no. 4: 548–550.
Passantino, Gretchen, Bob Passantino, and Jon Trott. 1989. "Satan's Sideshow." *Cornerstone* 18, no. 90: 23–28.
Phillips, Phil. 1986. *Turmoil in the Toybox.* Lancaster, PA: Starburst Publishers. .
Poole, W. Scott. 2010. *Satan in America*. Lanham, MD: Rowman & Littlefield.
Rabinowitz, D. 1995. "The Amirault Case—A Darkness in Massachusetts." *The Wall Street Journal*, January 30, 1995. https://cltg.org/cltg/amirault/Rabinowitz-95-01-30.htm.
Richardson, James T., Joel Best, and David G. Bromley. 1991. "Satanism as a Social Problem." In *The Satanism Scare*, edited by James T Richardson, Joel Best, and David G. Bromley, 3–17. New York: Aldine de Gruyter.
Robbins, Susan P. 2002. "Social and Cultural Forces Were Partially Responsible for Satanic Panic." In *Satanism*, edited by Tamara L. Roleff, 91–102. Greenhaven Press.
Romano, Aja. 2021. "Why Satanic Panic Never Really Ended." *Vox,* March 31, 2021.
Ross, Tamie. 2000. "Laughs Stopped for Christian Comic Mike Warnke Offers Fans New Outlook After Ministry's Crash." *The Oklahoman*, September 30, 2000.
Rothschild, Zachary. K., Mark J. Landau, Daniel Sullivan, and Lucas A. Keefer. 2012. "A Dual-Motive Model of Scapegoating." *Journal of Personality and Social Psychology* 102, no. 6: 1148–1163.

Rundle, Lisa Bryn. 2020. *Uncover*. Season 6, episode 5. "The Many Martensvilles." Released April 29, 2020. CBC https://www.cbc.ca/radio/uncover/transcripts/transcript-uncover-satanic-panic-ep-5-1.5549041.

Scherer, Klaus. R. 1984. "Emotion as a Multicomponent Process." *Review of Personality and Social Psychology* 5: 37–63.

Shewan, Dan. 2017. "Conviction of Things Not Seen." *Pacific Standard,* June 14, 2015.

Sidey, Ken. H. 1990. "Publisher Withdraws Satanism Story." *Christianity Today*, February 19, 1990.

Simmons, Gene. 2001. *KISS and Make-Up*. New York: Crown Publishers.

Simonov, P., M. Frolov, V. Evtushenko, and E. Sviridov. 1977. "Effect of Emotional Stress on Recognition of Visual Patterns." *Aviation, Space, and Environmental Medicine* 48: 856–858.

Sipchen, Bob. 1993. "Looking for Satan in All the Wrong Places." *Los Angeles Times,* May 20, 1993.

Smith, Michelle, and Lawrence Pazder. 1980. *Michelle Remembers*. New York: Congdon & Lattes.

Stevens, Phillips, Jr. 1990. "The Dangerous Folklore of Satanism." *Free Inquiry* 10, no. 3: 28–34.

Sullivan, Daniel, Mark J. Landau, and Zachary K. Rothschild. 2010. "An Existential Function of Enemyship." *Journal of Personality and Social Psychology* 98, no. 3: 434–449.

Thompson, Don, and Linda Deutsch. 2013. "California serial killer Richard Ramirez dies." *Las Vegas Sun*, June 7, 2013.

Trott, Jon, and Hertenstein, Mike. 1992. "Selling Satan: The Tragic History of Mike Warnke." *Cornerstone Magazine* 21, no. 98: 7–19, 30, 38.

Victor, Jeffrey. 1990. "Satanic Cult Rumors as Contemporary Legend." *Western Folklore* 49, no.1: 51–81.

Victor, Jeffrey. 1991. "The Dynamics of Rumor-Panics About Satanic Cults." In *The Satanism Scare*, edited by James T. Richardson, Joel Best, and David G. Bromley, 221–236. Aldine de Gruyter.

Victor, Jeffrey. 1998. "Moral Panics and the Social Construction of Deviant Behavior." *Sociological Perspectives* 41, no. 3: 541–565.

Wade, Ronald M. 1999. "When Satan Came to Texas." *Skeptic* 7, no. 4: 40–44.

Whitson, Jennifer A., and Adam D. Galinsky. 2008. "Lacking Control Increases Illusory Pattern Perception." *Science* 322, no. 5898: 115–117.

12

Biased Fear

Implicit Bias, Responsibility, and Emotion

Kris Goffin

The focus of this chapter is biased fear. *Biased fear* is the term I use for experiences of fear which are implicitly biased (see also Goffin, 2023). Consider the following example:

> *Jan is a white man. He thinks that "Black men are criminals" is a harmful stereotype. At a subway station, Jan sees a Black man and startles. Jan's fear seems to tell him that he is in danger. He does not experience fear of any of the other people at that subway station, who are all white. Explicitly Jan disapproves of stereotyping Black men. Implicitly however, his fear seems to suggest that he somehow does endorse this stereotype.*

Jan's fear and behavior seem to contradict his beliefs. His "explicit" beliefs reject the idea that Black men would be dangerous. He even calls it a dangerous stereotype. Yet his fear seems to link "Black man" with "danger."

This is an example of what is described in social psychology as having an "implicit bias" and "implicit attitude" (Banaji and Greenwald 2013; Eberhardt 2019). Implicit bias can be defined as an unconscious bias that affects the way we see or judge people from a particular social group (Saul 2013, 40). Implicit bias can also influence our behavior. Often this behavior is a subtle form of avoidance. The subject of the bias is often a minority group, such as Black men, in the example of Jan's biased fear. What is remarkable about implicit bias is that implicit attitudes often contradict our explicit or conscious beliefs (Greenwald, McGhee and Schwartz 1998). For example, Jan claims that racism is terrible and that it is racist to think that all Black men are violent. This is Jan's "explicit" attitude because he is aware of this and because he would tell you this should you ask him about his beliefs regarding racism and Black men. However, his "implicit" attitude seems to contradict this. Unconsciously, Jan seems to associate "Black man" with "danger" or "threat." This process by which implicit assumptions contradict explicit beliefs is a widespread phenomenon (Banaji and Greenwald 2013; Eberhardt 2019). There are different forms of implicit bias. Jan's fear is an example of the emotional variant of implicit bias which is sometimes called "intergroup *anxiety*" (Amodio and Hamilton 2012). I will call Jan's emotion "biased fear" in this chapter. This term is related but distinct from the older term of "intergroup anxiety," in that it is defined more broadly as fear which is implicitly biased. Biased fear is fear that reflects an unconscious bias; in this case, the association between "Black man" and "dangerous" or "threat." Jan's biased fear contradicts his explicit beliefs.

The moral question that comes to mind here is: Is Jan responsible for this emotion and for the actions that result from this emotion? Can Jan distance himself from the emotion and say, "This is not the real me; I acted out of fear"? As a matter of fact, in many court cases regarding racialized police shootings, "the police officer acted out of fear" is often used as a reason not to condemn the officer for their actions (see, e.g., Eberhardt 2019). Acting out of fear is seen as a reason to not be responsible for one's action.[1] In this chapter, we will explore whether actions driven by "biased" fear are properly ones for which we should not be held responsible.

I will argue that the idea that action out of emotion exempts one from responsibility stems from so-called dual process models in psychology. I will criticize dual process thinking of biased fear and present an alternative. The alternative I present stems from the ideas of philosopher Robert Solomon (2001), who believes that emotional actions are to be located in the "grey zone" between reflexes and deliberative actions, as well as by psychologist Agnes Moors's claim (Moors et al. 2017) that emotional behavior is "goal-directed," a concept which I will explain later in the chapter. However, the basic idea is that biased emotion is not a "System 1" or a "System 2" process. So it is not part of one of the two processes described by so-called dual process models. It is somewhere in the "grey zone" between them, which Solomon also discusses: it is somewhere in between mere reflexes and intentional action. What it has in common with intentional action is that it takes into account your "goals," albeit unconsciously.

First, I will discuss the ideas of Solomon. Then, I will explain and critique the aforementioned dual process models to then provide an alternative based on a critical discussion of Agnes Moors's goal-directed account. I will consider an objection to the alternative I present. In the last section, I will discuss the implications of the view for debates about moral responsibility for biased fear.

Emotions and Responsibility: The Grey Zone

Robert Solomon (1973, 1976) claimed that we are responsible for our emotions because they are, in some sense, the result of our own choices. This idea sounded very controversial when he published it but may now be regarded as more plausible within the context of implicit bias research. Solomon argues that emotions are not just feelings or sensations. Emotions tell us something about the world. An emotion is a mental state with a particular meaning. Solomon argued that emotions are essentially evaluative judgments. For example, fear "tells" us that a certain threat or danger is present. Moreover, Solomon claimed that if emotions are judgments, they are not merely passive. Making a judgment is something you do; it is active and therefore a choice. Just because emotions imply choice, they are an "action" for which we are responsible (Solomon 1973, 1976).

At first glance, this statement seems very counterintuitive. Intuitively, emotions seem to be a passive phenomenon. It does not seem to follow from the fact that emotions tell us something about the world that we ourselves decide to think that way about the world.

In later work, Solomon (2001) downplayed his claims, as a response to the criticisms his view received. He qualified the idea that emotions are a choice yet continued to defend the idea of responsibility for emotions. He held that the idea of responsibility has been applied mainly to intentional action, while actions that are neither purely intentional nor purely passive (e.g., emotional actions) are ignored. He argued that between intentional action (such as deliberately raising your hand) and total passivity (such as someone grabbing you by your hand and raising your hand themselves), many actions do not belong to either pole of the spectrum, but still, it makes sense to talk about responsibility for them (Solomon 2001).

Solomon held that even if we were to abandon the idea of *emotions as choices*, we can still assume that we are responsible for our emotions. It is too easy to say, "I did this out of fear, so I am not responsible for that" or "It was just a feeling, so I am not responsible for that." According to Solomon, these are mere excuses to avoid responsibility. Even though emotions are not a choice, it seems too easy to blame all behavior out of emotion on something external to yourself. Solomon claims that we have the choice to engage in self-reflection, questioning our judgments and emotions. Emotions, which Solomon says are judgments, are related to larger complexes of different judgments. Fear, for instance, includes a complex of judgments such as the judgment that one values one's life, the judgment that a particular event might endanger our life, and the judgment that the perception of an occurrent event is such a thing that might endanger one's life.

Emotions are an expression of various beliefs you hold, as well as what you value and to what degree. An emotion that triggers an action you regret should be an invitation to self-reflection. Perhaps you hang onto beliefs that, after self-reflection, you decide you would be better off not having. In this way, self-reflection can prevent future actions and emotions you would regret in retrospect.

One can also apply Solomon's intuition that it is too easy an excuse to claim that one is not responsible because one was "emotional" to Jan's biased fear. Although it was not Jan's "choice" to feel fear of the Black man, it still seems inappropriate to distance oneself entirely from that emotion. More appropriate would be that this emotion would invite Jan to self-reflect. Perhaps Jan will realize that somewhere, he still carries with him the stereotypical prejudices that live within his culture and society. Jan can also take responsibility and try to ensure that these implicit prejudices no longer influence his behavior.

So, Solomon argues that between a conscious intentional act, such as intentionally raising your arm, and a completely passive movement, such as your arm being pulled up by someone else, there is a grey zone about which little is reflected. Emotions belong to this grey zone.[2]

In implicit bias research, some have also argued that biased behavior is somewhat in between mere reflexes and conscious intentional actions. Consequently, some (Mandelbaum 2016; Moors 2014) have criticized most implicit bias research as approaching the mind with overly dichotomous thinking. In this chapter, I will develop a view of biased fear, locating it in this "grey zone." However, first, we need to discuss a central way of thinking about implicit bias that sees everything in black and white: the dual process theory.

Dual Process Theory

Most cognitive models of implicit bias are dual process models. Popular theories of behavior causation include the Reflective-Impulsive Model (RIM) (Strack and Deutsch 2004) and the Associative-Propositional Evaluation (APE) Model (Gawronski and Bodenhausen 2006; Gawronski and Bodenhausen 2011). These theories make a clear distinction between the two systems. System I is supposed to involve the activation of pre-established stimulus-response associations (i.e., stimulus-driven processes) in an automatic way (i.e., quick, unconscious, efficient, unintentional, and/or difficult to control). System II involves propositional processing of the expected utilities of various action options (i.e., goal-directed processes) in a non-automatic way (slow, conscious, effortful, intentional, and/or easy to control). These models are default-interventionist. System I is the default, which will guide behavior automatically. System II can intervene; it can stop one from behaving in a way that System I tells you to behave.

According to RIM and APE, implicit measures are not direct indicators of implicit attitudes. What implicit measures assess is rather the result of the interaction between two processes: one associative/impulsive (SI) and the other propositional/reflective (SII). Implicit stereotypes and prejudices are supposed to be System I, whereas explicit stereotypes and prejudices are supposed to be System II. Performances on implicit measurement tasks and biased behavior are the result of the interaction between System I and System II. It is considered to be the default mechanism unless it is prevented or overridden by System II. So suppose that Jan sees the Black man at night: System I represents the Black man as dangerous, which evokes the action tendency to avoid the Black man. This is what will happen if Jan does not intervene. He can consciously and intentionally repress this tendency to behave in that way. In these dual process models, System I is often seen as "emotional" and "affect" and System II as "rational" and "cognitive." Likewise, in dual process models, "implicit bias" is often seen as an emotional and affective state to be contrasted with rational cognition (e.g., Gawronski and Bodenhausen 2011; Niedenthal 2005; Corneille and Hütter 2020). So biased fear can be seen as an example of a System 1 response in these models.

However, these dual process models have been criticized. Some of these criticisms have been called "the mapping problem" (Moors 2014) or "the alignment problem" (Keren and Schul 2009; Melnikoff and Bargh 2018; a similar objection has been proposed by Mandelbaum 2016). All these criticisms boil down to the same argument:

many dual process models assume that if a mental phenomenon has one characteristic associated with one system, it can be inferred that it has all the characteristics of that system. In other words, it is assumed that various dichotomies (associative vs. propositional; automatic vs. non-automatic; stimulus-driven vs. goal-directed) are mapped or aligned. For instance, if a process is found to be unconscious and quick, it is often concluded that this system is also associative and stimulus-driven. By contrast, several lines of empirical research show that various dichotomies do not map neatly onto each other. For instance, implicit attitudes may be automatic in the sense that they are unconscious or unintentionally activated, but they do not have to rely on associations and can also have a propositional structure (De Houwer 2014; Hughes et al. 2011).

Likewise, one can think of biased behavior as involving a mixture of features that have been associated with the two features of the two systems. Default-interventionist dual process models simply rule this out as a possibility. If this is, however, possible, then we can think of biased behavior as a kind of behavior with mixed features. The goal-directed model, which we will discuss in the next section, is an example of an understanding of biased behavior along these lines.

Applied to moral responsibility, strict dual process theories might imply that we are responsible for System-II-induced behavior but not for System I behavior. System I is automatic and not reflective of our real selves. System II is who we are. The dichotomy of responsible vs. not responsible "maps" onto other distinctions. Because System I is unconscious and automatic, we are not responsible for this kind of behavior. However, as mentioned before, a number of critics (Mandelbaum 2016; Moors 2014) have argued that these distinctions cannot be mapped onto each other. The same thus holds for the distinction "responsible" vs. "not responsible."

A Goal-Directed Account of Biased Fear

Agnes Moors has criticized dual process theories. She presents an alternative account of several mental phenomena which are traditionally seen as "System I," such as emotion (Moors et al. 2017) and implicit bias (Moors and Köster 2022). The central idea of her account is that mental processes like emotions can take into account your goals, albeit unconsciously. So these mental processes are neither reflex-like nor conscious and deliberative. I will suggest this account be seen as the basis of a non-dual process theory account of biased fear.

One of the standard dichotomies in dual process thinking is the dichotomy between stimulus-driven (System I) and goal-directed (System II). In a stimulus-driven process, the perception of a stimulus directly activates a specific response. This is based on an association between the stimulus and a specific behavior. For instance, we see a snake (stimulus) which is associated with "run!" (association). So, a stimulus-driven behavior in this context means that when we see a snake, we immediately start running and the mental process in between these two events is an internal representation of the association between the stimulus ("snake!") and response ("run!").

In a goal-directed process, one considers different action options and one decides which action would be best to achieve one's goals in the current circumstances. For instance, when seeing a snake, one would consider what is best to achieve one's goals of safety and avoiding harm. Would it, in this context, be best to run away or to attack the snake? One would calculate both whether the outcome of a possible action would be good or bad to achieve that goal as well as how likely it would be that one succeeds in achieving one's goals if one performs this behavior. Based on these calculations, one might decide to run away from the snake.

According to the aforementioned dual process models (Strack and Deutsch 2004; Gawronski and Bodenhausen 2006), implicitly biased behavior is a stimulus-driven process. Moors and Köster (2022), however, present an argument in favor of a goal-directed account of implicit bias (see also Moors et al. 2017). The reason to think of implicitly biased behavior as stimulus-driven is because "goal-directed" behavior implies "slow" and "optimal behavior," while "stimulus-driven" behavior implies "quick" and "suboptimal" behavior. Optimal behavior (as opposed to suboptimal behavior) in this context means the behavior which is more effective in achieving your goals. A goal-directed process will be more optimal because it takes into account various action possibilities and how they might align with achieving your goals in this context. However, this calculation will take time. Therefore, goal-directed behavior is slower than stimulus-driven behavior. This argument is based on the dual systems approach. Dual process models rule out the possibility of behavior and preceding mental processes which have a mixture of the features typically associated with both systems. It is presupposed that if a kind of behavior is "suboptimal," then it is not goal-directed. For instance, Jan's behavior is suboptimal because it is unconscious and automatic. It does not take into account Jan's goals and beliefs, but it is just an impulse, based on certain associations.

However, this line of reasoning presupposes the problematic idea which is addressed in the "mapping problem" and the "alignment problem," namely that it is presumed that if a process has one of the features associated with one of the two systems, it also has all the other features associated with that system. For instance, because a system is "unconscious" and "quick," it is therefore "suboptimal" and not "goal-directed." But this is not necessarily the case. It could be that a process has a mixture of features that are associated with the two systems. Therefore, one cannot simply infer from the fact that something is unconscious and quick that it therefore also not goal-directed. Moors argues that processes can be goal-directed but still suboptimal, fast, and perhaps unconsciously triggered.

There is also empirical evidence that supports this claim (Krieglmeyer et al. 2013). In their experiments, participants were presented with a series of stimuli: some were "positive" and other stimuli were "negative." The task was to either bring the stimulus closer (approach) or to push it away (avoidance). It turns out that this behavior could be manipulated according to one's goals (by giving additional instructions), without making the behavior less "quick and dirty," proving that it is possible that an unconscious goal-directed process precedes a "quick and dirty" behavioral response.

I believe that Moors's account of both emotions and biased behavior provides a good foundation for understanding the phenomenon of biased fear, and one which aligns with what Solomon was pointing out in his later work: that emotions are somewhat "in-between" reflexes and conscious intentional action. In my view of biased fear, Jan's behavior toward the Black man will be determined by which of his goals is the most prevalent. If Jan tries to avoid the Black man, then he (unconsciously) calculates that the Black man is a threat to achieving his goal of safety. The best way to achieve the goal of safety would be to avoid that Black man. Jan's behavior was triggered by a quick and unconscious, but nevertheless goal-directed process. Jan tries to behave according to what is best to achieve his goals. Jan's biased emotional fear is not simply associative, automatic, and so on; nor is it a fully conscious and intentional action. Instead of thinking of this emotion as either a System I or a System II mental process, we need to acknowledge that this mental state has features that are a mixture of processes traditionally associated with the System I and System II dichotomies. Biased fearful behavior is goal-directed, but the processes that give rise to the behavior are unconscious. It takes into account your goals, but you are not aware that you are making these goal calculations and decisions.

One could note that we all have the basic goal to be safe. However, we still act in various ways in different situations. Moors (2022) points out that we have to understand goals as standing in a "goal hierarchy." So there is a fundamental goal such as safety, and people create different sub-goals to achieve that goal, for instance, "be healthy." And one creates further sub-goals such as "go to the gym regularly," to "go to the gym now," and to "cross the street" (to go to the gym). In this model, basic needs to desires to motor representations are all "goals" that are part of different goal hierarchies. So everybody has the goal of safety but not everybody has the sub-goal to avoid Black people at night to be safe.[3]

We have to understand the unconscious calculation here as an unconscious mental process that underlies Jan's experience of fear. It is the mental process that connects the stimulus (seeing the Black man) to the fearful avoidance behavior Jan displays. It is the cognitive process that goes on in his mind, of which he is probably not aware. Moors (2022) describes such cognitive processes in detail. How these cognitive processes relate to neural processes is another question. I remain neutral as to how this cognitive model is implemented in neural processes. A good place to start, to see how such implementation would work is LeDoux's work (2015, 2020). LeDoux distinguishes in his later work between the conscious experience of "fear" and the mental process of "threat detection." What I describe in this chapter focuses on "threat detection" in LeDoux's terms. It is a mental mechanism which operates largely unconsciously, detecting threats and calculating how one should respond to them quickly. The conscious experience of fear often accompanies this process, but it is not essential to it. My view is compatible with this view, and LeDoux's work is a way to connect the claims I make in this chapter to neuroscientific research.

An Objection: Action Tendencies

One could argue that the goal-directed account of biased fear misses what makes an action "emotional." According to this account, emotional behavior is just like regular behavior: it is goal-directed. The goal-directed model thus states that it is the same mental process that explains both emotional behavior and non-emotional behavior. All types of behavior are the result of an unconscious goal calculation. The relevant goals in cases of biased fear, like Jan's case above, might be unconscious but they are still goals, and they are still prompting goal-directed action.

Most emotion theorists, however, have argued that emotional behavior is characterized by "action tendencies" (Deonna and Tarantino 2021; Frijda 1987; Scarantino 2017). This notion was coined by Magda Arnold (1960). An action tendency is—simply put—the tendency to act in a certain way. Each emotion has a specific type of action one is inclined to perform when one experiences this emotion. It is often said that the action tendency of fear is "avoid." This is the behavior that Jan is displaying as well. In the standard implicit bias literature, it is also said that a negative implicit attitude leads to avoidance behavior (Chen and Bargh 1999). So this would be an easy match. An action tendency could be understood along the lines of dual process theory as stimulus-driven rather than goal-directed behavior (Moors et al. 2017). This tendency to act could be seen as the "default" choice of action. One feels the impulse to "avoid," which can be overridden by the System II mental state of goal-directed behavior. But the action tendency is what we initially feel: it is "automatic" and reflex-like. No calculation of one's goals is taken into account, neither consciously nor unconsciously. It is a stimulus-driven response that goes from a stimulus perception to the tendency to act in a certain way: "avoid!"

However, I believe that this is wrong. If you agree with the statement that each emotion essentially has an action tendency, and that the action tendency of fear is avoidance, it still does not follow from this that biased fear is not goal-directed. There are two reasons to not think of the mental process that gives rise to emotional behavior as a mental process that has all of the System 1 characteristics.

The first reason is that "avoidance" is not an action, but a type of behavior. The actual action you perform out of fear needs a further decision process. Do you run away? Do you hide? One could argue that an action tendency hints at a range of options of possible actions, but a mental process still has to decide which specific action you will perform (see Scarantino 2017). This mental process will have to take into account at least some of your goals regarding the specific circumstances in which you find yourself. Hence, emotional behavior is not fully stimulus-driven or a pure "System I" process.

Second, one might believe that behavior out of fear is fully "System I" because fear comes with a certain "urgency" and this feels like a reflex. If you are overwhelmed with fear, you instinctively feel: "I need to run away" without thinking about it. However, this felt urgency is not the same thing as a System I process, with all the features of System I. It can be argued that this feeling of urgency is what sets apart an emotionally charged action from an action based on cold deliberation. However, this felt urgency says something about the structure of the phenomenological quality of the emotional experience. It would be wrong to conclude anything more about the underlying process: whether it is goal-directed or not. Once again, the mapping problem teaches us that it would be wrong to conclude from an experiential feature that a mental process cannot be goal-directed. Moreover, Moors (2022) provided an account of the physiology of "high urgency" emotional behavior. This physiology provides an explanation of the "high urgency" phenomenology without referring to System 1 processes. Instead, urgency phenomenology is consistent with goal-directed phenomenology.

Hence, I suggest that we reject the claim that what distinguishes emotional behavior from non-emotional behavior is that emotional behavior is the result of a "System 1"—process. I have suggested that the feeling of urgency sets apart emotional behavior from non-emotional behavior. What both types of behavior have in common is that they are both goal-directed. Jan's biased fear might thus be accompanied by a feeling of urgency. It is nevertheless, a goal-directed process.

Moral Implications

I have argued that biased fear is indeed to be located in what Solomon called the grey area between intentional action and passive reflexes. I will now conclude by presenting some considerations as to the extent to which we can be held accountable for biased fear.

Solomon (2001) argues that it is too easy not to claim responsibility for these emotions. In his early work, he claimed that we are responsible for our emotions because they are a "choice." Interestingly, traditional moral theory often presupposes that we are only responsible for actions that are the result of conscious choices. Recently, alternative theories have put this hard requirement into question. For instance, Michael Brownstein (2016, 2018) defends the proposition that we are morally responsible for behavior that results from implicit bias because it reflects our "deep self" ("*deep self*"). I will call this view "the deep self account." According to Brownstein, we are morally responsible for behavior that is biased if it is an expression of who we really are. The "deep self" should be understood as consisting of stable mental attitudes that constitute a person's identity. Brownstein follows other ethicists (Jaworska 2007; Shoemaker 2003; Sripada 2015) in claiming that we should understand the deep self as that which we care about. A distinction can be made between the deep self and a more superficial self. The deep self is about our fixed values and deep beliefs. This is strongly distinguishable from more superficial desires and pragmatic decisions. We are responsible for the actions that come from the deep self.

It is a matter of debate what counts as the "deep self" and what counts as a superficial desire. Frankfurt (1971, 1999) is very strict and would only count certain values that we are fully aware of and intellectually agree with as part of the deep self. We want to want these things. For instance, an alcoholic might crave a drink but at the same time, they do not want to want a drink. In this case, it could be argued that the non-willing alcoholic's craving for alcohol is not part of their deep self.

Most deep self-accounts (Jaworska 2007; Shoemaker 2003; Sripada 2015) are less strict than Frankfurt's. It is not necessary that you are aware of or intellectually agree with every stable attitude that constitutes your deep self. An argument in favor of the fact that in order for something can count as your deep self could be that people can deceive themselves. One could believe that one is a "good person" but nevertheless act in unethical ways. Self-deception does not give you a pass to do unethical things.

Nevertheless, according to most models of the "deep self" (Jaworska 2007; Shoemaker 2003; Sripada 2015), Jan's biased emotion would fall outside of this. His "deep" self consists of egalitarian values and the belief that racism is terrible. Jan's belief that it would be racist to think that all Black men are dangerous is his "real" belief. This belongs to his deep self because it is part of the beliefs held by his reflective self. Jan's deep self is egalitarian and anti-racist. His biased fear is merely an impulsive reflex. This is not who he "really is." It is a superficial and thoughtless reaction. Jan can distance himself from this emotion and consider it external because it does not reflect his deep self.

Brownstein takes this even further and argues that implicit biases do belong to the deep self. Brownstein (2016, 2018) argues that implicit biases do represent stable attitudes and thus are not merely "superficial." Brownstein's argument is based on several studies of implicit bias. He claims that if a person exhibits a particular bias, that bias remains stable in different contexts. For example, studies indicate that many people associate pictures of Black men with negative words, or more specifically with the concept of "dangerous"; this is demonstrated in the "Implicit Association Test" (Greenwald, McGhee and Schwartz 1998). In another series of studies, participants have to play a kind of shooting game: you see several people with a hard-to-identify object in their hands; this is known as the "First Person Shooter Task" (Correll et al. 2007). You have to shoot the people with a gun and not the unarmed people. If you score high on the association between Black men and danger in the implicit association test, you are also more likely to make mistakes with unarmed Black men in the shooting test. What remains stable in all these tests, according to Brownstein, is that you are concerned that Black men have violent tendencies.

According to Brownstein, this proves that implicit bias is a stable attitude and belongs to your deep self. Jan may also share this implicit concern about the supposed violent tendencies of Black men. If this is the case, then Jan cannot distance himself from this emotion.

Brownstein also claims that this implies that we are responsible for the actions influenced by implicit bias. This sounds radical, but one must keep in mind that Brownstein makes a distinction between different types of moral responsibility. He follows Shoemaker (2011) who distinguishes between responsibility in the sense of "attributability"; responsibility in the sense of "answerability"; and responsibility in the sense of "blameworthiness." "Answerability" has to do with the ability to give reasons for a particular action. Brownstein only talks about "attributability." "Attributability" means that we can attribute actions to a person because they stem from her deep self.

This is a form of responsibility distinct from the stronger variant of responsibility that can be described as having "guilt."

Some philosophers argue that belonging to the deep self ("attributability") is a necessary condition for moral responsibility but not a sufficient condition. For example, Neil Levy (2016) argues that "attributability" alone is not enough to speak of moral responsibility. One can, for instance, argue that Jan is not in control over his fear and that he is therefore not responsible for his biased emotion. Brownstein, on the other hand, claims that "attributability" does constitute a full-fledged form of moral responsibility in itself.

Applying Brownstein's idea to emotions, we can argue that we are responsible (in the sense of "attributability") for an emotion if the emotion is an expression of a stable attitude. Jan may not be "blameworthy" but is to some extent responsible for his biased emotion if it is an expression of a stable concern that Black men have violent tendencies.

The goal-directed account of biased fear can provide support for Brownstein's claims. According to this theory, biased fear is not merely a reflex-like reaction to a stimulus. Actions out of biased fear involve an unconscious consideration of one's "goals." Goals seem to fit the characterization of the stable attitudes that Brownstein claims are constitutive of the deep self (see Goffin 2023). We could thus argue that it follows from the goal-directed account of biased fear that actions out of biased fear are attributable to one's self. We are, in this sense, responsible for these behaviors.

A counterargument one might formulate against Brownstein's theory is that the notion of the "deep self" loses meaning in this context. The distinction between the deep self and the superficial self is an important distinction for Brownstein, as it is supposed to demarcate the difference between what is attributable to us and what is not. However, if behavioral expressions of implicit bias are attributable, a great number of mental states would be part of the deep self. Not just conscious, rational, intentional states, but most mental states which cause one to act in one way or another would belong to the deep self. The only cases that would belong to the superficial self, according to Brownstein, would be behavior caused by having a stroke or actual reflex movements, such as pulling away your hand from a hot stove. These actions do not require any stable mental attitudes. However, most actions, even unconsciously triggered, would be part of the deep self. One could use this criticism as a *reductio* against Brownstein's claim (see Goffin 2023). If Brownstein is right, then almost everything belongs to the deep self, and then the distinction between the deep self and the superficial self becomes meaningless.

One could also go another way. Rather than arguing that implicit attitudes belong to the deep self, I would argue that implicit bias challenges the distinction between the deep and superficial selves. Following Solomon, we could argue that on this account of moral responsibility, actions out of biased fear are in the "grey zone," between actions which arise out of the deep self and actions which arise out of the superficial self. One could, however, say that it is "too easy" for Jan to just say: "I have zero responsibility for this because this fear has nothing to do with me. It does not belong to my deep self. It is not who I really am."

This provides us with a reinterpretation of Solomon's claim that emotional behavior, which is in the "grey zone" between intentional action and passive reflexes, is also open to moral evaluation. The goal-directed account describes why biased fear is located in the grey zone: it is a goal-directed mental process, even though this goal calculation happens unconsciously. Biased fear, therefore, has features that are associated with System I and features that are associated with System II.

Thinking of the mind in terms of the "deep self" versus the "superficial self" resembles the dichotomies that dual processes think about. Biased fear could be conceptualized as a mental state in the "grey zone" between the deep self and the superficial self. Likewise, responsibility for biased fear can also be located in the "grey zone" between fully responsible and not responsible. Thus, I do not intend to conclude the discussion on moral responsibility for implicit bias here. However, I do claim that all instances of biased fear fall within the "grey zone." This doesn't imply that each case of biased fear warrants the same moral blame, as there is more to discuss. However, I do hold that because biased fear is in the grey zone, it is a far too easy excuse to say, "I did it out of fear; I'm not responsible."

Acknowledgment

Funding provided by Research Foundation—Flanders (FWO) Junior Postdoctoral Fellowship 1217120N.

Notes

1 In this chapter, I will use "action" and "behavior" interchangeably. The reason for this is that often "action" is distinguished from "behavior," to mark the difference between things we are responsible for and things we are not responsible for. But in this chapter, I am investigating whether we are in fact responsible for emotional behavior/action.

2 In this chapter, I will limit myself to cases of implicit bias. It could be argued that implicitly biased fear is similar to PTSD-related fear. One could argue that PTSD-related fear is not to be understood as part of the "grey zone" I describe here. One could, however, also argue that dual-process theory is equally inapt to understand these kinds of emotions. I am neutral about this, as I merely want to focus on implicit bias.

3 See Goffin 2023.

Bibliography

Amodio, David M., and Holly K. Hamilton. 2012. "Intergroup anxiety effects on implicit racial evaluation and stereotyping." *Emotion* 12, no. 6: 1273.

Arnold, Magda. 1960. *Emotion and Personality*. New York: Columbia University Press.

Banaji, Mahzarin R., and Anthony G. Greenwald. 2016. *Blindspot: Hidden biases of good people.* New York: Bantam.
Brownstein, Michael. 2016. "Attributionism and moral responsibility for implicit bias." *Review of Philosophy and Psychology* 7: 765–786.
Brownstein, Michael. 2018. *The implicit mind: Cognitive architecture, the self, and ethics.* Oxford: Oxford University Press.
Chen, Mark, and John A. Bargh. 1999. "Consequences of automatic evaluation: Immediate behavioral predispositions to approach or avoid the stimulus." *Personality and Social Psychology Bulletin* 25, no. 2: 215–224.
Correll, Joshua, Bernadette Park, Charles M. Judd, and Bernd Wittenbrink. 2007. "The influence of stereotypes on decisions to shoot." *European Journal of Social Psychology* 37, no. 6: 1102–1117.
Corneille, Olivier, and Mandy Hütter. 2020. "Implicit? What do you mean? A comprehensive review of the delusive implicitness construct in attitude research." *Personality and Social Psychology Review* 24, no. 3: 212–232.
De Houwer, Jan. 2014. "A propositional model of implicit evaluation." *Social and Personality Psychology Compass* 8, no. 7: 342–353.
Deonna, Julien A., and Fabrice Teroni. 2021. "Which attitudes for the fitting attitude analysis of value?" *Theoria* 87, no. 5: 1099–1122.
Eberhardt, Jennifer. 2019. *Biased: The New Science of Race and Inequality.* London: William Heinemann.
Frankfurt, Harry. 1971. "Freedom of the Will and the concept of a person." *The Journal of Philosophy* 68, no. 1: 5–20.
Frankfurt, Harry. 1999. *On Caring. Necessity, Volition, and Love.* New York: Cambridge University Press.
Frijda, Nico. 1987. "Emotion, cognitive structure, and action tendency." *Cognition and Emotion* 1, no. 2: 115–143.
Gawronski, Bertram, and Galen V. Bodenhausen. 2011. "The associative–propositional evaluation model: Theory, evidence, and open questions." *Advances in Experimental Social Psychology* 44: 59–127.
Goffin, Kris. 2023. "Biased emotions: Implicit bias, emotion & attributability." *Review of Philosophy and Psychology* 14, no. 4: 1237–1255.
Greenwald, Anthony G., Debbie E. McGhee, and Jordan LK Schwartz. 1998. "Measuring individual differences in implicit cognition: the implicit association test." *Journal of personality and Social Psychology* 74, no. 6: 1464.
Hughes, Sean, and Dermot Barnes-Holmes. 2011. "On the formation and persistence of implicit attitudes: New evidence from the Implicit Relational Assessment Procedure (IRAP)." *The Psychological Record* 61: 391–410.
Jaworska, Agnieszka. 2007. "Caring and internality." *Philosophy and Phenomenological Research* 74, no. 3: 529–568.
Keren, Gideon, and Yaacov Schul. 2009. "Two is not always better than one: A critical evaluation of two-system theories." *Perspectives on psychological science* 4, no. 6: 533–550.
Krieglmeyer, Regina, Jan De Houwer, and Roland Deutsch. 2013. "On the nature of automatically triggered approach–avoidance behavior." *Emotion Review* 5, no. 3: 280–284.

LeDoux, Joseph. 2015. *Anxious: Using the Brain to Understand and Treat Fear and Anxiety.* New York: Penguin.
LeDoux, Joseph. 2020. "Thoughtful feelings." *Current Biology* 30, no. 11: R619–R623.
Levy, Neil. 2016. "Implicit bias and moral responsibility: Probing the data." *Philosophy and Phenomenological Research* 93, no. 3: 3–26.
Mandelbaum, Eric. 2016. "Attitude, inference, association: On the propositional structure of implicit bias." *Noûs* 50, no. 3: 629–658.
Melnikoff, David E., and John A. Bargh. 2018. "The mythical number two." *Trends in Cognitive Sciences* 22, no. 4: 280–293.
Moors, Agnes. 2014. "Examining the mapping problem in dual process models." In J.W. Sherman, B. Gawronski, and Y. Trope (eds.) *Dual Process Theories of the Social Mind.* New York: Guilford Press: 20–34.
Moors, Agnes. 2022 *Demystifying Emotions: A Typology of Theories in Psychology and Philosophy.* Cambridge: Cambridge University Press.
Moors, Agnes, and Massimo Köster. 2022. "Behavior prediction requires implicit measures of stimulus-goal discrepancies and expected utilities of behavior options rather than of attitudes toward objects." *Wiley Interdisciplinary Reviews: Cognitive Science* 13, no. 5: e1611.
Moors, Agnes, Yannick Boddez, and Jan De Houwer. 2017. "The power of goal-directed processes in the causation of emotional and other actions." *Emotion Review* 9, no. 4: 310–318.
Niedenthal, Paula M., Lawrence W. Barsalou, Piotr Winkielman, Silvia Krauth-Gruber, and François Ric. 2005. "Embodiment in attitudes, social perception, and emotion." *Personality and Social Psychology Review* 9, no. 3: 184–211.
Saul, Jennifer. 2013. "Implicit bias, stereotype threat, and women in philosophy." In F. Jenkins and K. Hutchison (eds.), *Women in philosophy: What needs to change.* Oxford: Oxford University Press: 39–60.
Scarantino, Andrea. 2017. "Do emotions cause actions, and if so how?." *Emotion Review* 9, no. 4: 326–334.
Shoemaker, David W. 2003. "Caring, identification, and agency." *Ethics* 114, no. 1: 88–118.
Shoemaker, David W. 2011. "Attributability, answerability, and accountability: Toward a wider theory of moral responsibility." *Ethics* 121, no. 3: 602–632.
Solomon, Robert C. 1973. "Emotions and choice." *The Review of Metaphysics* 21, no. 1: 20–41.
Solomon, Robert C. 1976. *The Passions.* Garden City, New York: Doubleday Anchor.
Solomon, Robert C. 2001. "On the Passivity of the Passions." In A. S. R. Manstead and Agneta Fischer (eds.). *Feelings and Emotions.* Cambridge: Cambridge University Press: 11–29.
Strack, Fritz, and Roland Deutsch. 2004. "Reflective and impulsive determinants of social behavior." *Personality and Social Psychology Review* 8, no. 3: 220–247.
Sripada, Chandra. 2016. "Self-expression: A deep self theory of moral responsibility." *Philosophical Studies* 173: 1203–1232.

13

Fear, Pathology, and Feelings of Agency

Lessons from Ecological Fear

Charlie Kurth and Panu Pihkala

This chapter examines the connection between fear and the psychopathologies it can bring, looking in particular at the fears that individuals experience in the face of the climate crisis and environmental degradation more generally. We know, of course, that fear can be a source of both good and ill. Fears of climate-change-driven heat waves, for instance, can spur both activism and denial (e.g., Mah et al. 2024). But as of yet, we don't have a very good understanding of *why* eco-fears, as we will call them, shape our thoughts and actions in the ways that they do. More importantly, we also don't really understand why some experiences of eco-fear can lead to depression, PTSD, and other psychopathologies. In an effort to make some progress on this front, we want to look more closely at the role that feelings of agency—our general feeling that we have enough ability to address the threats and challenges we face—play in shaping our fears.

Our discussion begins with some examples of fears felt in the face of ecological threats like climate change. These cases serve as the launchpad for our account of how feelings of agency can affect when and how we feel afraid. We then turn to develop an empirically informed model of the ways in which fear and feelings of agency interact, highlighting how our proposal enriches our understanding of when—and why—our fears develop into pathologies. With this done, we then discuss two normative implications that we believe follow from our model. The first concerns environmental education. Here we position ourselves against those who advance a "don't scare the kids" approach to discussions of the destruction that anthropocentric ecological violence will continue to bring. Rather than shielding students from the fear that facts about climate change so often bring, we should be—in a broadly Aristotelian manner—helping students mold their fears into eco-courage. The second normative upshot concerns the growing tendency to pathologize fear in ways that can further harm already vulnerable individuals. Looking at how this issue manifests itself in the context of our model of (eco-) fear and its ties to feelings of agency not only allows us to better understand the harms that this pathologizing can do but also how we can combat it.

Before beginning, a brief comment on our terminology. Discussions about threat-related eco-emotions have focused mainly on eco-anxiety and worry (see Ojala et al. 2021 for a review of the relevant literature). However, there's often been conceptual confusion about what phenomenon these "eco-emotion" labels pick out. For example, while many scholars purport to be talking about eco-anxiety, their discussions seem better understood as focused on our general negative emotional responses to climate change—not just anxiety, but sadness, fear, guilt, and more (e.g., Clayton and Karazsia 2020). Others use the label "eco-fear," but seem to actually be focused on eco-anxiety (e.g., McQueen 2021). In this chapter, the term eco-fear is used to refer to the emotion that is experienced in response to *imminent threats* of ecological damage, where this contrasts with eco-anxiety, which we understand as the emotion experienced in response to *uncertainty about (non-imminent) threats* to the environment (see Kurth and Pihkala 2022; Pihkala 2022 for elaboration). When needed, we distinguish between fear, anxiety, and worry, but our focus is on eco-fear.

A Puzzle about Eco-Fear: The Good, the Bad, and the Pathological

We can begin with some examples of how eco-fear can bring not just important benefits, but also real trouble. We do this in order to draw out the question that is our focus: how can we better understand why eco-fears become overwhelming or otherwise problematic?

We can start by considering the good that eco-fears can do. On this front, social scientists have studied how individuals respond when they experience, or even just learn about, the devastation that climate change is bringing. They have found not only that people feel threatened—and so afraid—but also that their fears can spur activism and efforts to combat global warming. Fear, for instance, can motivate individuals to refrain from air travel and other environmentally destructive behaviors. In this vein, reports from sociologists are rich in examples of people saying things like: "Greta made me raise my ambitions because she made me *dead scared for my future*. And I am grateful for that . . . I can still say to the next generation that *I did all I could* before it was too late" (quoted in Wormbs and Söderberg 2021, 320, emphasis added).

But, alas, not all occasions of eco-fear have happy endings. For instance, the sociologist Stuart Tannock has examined how individuals respond to ecological fears, finding that "one of the strongest forms of climate denial now is based not on the claim that the climate crisis does not exist, but rather on the feeling that it is *too overwhelming to think or do anything about*" (2021, 98, emphasis added). Empirical work confirms this. We see, for instance, that in comparison to liberals, conservatives who experience negative emotions like fear when hearing about climate change tend to respond with greater disengagement via denial, self-distraction, and substance abuse (Mah et al. 2024). Additionally, some may fear things which they associate with climate awareness, like having to give up fossil-intensive lifestyles, but these fears then *prevent* them from engaging more deeply with climate change. People may even fear experiencing climate emotions. As the climate activist Jack Weber explains, "fear is the primary emotion underlying climate denial and inaction. We are afraid of the anxiety we would feel if we paid attention to climate news" (2020, 77).

What's worse, in some cases, eco-fears don't just block pro-environmental engagement but actually harm the individual who experiences them. Consider, for example, the bushfires that raged through Western Australia in 2019–2020. The fires burned 24.3 million hectares (an area larger than Finland), destroyed over 2,750 homes, and killed at least 34 people, not to mention *three billion animals* (that's not a typo: Slezak 2020). Individuals whose lives were upended by the destruction—and the intense fear they experienced as everything around them burned—are now being diagnosed with PTSD. For them, even seemingly innocent things like raindrops are triggering events that can leave them incapacitated (Schlosberg 2024).

We see similar trouble in more mundane cases, especially among young adults. As an example, consider the following excerpts from interviews conducted by the psychologist Michalina Marczak and her colleagues: "I have been quite good at not getting scared before, but in the recent months I get more scared. I don't exactly know why, but maybe because time goes by and nothing is happening. Maybe it just takes a toll on you, after some time. So, yeah, when I think about it now, I feel unrest and scared" (Marczak et al. 2021, 10). It's not just that individuals experience persistent, compounding fears about the climate crisis but that these fears bring feelings of hopelessness, powerlessness, and dismay. Witness: "When I think about the climate situation, it's just like . . . it's so sad that we reached this stage that's just slipping off a cliff, or running off a cliff, yeah, and it makes me question the human goodness . . . But then this whole situation is just kind of . . . it's easier to . . . to . . . to slip into [sighs heavily] maybe despair and . . . losing . . . trust in human nature or human beings" (10–1).

So we're left with a puzzle. While eco-fears can be a source of significant good, they can also bring not just indifference and inaction but profound harm—depression, hopelessness, PTSD, and the like. Why is this?

Getting Some Clarity: A Model of Fear and Its Connections to Feelings of Agency

As a start to an answer, let's return to Australia, this time to the floods that devastated large parts of New South Wales in 2017. Here's how one survivor—let's call her Sandra—described her experience:

> I got no warning but *the TV said evacuation* for Lismore [the area of NSW where she lived], and when I rang SES for information *I could not get through*. I needed clarification for my family and *I have three special needs kids* and *I needed help* to evacuate . . . *I was getting more scared* and finally got hold of SES who told me

> *leave now* as "we expect catastrophic loss . . . *your house will collapse* because it's in direct path of flood when the levy tops." I said I need help! *I was told no help for me* . . . [We were] condemned [to] a *horrific night of hell.* (quoted in Bailie et al. 2021, emphasis added)

While there's much to note in Sandra's comments, we want to focus on how her fears about her safety and the safety of her special needs children were exacerbated by her inability to get help. She wasn't just scared, but *felt she had no* agency—no ability to manage in the situation she was in. This feeling of lost agency then led to a vicious cycle of increased fears and a deepening feeling that the situation exceeded her ability to cope with it.

Given the extent of the fears and lost feelings of agency that people like Sandra experience, it's no surprise that we see higher levels of PTSD, anxiety, distress, and depression in the NSW residents whose lives were upended by these events. For instance, 45 percent of NSW residents impacted by the flood reported probable PTSD compared to only 12 percent of those who were not affected (Longman et al. 2023). This isn't an isolated feature of the NSW floods, but rather a general finding that researchers see when they study the mental health impacts of natural disasters (e.g., Waite et al. 2017). But it's also important to note that the combination of fear about environmental threats and compromised feelings of agency can be problematic even when an individual's condition wouldn't meet a clinical definition of psychopathology. For instance, the political scientist Sarah Pickard interviewed fifty young environmental activists about their emotional responses to the climate crisis. She found that feelings of fear and anxiety—when combined with a sense of being overwhelmed (i.e., a feeling of compromised agency)—lead to disengagement: these experiences "prevented them from taking action" (2021: sec 3a).

What examples like these suggest is that fears are more likely to bring trouble—to, for instance, trend toward pathology—to the extent that they are accompanied by compromised feelings of agency. In what follows, we develop a model of fear and its central connections to feelings of agency. While our proposal is far from a complete account, it nonetheless sheds light on an important route by which fears can become pathological.

We start with the emotion fear, which we understand as a response to imminent threats to things we care about. When afraid, we typically undergo a strong, aversive experience that presents the target of our fear in an evaluative light—what we're afraid of is seen *as threatening*. But fear doesn't just alert us to threats; it also prompts motivations aimed at helping us *neutralize* the threat at hand. While this motivation most often manifests as the familiar fight/flight/freeze response, it can also take different forms (e.g., tonic immobility), and the resulting behavior will be shaped by, among other things, one's perception of situational factors like the details of what's threatened, how soon the threat will arrive, and what routes of response are available (Kurth 2018a). Moreover, while the behaviors that fear prompts will often be helpful, they can also be problematic. We might fight when fleeing would be the better option.

Or we might find ourselves paralyzed, unable to act at all. Here, the paralysis is not the "freeze" of the fight/flight/freeze response, but rather a consequence of us being so overwhelmed by the threat that we're not able to engage the behavioral response (fleeing, say) that our fear cues up.

Next, there's what we will call our feeling of agency—our perception of our ability to effectively engage with our environment. As we're understanding it, feelings of agency are part of a metacognitive mechanism that helps us (non-cognitively) assess whether we are succeeding as agents within our environments. More specifically, this mechanism is metacognitive and epistemic in the sense that it monitors our progress with regard to our goals, providing feedback in the form of affect that helps us recognize occasions where we should tweak or even change the strategies we are pursuing (Moscarello and Hartley 2017). So, roughly speaking, when our feelings of agency are high, our actions seem (largely) effortless and error free; we feel confident in our ability to accomplish our goals and respond to challenges. By contrast, when our feelings of agency are compromised, we feel less confident—perhaps overwhelmed, even helpless—about our ability to effectively operate in the circumstances we're in. Putting this into the context of danger and the fear it provokes, one's feeling of agency is one's affectively delivered assessment of whether one has the resources and ability to address the threat at hand (where this may include one's sense that one can control not just the threat, but also the fear one feels).[1]

Here's why this matters for our understanding of fear and pathology. First, given that fear presents us as facing an imminent threat to something we care about, it will (other things equal) tend to undermine our feelings of agency. Of course, fear is not the only emotional response to ecological crises that can affect our feelings of agency—frustration, sadness, and the like can too. But given examples like those from Australia with which we began, fear clearly plays a significant role. Second, our feelings of agency (and their trajectory: strengthening, weakening, or holding steady) will affect our ability to effectively channel the fear we experience. In particular, to the extent that our feelings of agency are compromised, not only will we tend to be less able to address the threat at hand, but it will also be more likely that our fears will trend pathological. So by understanding the connections between fear and feelings of agency, we get a better (if only partial) understanding of how fears can become pathologies.[2]

Our model of fear, feelings of agency, and their connections to pathology is supported by several lines of empirical work. While none of these is decisive, the combination licenses optimism in the plausibility of our model. To see this, first consider work investigating "fear appeals"—that is, communications aimed at arousing fear in order to promote caution. The most familiar examples are public service advertisements aimed at combating drunk driving. These ads aim to elicit fear through images and audio of a terrible auto accident, with beer cans scattered in the street in order to implicate alcohol as the cause. While some work suggests fear appeals like these are not effective, the bigger picture tells a more interesting story (e.g., Tannenbaum et al. 2015). In particular, a closer look at studies of the effectiveness of fear appeals indicates not only that they can work but that they tend to work best when they succeed in both eliciting fear *and offering individuals information about how to avoid the feared outcome* (e.g., an image of an intoxicated person calling a cab). That is, fears are unlikely to be helpful when they are accompanied by diminished feelings of agency regarding the threat at hand. But they are more likely to be useful when one is afraid and feels one can take effective action. Granted, drunk driving fear appeals might seem to offer thin support for our model—after all, we know more about the dangers of drunk driving and how to avoid them. So, it's worth noting that we find similar results for climate-change-focused fear appeals: efforts to elicit fear as a way to promote pro-environmental behavior are undermined to the extent that the communications leave their target audiences with compromised feelings of agency but can be effective if suitable options for pro-environmental behavior are offered (e.g., Reser and Bradley 2017).[3]

The second line of support for our model comes from findings in trauma research. This work indicates that the combination of self-reported fear about one's safety, feelings of helplessness, and a felt lack of agency with regard to one's situation are better predictors of PTSD and depression than assessments of the objective severity of the harms experienced. This result has been found not just in the context of trauma from natural disasters but also in the experiences of survivors of domestic violence (Salcioglu et al. 2017), torture (Basoglu and Salcioglu 2011), and war (Basoglu et al. 2005). Additional research shows that interventions aimed at helping trauma survivors restore their sense of agency are effective ways to address PTSD and depression (e.g., Basoglu and Salcioglu 2011). While these trauma findings are based on correlational studies, the combination of them suggests that there's a *causal* role for compromised feelings of agency in the development of psychopathology. These trauma examples (especially war and natural disasters) are also structurally similar to fears about ecological crises with regard to the underlying uncertainty about both the threat and how to respond to it. So the lessons learned from this work lend support to our proposal.

Finally, research looking at what's called one's "sense of agency" enriches the picture by pointing to a causal connection that runs in the opposite direction: from fear to feelings of agency. More specifically, this work focuses on understanding our automatic, implicit feeling that the (physical) actions we initiate, and the outcomes they have, are things we produce. In the current context, this work is interesting because research has explored how emotions affect our feeling that we are the causes of what we do and what happens. These studies suggest that, in comparison to control conditions, individuals who are made to feel afraid by the threat of a painful shock or a fear-inducing vocalization (e.g., a recording of someone saying, "Yikes!") show a significantly degraded sense of agency (e.g., Christensen et al. 2019).

Taken together, these results sharpen our understanding of the relationship between fear, feelings of agency, and pathology. More specifically, we can understand fear as a distinctive danger-avoidance mechanism, one that attunes us to imminent threats to things we care about. Feelings of agency can then be seen as a more general tool for assessing our ability to interact effectively in our environment. Combining this suggests that when fear is combined with moderate to high feelings of agency, it will tend to be healthy (i.e., non-pathological) and instrumentally valuable. But fear and *low/decreasing* feelings of agency are a sign that things have taken a turn for the worse. Moreover, while the two systems are distinct, they also interact. Fear—as a signal of imminent threats—will tend to weaken feelings of agency. Similarly, while strong feelings of agency will tend to help one effectively direct one's fear response, compromised feelings of agency will generally undermine effective fear-driven responses.[4]

All this raises questions about what we can do to encourage better fear experiences, an issue that we will discuss in the next section. But before getting to that, it's worth pausing to consider how our model helps us make sense of the puzzle from the last section. More specifically, our model predicts that when eco-fears are accompanied by positive feelings of agency—feelings that one can do something about the environmental threat faced—they will tend to promote pro-environmental attitudes and actions. But to the extent that one's feelings of agency are compromised, one's eco-fears will be more likely to be sources of trouble, even pathology. Moreover, what people fear in the face of ecological issues will be impacted by individual personality differences and social/cultural influence (e.g., Crandon et al. 2022). Here too there's the potential for trouble as when, for instance, a climate denier's feelings of agency are undermined because they feel it's impossible to engage with climate matters in the social groups they are a part of. With this progress in hand, the balance of the chapter discusses two normative implications that we think follow from what we've learned so far.

From Eco-Fear to Eco-Courage

Within environmental education circles, researchers are increasingly concerned about both how to inform children about the climate crisis and what should be done to help them manage the strong negative emotions—fear, anxiety, guilt, anger, and more—that often emerge as they come to understand the threats that anthropocentric climate change poses (Pihkala 2024; Atkinson and Ray 2024). A prominent, early line of thought on this front emphasizes the need for a protective approach. Advocated perhaps most forcefully by the environmentalist David Sobel (1996), the basic idea is that because the truth about environmental problems like climate change is so likely to elicit strong negative emotions, and because children are so unprepared to deal with these emotions, we need to approach climate change education in a distinctive and cautious manner.

More specifically, Sobel maintains that rather than presenting children with fear-inducing facts about climate change (as is typically done), we should be working to get children more engaged with—and in—the environment. According to this thinking, adults presume that if children are exposed to bad environmental news before they are able to deal with it and before they have a strong connection with the environment, they will start to avoid environmental issues and natural environments altogether. Sobel calls this "ecophobia." Although many have questioned Sobel's presumption that it's possible to shield children from distressing ecological information (e.g., Kelsey and Armstrong 2012), his proposal has been internalized by many classroom teachers. For instance, Maria Ojala has examined teachers' attitudes toward the climate change emotions felt by their students. She's found that the vast majority see these emotions, especially negative emotions like fear, anxiety, and anger, as *irrational*—responses that should not only be discouraged, but silenced or ignored when felt (Ojala et al. 2021).

Of course, there's much that this line of thinking gets right. Our emotions can get the better of us. And we know that immersing children (and adults!) in the outdoors can help foster interest in—and concern for—the environment (e.g., Chawla 2020). But while Sobel and others are correct to emphasize these points, their alternative is too extreme. Implicit in their thinking is the assumption that fear is deeply, even inherently, problematic. We disagree. And we're not alone—the core of our concern goes as far back as Aristotle.

More specifically, on Aristotle's account, emotions undergird virtues, and fear is the emotion that undergirds courage. As he sees it, one cannot be truly courageous without also being afraid: the courageous person not only fears "things that are painful and destructive" (*EE* 1229a32–40) but "will face them because it is noble to do so and base not to" (*NE* 3.9.2–4). Moreover, facing our fears—learning to grapple with and productively channel them—is central to how we learn to be courageous. This is just the general Aristotelian maxim of learning by doing:

> What we need to learn to do, we learn by doing; for example, we become builders by building, and lyre-players by playing the lyre. So too we become just by doing just actions, temperate by doing temperate actions and courageous by courageous actions. (*NE* 1103a32–b2)

Developing this a bit, Aristotle's idea seems to be that by learning to act in the face of fear, one comes to *understand* one's fear. One comes to understand not just *when* one will be afraid, but also *how* fear affects one's attention, thoughts, and actions, as well as *what* one can do to enhance or better direct its influences. Crucially, in this picture, fear is not something that one *overcomes* or gets rid of as one becomes courageous. Rather, one's fear *remains there* as an essential component of courage. What changes is one's understanding of one's fear and one's ability to better harness its effects on one's thoughts and actions. Finally, on Aristotle's account, we will often need to not only learn to temper the fears we actually experience, but also encourage fears that we don't (typically) feel. This, too, is essential to forging the right kind of link between fear and courage—these newly developed fears are essential to helping us, for instance, better appreciate unnoticed dangers or avoid acting from a foolish fearlessness.

Moving from the Aristotle of the past to the eco-emotion scholars and environmental activists of today, we see others emphasizing the importance of developing courage in the face of environmental threats. For instance, the legal scholar Valeria Vegh Weis and the sociologist Rob White note that "standing up and speaking out, especially when the protagonists are rich, powerful and dogmatic, is always going to be hard and this includes for those involved in resisting ecocide . . . All these struggles *require considerable courage*" (2020, 310, emphasis added). Similarly, the Extinction Rebellion activist Susie Orbach writes that "we need to accept our own feelings of grief and fear . . . In doing so we will build a movement that can handle the horrors we are facing" (in Stuart 2020: 494), and as the NASA climate scientist Kate Marvel maintains, "We need courage, not hope. Grief, after all, is the cost of being alive. . . . Courage is the resolve to do well without the assurance of a happy ending" (in Wiseman 2021, 10).

Though not typically made explicit, observations like these clearly bring a broadly Aristotelian account of courage into the conversation about how we should respond to pressing environmental threats like climate change. But while noting the importance of "eco-courage" (as we will call it) is important, this is typically where the conversation stops.[5] That's a problem. Without a better understanding of what eco-courage is, how it is related to emotions like fear, and what we can do to cultivate it, we're missing what really matters. As a first step toward a more complete account of eco-courage, we aim to combine insights from Aristotle's account of courage with our model of fear and feelings of agency. Not only does this help us fill in some of the gaps in current thinking about eco-fear and eco-courage, but it also provides an alternative to the "don't scare the kids" proposal that we get from Sobel and others.

We begin by endorsing two Aristotelian ideas.[6] First, we agree not just that fear is central to what eco-courage is, but also that being afraid in the face of things like the climate crisis is central to our ability to become more eco-courageous. Second, we also agree that in order to become more eco-courageous, we need to engage with our fears. That said, we find that Aristotle's "learn by doing" maxim and the quick examples he gives to illustrate the idea don't say enough about how we should go about engaging with our fears. It's here that our model can help. As we've seen, the way that we respond to imminent threats is shaped by both our fear and our feelings of agency. This, in turn, suggests that there are two (complementary) ways that engaging with our fears can promote courage. First, we can work to shape our emotion—our fear—for the better. Second, we can work to enhance the resilience of our feelings of agency.

In order to better see what deploying these strategies might look like, consider some examples where one would want to become more eco-courageous.

(1) Situations where *intense climate fears* leave one so overwhelmed that one is unable to engage in pro-environmental action (e.g., protesting, encouraging collective action).
(2) Situations where climate fears, in combination with *feelings of hopelessness or powerlessness*, leave one unable to engage in pro-environmental action.
(3) Situations where, because of a *lack of fear* or a *mutation of one's fears into vices* like cowardice or denial, one fails to recognize (much less act to address) the imminent danger posed by, say, a new plan to lower fuel-efficiency standards.

With these cases in hand, we're now positioned to see how the two strategies for developing eco-courage—efforts aimed at fear or feelings of agency—differ.

Deploying the first strategy. In cases like (1) and (3), we have situations conducive to the first strategy where we aim to shape our fear for the better. More specifically, the idea is that by (say) exposing oneself to news of imminent climate threats, one can come to better understand not just what one will be afraid of, but also how one's fear affects one's attention, thoughts, and actions. One can (perhaps with the help of others) then use this understanding to help oneself assess things like whether one's fears are outsized and, if so, how to address them. In so doing, one is working to change one's emotional disposition—one is working to *change fear itself.*

At a practical level, there are various (complementary) ways that this could be done. For type-(1) cases, where intense fears block action, reappraisal techniques that help individuals down-regulate their fear show promise as a way to avoid paralysis that blocks pro-environmental motivations (Hamilton 2020). In a similar way, simpler efforts to engage in, say, breathing exercises to dampen intense fear can help (Doppelt 2016), as can journaling activities where one both writes about past episodes of intense eco-fears and reimagines how one could have acted more courageously (Weber 2020). Often a prerequisite for these kinds of methods is work which helps people to receive validation for their fear, normalize it, and explore it with trusted others (Greenspan 2004; Weber 2020).

But efforts to change when and how one feels eco-fear can also be used in type-(3) cases where one fails to be afraid when one should. Here, traditional eco-emotion-framed "fear appeals" can help, especially (as we saw) when they include actionable suggestions about how to respond to an environmental threat (e.g., providing information about how to get involved in a climate change advocacy group). More technologically sophisticated versions of this could be developed by following in the footsteps of efforts that use VR simulations to induce fear in order to combat aggressive driving (Cutello et al. 2021). Additionally, psychosocial support groups could help people to move from, for instance, more socially focused climate fears (e.g., fearing that one's denialist friends will treat you badly if you show climate awareness) to engaging with the fundamental climate impacts (e.g., the fires and floods that have recently plagued Australia) (Lertzman 2019; Weber 2020). Techniques like these can also encourage pro-environmental action in individuals who aren't concerned—aren't scared enough—to act in meaningful ways (recall Thunberg from the epigraph).

Deploying the second strategy. In type-(2) cases—where the culprit is less the fear and more a compromised sense of agency—the second strategy seems a better fit. Here, the aim is not to change the fear (at least not directly), but rather to focus on enhancing feelings of agency. As we saw above, work with trauma victims suggests that forms of what's called Control-Focused Behavioral Therapy (a treatment protocol that uses a distinctive type of guided exposure) can help individuals regain a sense of agency with regard to their fears. For instance, someone with PTSD from an earthquake can, through guided practice, come to see that they have the power not just to leave the room they were in when the earthquake occurred but also the power to *come back in* (Basoglu and Salcioglu 2011). While strategies of this sort have not received much attention in the context of shaping eco-fears for the better, the work of the environmental activist Jack Adam Weber emphasizes the importance of raising what he calls one's "fear-mark"—one's ability to retain a sense of agency in the face of climate fears. As he explains, "the higher our fear-mark, the more effective we are at interfacing with climate chaos. Such courage grows with practice and support" (2020, 75). Here, too, techniques that help mellow intense fears can be helpful insofar as they can help individuals shore up their feelings of agency (e.g., breathing exercises or saying to oneself: "It's understandable that I'm afraid, but I can handle it") (Weber 2020, 75–102; Greenspan 2004, 197–203).

In a similar vein, strategies that seek to leverage the power of group dynamics can also be effective. We see this in the observations of the climate activist Anna Rose: "courage inspires courage. . . . So many people I meet have become active on climate because they saw someone step out of their comfort zone and risk something" (Newby 2021: 42). While Rose seems to be focusing on serendipitous occasions of courage prompting more courage, there are likely ways that occasions like these can be more actively promoted. For instance, strategies within the "pedagogies of discomfort" paradigm encourage students to move outside their comfort zones, but do so within structured, supportive environments that allow them to critically engage with their thoughts, feelings, and inclinations (Boler and Zembylas 2003). So, for instance, the social work scholar Vivienne Bozalek and her colleagues developed a set of conversations about the legacies of apartheid among a group of racially and socio-economically diverse university students in South Africa. They found that by encouraging students to reflect on and talk about their hopes and fears for post-apartheid South Africa, many were able to "develop a sense of . . . agency" (Bozalek et al. 2013, 9). While pedagogies of discomfort have traditionally been focused on educating for social justice, there's increasing interest in deploying these tools in the context of climate change education and advocacy (Kurth and Pihkala 2024; Ojala 2016).

Summing up, we can now see how thinking about eco-fears within a broadly Aristotelian framework provides an attractive alternative to the more skeptical, cautious approach of scholars like Sobel. Moreover, combining Aristotelian insights about how to develop courage from fear with our empirically informed model of fear delivers a richer account of how we might structure efforts to promote eco-courage in our children and in ourselves. This, in turn, could launch a virtuous cycle where, as the activist Anna Rose points out, occasions of eco-courage can inspire more.

A Looming Threat: Pathologizing Eco-Fears and Stigmatizing the Vulnerable

Even if we agree that the link between *experiences* of fear and pathology is weaker than researchers like Sobel suggest, the connection between *labeling* fears as pathological and subsequent harms represents a more significant source of concern. After all, it's well known that marking someone as, say, a depressive, can bring painful stigmatization, as can less direct labeling of individuals of the sort that we see when a person's fears or anxieties get marked as "inappropriate," "excessive," or otherwise misplaced (Kurth 2022a). But our discussion here suggests a further cause for concern: pathologizing fears, especially in ways that stigmatize, can undermine feelings of agency.[7]

As with the above, looking to eco-fear is instructive, for there's no shortage of examples where pathologizing language is used to describe eco-fears. And in many cases, this pathologizing talk seems *intended* to stigmatize the individuals it's directed toward. For instance, we have editorials in prominent newspapers with titles like this one from *The Telegraph*, "Climate Anxiety is Driving the West into Dangerous Mass Hysteria," which was accompanied by the pull quote: "Enough with the fear and loathing. If this is indeed a crisis, we should deal with it like grown ups" (Daley 2020). Moreover, recall the research of the psychologist Maria Ojala discussed above; it reveals that skepticism is the *prevailing response* that many of the classroom teachers she has studied have to the fears that their students experience when learning about the climate crisis.

This pathologizing is problematic in a variety of ways. More obviously, these labels—however mistaken and misapplied—can still be internalized in ways that spur the development of pathologies or non-pathological, but nonetheless difficult, feelings. These labelings can also lead others to develop negative attitudes toward those who are the targets of the labeling.[8] On this point, consider how the climate activist Tori Tsui describes her experiences. She found not only that she was frequently ridiculed, scapegoated, and criticized for campaigning against the injustices of climate change but also that this targeting severely undermined her mental health (Tsui 2023). Our account sheds light on a probable driver of her troubles: being constantly "branded disruptive, dangerous, delusional and irrational" (2023, 39) undermined her feeling of agency, her sense that she could accomplish her goals.

So, what can be done? At one level, the problems here reflect deep, systematic issues—sexism, racism, politics of hate, and the like—and so call for large-scale structural solutions. We don't intend to enter that discussion here (but see Kurth 2022a; Kurth and Pihkala 2024, and Raymond et al. 2014 for discussion of how progress might be made). Rather, in what follows, we focus on a few strategies that have promise for bringing local change by bolstering feelings of agency.

As an easy first move, we can do more to publicly acknowledge occasions of well-attuned eco-fear and eco-courage, and to testify to the interconnections of fear, courage, and agency (noting, for instance, that courage is not the absence of fear, but rather the ability to *withstand and act on it*). Public affirmations of this sort not only function to commend the individual whose fear or courage is highlighted, but also work to both challenge problematic beliefs and norms about what the "appropriate" emotion is and offer a better, agency-affirming model. Here, consider the environmental studies scholar Jennifer Atkinson who has published essays with titles like "Addressing climate grief makes you a badass, not a snowflake" (2018).

Conclusion

While our focus has been on eco-fear, much of what we say presumably holds for fear more generally. If that's right, then how we experience fear (in general) is intimately connected to the agency that we feel we have in the situation we're in. This would then have corresponding normative implications for how we ought to cultivate courage by engaging with our fears as well as the strategies we should adopt in order to undercut the damage that pathologizing our fears can do.

Acknowledgments

We'd like to thank Ami Harbin, Robert Wallace, Tim Kearl, and David Schlosberg for their insights on earlier versions of this chapter.

Notes

1 So understood, feelings of agency are part of a larger set of metacognitive feelings (e.g., feelings of doubt, feelings of knowing) that work to assess and regulate our thoughts and actions. For discussion, see Proust 2009; Kurth 2018b.

2 Two points of elaboration. First, we take fear and feelings of agency to be *distinct* elements of fear experiences. In so doing, we differ from Frédérique de Vignemont (2024) and others who understand the content of fear as (roughly): I'm in danger and lack agency. We think our model (where fear is just about danger) fits better with research on fear—for example, fear is a domain-specific response, but feelings of agency are domain general; fear and feelings of agency appear to be underwritten by distinct neural mechanisms (Kurth 2018a). Second, Innocenti et al. (2023) develop a model of the connections between eco-*anxiety* and *feelings of self-efficacy* that not only complements our proposal about (eco-) *fear* and feelings of agency, but also meshes with findings about the close connections that we see between (eco-) anxiety and (eco-) fear (e.g., Kurth 2018a, Kurth and Pihkala 2022, Pihkala 2022; Pihkala 2020).

3 Of course, the fact that a fear appeal succeeds in motivating pro-environmental behavior does not mean that the resulting action is enough, even if shared by others, to address climate change. However, if there are pathways to agency, people are at least more likely to act and to be able to channel their fear constructively.

4 The relevance of compromised feelings of agency for our understanding of pathology is unlikely to be just a feature of fear. Lost feelings of agency—and the desire to regain it—are a mark of other conditions like eating disorders. Speaking of her own battles with bulimia, the world champion cross-country skier Jessie Diggins explains that the disorder is "not at all about food or your body. It's about looking for a feeling of control when you feel like you have none in your life" Graham (2024).

5 The works of Miriam Greenspan (2004), Jo Hamilton (2022), and Jack Adam Weber (2020) are notable exceptions, and our thinking on these matters has benefited from the insights of these authors.

6 While one could accept the whole of an Aristotelian account of virtue and its development, we do think that it is neither necessary nor advised. See Kurth 2021, Kurth 2022: chapter 8 for discussion.

7 Intense ecological emotions are real and often debilitating; they are experiences that need to be addressed carefully and respectfully, not dismissed (as is too often the case) as irrational or insignificant. Though it won't be our focus, it is also worth noting that having a label like eco-fear or eco-anxiety can be extremely beneficial—a tool that helps individuals better understand and cope with what they're feeling.

8 There are further problems. Calling a distressed climate activist a "snowflake" or saying she should just "get over" her fear can—and often does—amount to a form of affective injustice (Srinivasan 2018) or emotional persecution (Kurth 2022a) where the person's emotions aren't taken seriously or are (deliberately) used against them.

Bibliography

Atkinson, Jennifer. 2018. "Addressing Climate Grief Makes You a Badass, Not a Snowflake." *High Country News*. May 29, 2018.

Atkinson, Jennifer, and Sarah Ray. 2024. *The Existential Toolkit for Climate Justice Educators*. Berkeley: University of California Press.

Bailie, Jodie, Jo Longman, Michelle Villeneuve, Ross Bailie, and Veronica Matthews. 2021. "Floods Can Worsen Inequality." *The Conversation*, April 15, 2021. https://theconversation.com/floods-can-worsen-inequality-here-are-4-ways-we-can-ensure-people-with-disabilities-arent-left-behind-157959.

Basoglu, Metin, Maria Livanou, Cvetana Crnobarić, Tanja Francisković, Enra Suljić, Dijana Durić, and Melin Vranesić. 2005. "Psychiatric and Cognitive Effects of War in Former Yugoslavia." *Journal of the American Medical Association* 294: 580–590. http://dx.doi.org/10.1001/jama.294.5.580.

Basoglu, Metin, and Ebru Salcioglu. 2011. *A Mental Healthcare Model for Mass Trauma Survivors*. Cambridge: Cambridge University Press.

Boler, Megan, and Michalios Zembylas. 2003. "Discomforting Truths." In *Pedagogies of Difference*, edited by Peter Pericles Trifonas, 107–130. Abingdon: Routledge.

Bozalek, Vivienne, Ronelle Carolissen, and Brenda Leibowitz. 2013. "A Pedagogy of Critical Hope in South African Higher Education." In *Discerning Critical Hope in Educational Practices*, edited by V. Bozalek, R. Carolissen & B. Leibowitz, 40–54. Abingdon: Routledge.

Chawla, Louise. 2020. "Childhood Nature Connection and Constructive Hope." *People Nature* 2: 619–642. https://doi.org/10.1002/pan3.10128.

Christensen, Julia, Steven Di Costa, Benjamin Beck, and Patrick Haggard. 2019. "I just lost it!" *Experimental Brain Research* 237: 1205–1212.

Clayton, Susan., and Bryan Karazsia. 2020. "Development and Validation of a Measure of Climate Change Anxiety." *Journal of Environmental Psychology* 69: 101434.

Crandon, Tara, James Scott, Fiona Charlson, and Hannah Thomas. 2022. "A Social–Ecological Perspective on Climate Anxiety in Children and Adolescents." *Nature Climate Change* 13: 123–131. https://doi.org/10.1038/s41558-021-01251-y.

Cutello, Clara, Michaela Gummerum, Yaniv Hanoch, and Elizabeth Hellier. 2021. "Evaluating an Intervention to Reduce Risky Driving Behaviors." *Risk Analysis* 41: 1662–1673.
Daley, Janet. 2020. "Climate Anxiety is Driving the West into Dangerous Mass Hysteria." *The Telegraph*, April 9, 2020. https://www.telegraph.co.uk/news/2022/04/09/climate-anxiety-driving-west-dangerous-mass-hysteria/.
de Vignemont, Frédérique. 2024. "Fear Beyond Danger." *Mind & Language*. [online-first] https://doi.org/10.1111/mila.12506.
Doppelt, Bob. 2016. *Transformational Resilience*. Routledge. https://doi.org/10.4324/9781351283885.
Graham, Bryan. 2024. "Jessie Diggins: 'Eating Disorders are About Control When You Feel Like You Have None.'" *The Guardian*, October 18, 2023. https://www.theguardian.com/sport/2024/mar/25/jessie-diggins-cross-country-skiing-eating-disorder-awareness.
Greenspan, Miriam. 2004. *Healing Through the Dark Emotions*. Shambhala Publications.
Hamilton, Jo. 2020. "Emotional Methodologies for Climate Change Engagement." Dissertation, Doctor of Philosophy, University of Reading.
Innocenti, Matteo, Gabriele Santarelli, Gaia Lombardi, Lorenzo Ciabini, Doris Zjalic, Mattia Di Russo, and Chiara Cadeddu. 2023. "How Can Climate Change Anxiety Induce Both Pro-environmental Behaviours and Eco-paralysis?" *International Journal of Environmental Research and Public Health* 20: 3085.
Kelsey, Elin, and Carly Armstrong. 2012. "Finding Hope in a World of Environmental Catastrophe." In *Learning for Sustainability in Times of Accelerating Change*, edited by A. Wals and P. Corcoran, 187–200. Netherlands: Wageningen.
Kurth, Charlie. 2018a. *The Anxious Mind*. Cambridge: MIT Press.
Kurth, Charlie. 2018b. "Emotion, Deliberation, and the Skill Model of Virtuous Agency." *Mind & Language* 33: 299–317.
Kurth, Charlie. 2022a. "Inappropriate Emotions, Marginalization, and Feeling Better." *Synthese*, 200: 155.
Kurth, Charlie. 2022b. *Emotion*. London: Routledge.
Kurth, Charlie, and Panu Pihkala. 2024. "Centering an Environmental Ethic in Climate Crisis." In *The Cambridge Handbook of Ethics and Education,* edited by S. Fraser-Burgess, J. Heybach, D. Metro-Roland, 734–757. Cambridge: Cambridge University Press.
Kurth, Charlie, and Panu Pihkala. 2022. "Eco-Anxiety: What it is and Why it Matters." *Frontiers in Psychology*. https://doi.org/ 10.3389/fpsyg.2022.981814.
Lertzman, Renée Aron. 2019. 'New Methods for Investigating New Danger'. In *Climate Psychology*, edited by P. Hoggett, 25–39. Cham: Palgrave Macmillan.
Longman, Jo, Kazi Rahman, Veronica Matthews, and James Bennett-Levy. 2023. "Flooding, Displacement, Peritraumatic Experience and Disaster-related PTSD in Northern New South Wales." *Australian & New Zealand Journal of Psychiatry* 57: 1580–1582.
Mah, Andrea, Brian Lickel, Ezra Markowitz, and Allecia Reid. 2024. "Climate Change Stress Leads to Diverse Coping Approaches Depending on Political Beliefs." *Ecopsychology*. https://doi.org/10.1089/eco.2023.0044.

Marczak, Michelina, Malgorzata Winkowska, Katia Chaton-Østlie, and Christian Klöckner. 2021. "It's Like Getting a Diagnosis of Terminal Cancer." *ScienceOpen* [Preprint]. https://doi.org/10.21203/rs.3.rs-224032/v1.
McQueen, Alison. 2021. "The Wages of Fear?" In *Philosophy and Climate Change*, edited by M. Budolfson, T. Macpherson, and D. Plunkett, 152–177. London: Oxford University Press.
Moscarello, Justin, and Catherine Hartley. 2017. "Agency and the Calibration of Motivated Behavior." *Trends in Cognitive Sciences* 21: 725–735.
Newby, Jonica. 2021. *Beyond Climate Grief.* Sydney: NewSoundBooks.
Ojala, Maria, Ashlee Cunsolo, Charles Ogunbode, and Jacquelie Middleton. 2021. "Anxiety, Worry, and Grief in a Time of Environmental and Climate Crisis." *Annual Review of Environment and Resources* 46. https://doi.org/10.1146/annurev-environ-012220-022716.
Ojala, Maria. 2016. "Facing Anxiety in Climate Change Education." *Canadian Journal of Environmental Education*, 21: 41–56.
Pickard, Sarah. 2021. "You are Stealing Our Future in Front of Our Very Eyes." *E-rea. Revue électronique d'études sur le monde anglophone* 18. https://doi.org/10.4000/erea.11774.
Pihkala, Panu. 2024. "Emotional and Affective Issues in Environmental and Sustainability Education." *Oxford Bibliographies Online in Education*. https://doi.org/10.1093/obo/9780199756810-0310.
Pihkala, Panu. 2022. "Toward a Taxonomy of Climate Emotions." *Frontiers in Climate* 3: 738154. https://doi.org/10.3389/fclim.2021.738154.
Pihkala, Panu. 2020. "Anxiety and the Ecological Crisis." *Sustainability* 12: 7836.
Proust, Joëlle. 2009. "Is There a Sense of Agency of Thought?" In *Mental Actions and Agency*, edited by L. O'Brien & M. Soteriou, 253–275. Oxford: Oxford University Press.
Raymond, Leigh, S. Laura Weldon, Dan Kelly, Ximena Arriaga, and Ann Clark. 2014. "Making Change." *Political Research Quarterly* 67: 197–211.
Reser, Joseph, and Graham Bradley. 2017. "Fear Appeals in Climate Change Communication." *Oxford Research Encyclopedias*. https://doi.org/10.1093/acrefore/9780190228620.013.386.
Salcioglu, Ebru, Sevim Urhan, Tugba Pirinccioglu, and Sule Aydin. 2017. "Anticipatory Fear and Helplessness Predict PTSD and Depression in Domestic Violence Survivors." *Psychological Trauma* 9: 117.
Schlosberg, David. 2024. "Climate Turbulence and Justice." *Public lecture*. 8 Feb. 2024. University of Helsinki, Helsinki, Finland.
Slezak, Michael. 2020. "3 Billion Animals Killed or Displaced in Black Summer Bushfires, Study Estimates." *ABC News*. https://www.abc.net.au/news/2020-07-28/3-billion-animals-killed-displaced-in-fires-wwf-study/12497976.
Sobel, David. 1996. *Beyond Ecophobia*. Great Barrington, MA: Orion Society.
Srinivasan, Amia. 2018. "The Aptness of Anger." *Journal of Political Philosophy* 26: 123–144.
Stuart, Diana. 2020. "Radical Hope." *Journal of Agricultural and Environmental Ethics* 33: 487–504. https://doi.org/10.1007/s10806-020-09835-y.
Tannenbaum, Melanie, Justin Hepler, Rick Zimmerman, Lindsay Saul, Samantha Jacobs, Kristina Wilson, and Dolores Albarracín. 2015. "Appealing to Fear." *Psychological Bulletin* 141: 1178.

Tannock, Stuart. 2021. "Pedagogies of Hope and Fear." In *Educating for Radical Social Transformation in the Climate Crisis*, 87–117. London: Palgrave Macmillan.
Tsui, Tori. 2023. *It's Not Just You*. New York: Simon & Schuster.
Vegh Weis, Valeria, and Rob White. 2020. "Environmental Victims and Climate Change Activists." In *Victimology*, edited by J. Tapley and P. Davies, 301–319. Cham: Palgrave Macmillan. https://doi.org/10.1007/978-3-030-42288-2_12.
Waite, Thomas, Katerina Chaintarli, Charles Beck, Angia Bone, Richard Amlôt, Sari Kovats, ... and Isabel Oliver. 2017. "The English National Cohort Study of Flooding and Health." *BMC Public Health* 17: 1–9.
Weber, Jack. 2020. *Climate Cure*. Woodbury: Llewellyn Publications.
Wiseman, John. 2021. "Hope and Courage in a Harsh Climate." In *The Palgrave Handbook of Climate Resilient Societies*, edited by R. Brears. Cham: Palgrave Macmillan. https://doi.org/10.1007/978-3-030-42462-6_130.
Wormbs, Nina, and Maria Söderberg. 2021. "Knowledge, Fear, and Conscience." *Urban Planning* 6: 314–324.

14

The Fear of Having Wasted One's Life

Christopher Cowley

In E. M. Forster's *A Passage to India*, an unmarried British headmaster named Cyril Fielding, working in colonial India at the start of the twentieth century, looks back on his life there:

> And he felt dubious and discontented suddenly, and wondered whether he was really and truly successful as a human being. After forty years' experience, he had learnt to manage his life and make the best of it on advanced European lines, had developed his personality, explored his limitations, controlled his passions—and he had done it all without becoming either pedantic or worldly. A creditable achievement, but as the moment passed, he felt he ought to have been working at something else the whole time—he didn't know at what, never would know, never could know, and that was why he felt sad. (Forster 1924)[1]

This is a striking passage, even without knowing anything about the plot or the characters. I want to describe Fielding as fearing that he might have wasted his life. I want to examine this fear in more detail and will argue that it is distinct from several experiences that might seem similar (especially since they might occur in the subject at roughly the same time). Part of the distinctiveness, I will argue, has to do with the fact that Fielding "never would know, never could know" what the "something else" was.

The first comparison we can make is between Fielding's fear and perhaps more familiar examples of people fearing that they have wasted their lives, such as Betty Friedan's (1963) bored suburban housewife ("the problem that has no name") or Willy Loman in Arthur Miller's *Death of a Salesman*. It is central to both the housewife's and Loman's experiences that it includes a positive judgment about the independent disvalue of their respective life projects. In addition, they both have doubts about the sub-autonomous manner in which they embarked on them. In contrast, Fielding has been a teacher and a headmaster, in other words, jobs where there is no immediate suggestion that he has been constrained by oppressive social attitudes or distracted by baser human motives, and indeed jobs that are defined by positive moral and social ideals, ideals that most of Forster's readers could be presumed to share. Fielding himself has not become cynical or jaded about those values, or even burned out by the job. This situation makes it much more difficult for Fielding to discover the specific cause of his sadness and to articulate it to himself, and more difficult for outsiders to understand it.

The bulk of this chapter will compare Fielding's fear with three other experiences: the fear of having been inauthentic; the fear of having been negligent; and the more general experience of long-term regret. Unlike the disappointment of Friedan's housewife and Loman, all three experiences are compatible with a lingering positive evaluation of one's major life projects. Nevertheless, the three experiences remain importantly different from Fielding's fear, and the hope is that spelling out the differences will reveal more about this fear.

I'm calling Fielding's experience a *fear* because it falls short of knowledge, and yet it is more than a suspicion because so much is at stake. And because of the "never," it is a permanent fear (albeit low-level most of the time) and never resolvable. By all conventional standards, Fielding has not wasted his life, and he knows it. He is not a failure, and his fear is not a fear of failure. Maybe he has not shone and dazzled, maybe he has not lived up to earlier promise, but his achievement has nevertheless been *creditable*. So the fear is that some of his identity-conferring commitments and relationships were not as suitable to the particular person he was and is (or they were not managed properly) when compared to some other commitments or relationships that he failed to invest in or cultivate (or opportunities he failed to notice), and now it is too late. Its being "too late" is not about any precise location in his life, as marked by his chronological age or by his career stage; rather, it is an intuitive sense that most of us have about the arc of our life and about our remaining resources of energy and confidence.

Such a fear has not been discussed much in the philosophical literature on emotions or on the meaning of life. The literature on mental illness, especially depression, perhaps comes closest to this topic, but I want to resist the conclusion that Fielding is depressed. Certainly, his fear does not seem, in the book, to meet common criteria for depression, to interfere with his ordinary life activities, or even to push him to seek therapy, for example. People with depression might recognize Fielding's fear, but the fear does not make him by definition depressed.

In what follows, I will not be discussing much of the details of Forster's plot and other characters—I only want to speculate about the Fielding character as revealed in the above quotation. I am certainly not aiming at anything like a systematic or comprehensive account of this fear, but I think that my adumbrations might reveal some interesting dimensions, not only about the nature of fear more generally but also about what it means to try to live a meaningful life and to reflect on that life.

The Object of Fear

Before we move to the comparisons, we need to say something about paradigmatic cases of fear and what we are afraid of—the object of the fear. (I will assume that objectless fear is better described as anxiety or dread.) The most obvious fearsome objects are external threats: dogs, thefts, car accidents, unemployment. Given my understanding of human bodies and their vulnerabilities, of cars and dogs and knives and their sharp bits, of human social lives and their vulnerabilities, I can adjust my behavior accordingly. Even when the threat is invisible and abstract, and internal to the body (cancer), it is still external to the self. I can intelligibly fear it, I can try to avoid it or prepare for it, and when I am assailed, and I can fight it. In all the above cases, the combat logic pits "me" against "it," without any room for doubt. Yes, cancer is not fun, and it may get worse, but at least my immediate task is clear, and I can re-orient my life around the task and control my fear as best I can. Importantly, I can also talk about the object with others. I can assume that most of us are afraid of broadly similar things. My friends can encourage me or console me, give me practical and psychological advice, and share their own experiences of combat and avoidance.[2]

A second class of external fearsome object is a hypothetical scenario which, should it come to pass, will predictably sadden me or harm things I care about. I fear my sister won't get the job; I fear our country's football team will lose this weekend; I fear the peace negotiations will break down again. In logical terms, this is not a fear *of x* but rather a fear *that p*. Such a hypothetical scenario might need more detail from me to get a third party to understand my relationship with the object, the exact nature of my fearful understanding, and the values and interests that seem to be threatened. Unlike with angry dogs, there is more room for errors that can be exposed in the conversation with the third party. In principle, however, I can aim to explain my fear, and I can reasonably hope to give you enough detail to bring you to understand it (and sympathize).

There are other classes of fearsome *external* objects, but this will do to make the contrast with what I tentatively call an *internal* object of fear. (Again, we're not talking about cancer here, which remains external in my sense.) Fear of an internal object is complicated by the lack of a clear conceptual boundary between the fearful subject and the fearsome object. For example, I might fear that I was in fact adopted (unbeknownst to me), or I might fear that I have dementia. In logical form, these look like fears of an external scenario (fear *that p*), but the scenario involves my very identity. Importantly, I don't yet *know* that I am adopted or have dementia, and my attitude will change when either is confirmed—until then, I fear that I am other than what I thought I was.

I am less interested in this kind of internal fear because the objects of fear (the fact of having or not having dementia) are out of one's control. Such a person might be able to "process" their fear by resigning themselves to some conception of fate. Instead, I am interested in a person like Fielding fearing an internal object, namely that he might have wasted his life, or that he did not notice or appreciate or anticipate something important that he should have noticed or anticipated or appreciated. Somehow his life has added up to less than he thinks it could have added up to, and therefore he's not who he thought he should have become by now, or he's not flourishing as he thought he could have been.[3] Where did he get that standard of flourishing from? Like Fielding, we are having difficulties spelling things out. At any rate, the fear is conditioned by his awareness that (i) he has in fact had a good life, with no grounds for complaint and that (ii) he has had a good deal of control over his life, with no excuse for having wasted it.

I suggest that a typical characteristic of such internal objects is that they are very difficult to *communicate* to others (when compared to external objects), and this prevents the kind of interpersonal recognition and endorsement and sympathy that we rely on in so many contexts to control or even dispel our fears. If I am afraid of dogs, I can explain this to you; it makes sense, and you can, for example, lock your dog outside during my visit or take steps to show me that the dog is tame and friendly. Fielding is, as it were, trapped in his fear because there is so little that he can think or say about it with any precision, and there is little others can do even if he did try to talk about it.

Although I am denying that Fielding is depressed, the incommunicability of Fielding's fear is analogous to the incommunicability of depression. Andrew Solomon (1998) calls depression "ridiculous": sympathetic listeners can believe *that* he is depressed, *that* he is suffering, but they cannot imaginatively identify with the precise experience of his suffering when he tries to describe it to them. Once the usual clumsy metaphors have run out, there is little more that he can say, and this failure and isolation can only make the depression worse, as the listeners resist the temptation to conclude that Solomon is somehow being self-indulgent. Similarly with Fielding. He fears that he ought to have been working at something else, but he cannot say what. What is a concerned friend meant to respond to that, if Fielding tried to articulate it? At most he can remind Fielding of his creditable achievements, but these are not enough to reassure him.

Not only is it difficult to precisely specify the object of Fielding's fear, but insofar as he "didn't know [. . .], never would know, never could know" the "other thing" he suspects he ought to have worked on, it might be tempting to call this something like a foreboding rather than a fear. If I am afraid of something rustling in the bush, at least it makes sense to call that fear not only because it is focused on the bush but also because I can in principle discover what is in the bush. But Fielding's fear "leads" nowhere, and the narrative seems to attribute to Fielding an awareness that it never would lead anywhere. In response, I would say that the object—the possibility that he has been wasting his life—is clear enough to raise the experience above mere foreboding. Since there is so much at stake, it makes sense to fear the object.

Surely what matters, in narrative terms, is what Fielding goes on to do as a result of his fear, that is, into the future. As such, the experience described in the quotation is essentially incomplete. True, Fielding might well take his fear and use it to make decisions about his immediate future. He might admit that he is presently unhappy in his job, that he should change careers if he can, or at least change to a different school, perhaps in a different country. He might admit that he is presently unhappy as a bachelor and seek more intimate companionship with someone. In response, it's important to see that this is a separate task for Fielding. It might rescue *some* of his remaining life from the sense of waste, but he will still fear that most of his life hitherto has been wasted because he was not doing "something else." The waste is not limited to a discrete time period in the past that can be cast off and forgotten, in a defiant spirit of "what's done is done," because the possibly wasted is large enough to color the whole of his single extended life, a life that will therefore never be fully reparable or redeemable.

Inauthenticity

Now that we have set the stage, we can press on with the comparison between Fielding's fear of having wasted his life and the first of three other experiences: the fear of having been inauthentic. Again, my aim is to use the three experiences to help define Fielding's fear negatively.

Authenticity is a tricky word in philosophy, with a long history. The most familiar definition, being "true to oneself," has a strong hold in the popular modern imagination as well, and would be good advice for someone, for example, whose practical reasoning was overly influenced by an authority figure or by oppressive social or institutional norms. However, Fielding seems to have been sufficiently free of such influences, both now and in the past, when deliberating about his major life decisions. In addition, he had a free enough choice between a range of middle-class careers, he thought about the choice seriously, and he was not unduly motivated by the three classic ills of money, fame, and power. Even if he was somewhat ignorant about the job and/or about himself when he made the choice, he gathered relevant knowledge about both as he settled into the career during his first year or two, he made allowances for good and bad outcome luck,[4] and he *repeatedly* chose not to leave—that's enough for an authentic life. Any lingering fears that he now experiences cannot compare to the relative certainty with which he chose and re-chose his career. (In this paragraph I've been referring to the character Fielding in the Forster novel; but the main point is that it is plausible to imagine someone of Fielding's age who has been authentic *enough* throughout his life, and yet who still fears that he may have wasted it.)

Another definition of authenticity involves the successful avoidance of self-deception. Self-deception is another tricky notion. If we look first at other-deception, that seems straightforward enough: the used car salesperson knows the truth about the car and lies in order to sell it to the ignorant buyer at a higher price. With self-deception, it is not clear who is lying to whom, or whether the self-deceived person knows or does not know the truth. The beginning of an answer relies on layers of the self, such that "deep down" the self-deceiver suspects the truth rather than being honestly mistaken. Eventually, the self-deceived person might discover the truth about herself and declare "what have I done?" In a splendid passage, Chappell elaborates:

> In a host of ordinary-life cases the question arises "What have I done?"; and as the posing of the question often contextually implies, the person who asks it is not always the one best-placed to answer it. One person says to another: "You intended X (adultery, to set the building on fire, to plagiarize another student's work, to get drunk). You *obviously* intended X, so don't bother denying it"—and is absolutely right to say so. Absolutely right, no matter what the accused claims to the contrary. Absolutely right, too, even if the accused quite sincerely *tells himself* that adultery or arson or plagiarism etc. was not his intention. He can make little speeches in his head if he likes: "I am comforting Jean after John's demise," "I am maximizing our insurance return," or whatever. These little speeches, if others get to hear them, are

> not irrelevant to determining the agent's exact set of mind; but as is obvious from the practice of law courts the world over, they are not the sole or even the main evidence of anyone's intentions. (Chappell 2018, 199)

However, this is not Fielding's experience. At least in the big career decisions, he did not deceive himself about what he was "really" doing nor would his self-description fail to cohere with the way others would describe him. Self-deception somehow has to benefit the self-deceiver (at the very least by protecting their vanity), and insofar as Fielding made the "wrong" choices, they yielded no obvious benefit, and he was not guilty of particular vanity. Rather, he suspects that there was "something else" that he should have been working on. But when he looks out into the world, or he looks into himself, he cannot glimpse what that something else might be. Although he might not be as self-transparent as he would like to be, he does not face the task of wading through the heavy rationalizations that prop up the self-deceiver's precarious self-image. In addition, Chappell points to the key role of the concerned friend, who can see the adultery better than the adulterer, and spell it out sympathetically but forcefully. Fielding has friends, but they do not see any self-deception, let alone the "something else" that Fielding is looking for.

Negligence

The second of the three alternatives is the fear of negligence. Again, the plan is to show that what Fielding experienced was not a fear of having been negligent, but a distinctive fear of having wasted his life. At first glance, this is a more plausible candidate than a fear of inauthenticity. Part of his fear that he has wasted his life might have to do with his fear of having failed to notice, appreciate or anticipate what he *should have* noticed, appreciated or anticipated.

The key component of negligence is the "should have." After all, there are plenty of things that one fails to notice, appreciate, or anticipate. But when an observer remarks that the subject should have noticed X, it means that, *given* the subject's status, role, prior knowledge, experience, and so on, the observer has a reasonable expectation that the subject should have noticed X, either because it was in the subject's interest or because the subject had a particular duty to notice it. Similarly, when the autobiographical subject reflects on her life, she reflects not only on her actions but also on any omissions resulting from her negligent cognitive failures. Sometimes this is a question of degree; the subject might have been dimly aware of X but not enough to have investigated further, let alone to act on it. There is also second-order negligence. Fielding is dimly aware *now* about what he should have noticed, appreciated, or anticipated *earlier*. But he's not sure how to investigate further. (And in cases other than with Fielding, both first- and second-order negligence are exacerbated by vanity and self-deception.)

What sorts of things might Fielding have missed which he should not have? Plenty. Perhaps a career opportunity; perhaps another place that he could have settled in;

perhaps a friendship that he could have cultivated. Importantly, at the time of the quotation, Fielding is unmarried, and so there might well have been some marital options that he also missed. (He does get married later in the book, but the union does not augur well.)

Negligence is distinguished in the law from an intentional choice as well as from a reckless choice. By definition, a reckless agent is aware of (and appreciates) a *risk* that things might not turn out as she plans, and she intentionally disregards the risk while pursuing a benefit. But the negligent person does not have the opportunity to intentionally disregard a risk that she is unaware of. There is a long-standing discussion in criminal law theory about whether negligence should be *blameworthy*. After all, blameworthiness seems to presuppose awareness and choice. When I blame you, I am implicitly saying that you had the choice—including the choice to weigh the risk—and you chose incorrectly. Some (such as Moore (2009)) would therefore refrain from calling negligence an *act* in the full philosophical sense of the word and "demote" it to the status of an innocent error that happened "through" the person, thereby relieving her of direct responsibility. In response to Moore, when we imagine a doctor negligently failing to notice what she should have noticed and thereby causing the death of a patient, the patient's family will probably find it difficult to accept this as an innocent human error. A doctor's job is partly defined precisely in terms of a set of norms that govern what she should notice, appreciate, and anticipate in any given medical situation when she is present as a doctor, treating this patient who has been properly allocated to her. The dead patient's family will be strongly inclined to blame the negligent doctor for failing to do her job properly.

Now, the possibility that Fielding has been negligent in choosing (and re-choosing) his significant life options is obviously different from the medical context, since nobody else has been demonstrably *harmed* by any of Fielding's putative negligence. One response to Fielding would be to say: as long as you did not infringe or neglect a duty of care to anyone else, then you cannot have been negligent. Does it make sense to say that Fielding infringed a duty of care *toward himself*? Not really. First, because it is not obvious that he has suffered from any of his significant choices, including his career choices. Any putative suffering is only in relation to how much better his life might have gone if he had recognized the "something else" and chosen it. But that's much too vague. Second, as long as Fielding thought about his significant choices *seriously* (i.e., absent the pressure of time and other people's expectations), then he will have chosen the option that appeared the best, given the values that were salient in his thinking at the time. If now, in his sixties, he fears that he might have negligently failed to explore a glimpse of "something else" twenty years ago, then this can be taken to mean that the "something else" was not that attractive at the time. In other words, the self-blame implicit in a fear (of having been negligent) is not well-grounded.

Angela Smith (2006) discusses a more subtle kind of negligence. She describes a friend of hers, someone who enjoys celebrating her birthday. Smith conscientiously sends a greeting every year, but this year she negligently forgot and learns about her omission later from a third party. Smith feels terrible and quickly sends apologies and belated good wishes to the friend, but the damage is done. Smith fears that the negligent forgetting reveals that she does not love her friend as much as she thinks she does, as much as she hopes she does. And although Smith can take care to make explicit entries in her diary to remind herself for next year, she now worries about whether the underlying loss of spontaneous affection will cause further unpredictable omissions in the future. So perhaps the "something else" that Fielding is searching for is an earlier relationship that he negligently allowed to atrophy, a friendship, a profitable professional relationship, indeed perhaps a marriage, that would have had a much greater impact on the meaning of his life.

The most important thing, however, is that Fielding has not (or not yet) come close to identifying his moment or locus of negligence. He does not have a friend who will warn him of what he missed all those years ago. And he does not have a clear enough sense of how his life would have been better if he had worked on a particular relationship. Again, the comparison is with the negligent doctor and Smith the negligent friend; the accusation (self-accusation) of negligence is the end result of a painful process of discovery, where the counterfactual present can be apprehended clearly enough. Indeed, Fielding seems happy to have "developed his personality, explored his limitations, controlled his passions." His fear is still too inchoate and too incommunicable to call a fear of having been negligent.

Regret

This is a third possible way to describe Fielding's experience. Might it be that Fielding's fear of having wasted his life is better described as regret? I will try to show that the two experiences are distinct. The problem not only has to do with the lack of any specificity about *what* Fielding could be described as regretting (as mentioned above), but more importantly, because of some internal conceptual problems in the very idea of long-term regret.

I want to adapt an example introduced by McQueen (2017). Let's imagine a different character named Schmielding, someone similar to Fielding in having spent a career as a schoolteacher and headmaster. However, Schmielding can recall very clearly a choice he faced when he was twenty, between a career as a schoolteacher and a career as a professional dancer (leading to other activities in the dance world, maybe choreography, maybe teaching). The point is that dance was his passion at that age. His parents, who were funding his education, considered dance frivolous and insecure, and insisted he train to be a teacher, which he did. He tried to keep dancing as a hobby but did not have the time or energy to achieve much in it and eventually dropped it. Now in his sixties, Schmielding regrets that he did not ignore his parents, reject their money, and at least have a go at a dance career.[5]

Schmielding (unlike Fielding) knows exactly what the "something else" was that he should have done. Not that he wasted his life by *being a teacher* and headmaster, but he wasted it by *not being* a dancer. The content of his regret includes the counterfactual career that he is now convinced would have made him better off today. But this simple picture conceals problems of personal identity.

What is regret, exactly? First, I am taking regret as being paradigmatically about past voluntary decisions. When it comes to sad states of affairs, for example, some fatal earthquake, I would say that one cannot regret that, but only *lament* it. The paradigm of short-term, trivial regret is betting on the wrong horse this morning. I put a tenner on Abigail, and she lost; I regret not putting the tenner on Bertha, since she went on to win. Even if Abigail appeared the best this morning, I also regret not doing my homework before this morning, since I would have realized that Bertha had a much better track record. Three things about this paradigm: first, I can "quantify" my regret precisely (I know exactly how much I would have won). Second, there is no doubt that the morning chooser is the same person as the afternoon regretter, just as the actual loser is the same person as the counterfactual winner (call this the "identity triangle"). Third, I can reassure myself that such short-term trivial regret is *useful*—I can learn from my mistakes and keep a closer eye on Bertha in the future, or at least resolve to do my homework more thoroughly next time.

With regret that is long-term and *momentous* (William James's term), this "identity triangle" no longer holds. Schmielding is sixty years old and very different from the twenty-year-old who embarked on a career of teacher and later headmaster. There is no way that the twenty-year-old could have known what he would turn into, and what his future self would come to think about the career. And there is no way that the sixty-year-old Schmielding could know what a forty-year dancing career would have been like, and what it would have turned him into in the counterfactual present. He can certainly remember being passionate about dancing at twenty, but who knows how long that passion would have lasted? By sixty, his counterfactual self might have been happier; it might have been sadder; it might have been demented; or he might have felt that he "ought to have been working at something else the whole time"—such as being a schoolteacher. ("Maybe my parents were right after all.") And even if long-term regret could be coherent, it is now too late for Schmielding to learn anything from his mistake of forty years ago—even if he quits his teaching job to work in the dance world from now on.

Indeed, I am oversimplifying by assuming that there was a *single* decision, at age twenty, about how to spend the following forty years. But the fact is that Schmielding, after choosing to go to teacher training college at twenty, could have decided afterward (at twenty-five, say) to give professional dance another go. So after college he decided again to be a teacher. And after his first five years in his first teaching job (at thirty, say), he again could have decided to give dancing a go, but did not. As he grew older (and his body grew older), his options in the dance world would have narrowed, but there were still options, and he rejected them again and again. The point is, it's more likely that Schmielding did exactly what he wanted at each choice juncture, *given* his ambitions and values at the time. The twenty-year-old Schmielding evidently wanted to please his parents more than to dance.[6] All of this would make it difficult for Schmielding to articulate and endorse a specific regret about having remained in his teaching and headmaster career right through to the present day.

I have stipulated that regret is about wishing to undo a voluntary choice, and I have been arguing that this is too problematic for momentous choices over the longer term. What if we consider a third person, the sixty-year-old Zielding, who sees himself not as choosing but as thwarted (in whatever way) *from actualizing his potential*. At twenty, Zielding had a keen sense of his potential, but he was prevented from trying to reach it, and that is what saddens him at sixty.

Michal Masny (2022) has a useful example to test intuitions on this. He takes the real historical example of Sophie Germain, a French mathematician at the beginning of the nineteenth century. Because of her sex, she was not admitted to any university or invited to any conferences, her work was not published, and generally wasn't taken very seriously. Nevertheless, because she came from a wealthy family, she was able to achieve a fairly comfortable life and even to find some channels for her mathematical work. She seemingly accepted the reality of the systematic sexism without frustration and without any inclination toward, for example, suffragette activism. Masny then invents a twin sister (who lacks mathematical interest or ability) and asks the following question: If both sisters experience the *same* well-being (however measured: subjectively, objectively, or both), must we then say that they had *equally* meaningful lives? And Masny answers no; for Sophie's life was undermined by the fact that it could have been so much better. Of course, it could not have been much better *at the time*, but if social attitudes toward women had been better, then it could have been so much better. Here I would reject Masny's claim. It is one thing for Schmielding to regret not choosing a dance career, since that situation was under his control. In contrast, Sophie's situation was not at all under her control, and it is plausible to say that she did the best she could under the circumstances.

Importantly, Schmielding's complaint about not choosing the dance career, or Zielding's complaint about being thwarted in actualizing his potential, both seem *idle*, almost a kind of daydreaming, one that does not add anything to one's self-understanding. This point recalls a famous passage by Sartre (1946):

> For many have but one resource to sustain them in their misery, and that is to think, "Circumstances have been against me, I was worthy to be something much better than I have been. I admit I have never had a great love or a great friendship; but that is because I never met a man or a woman who were worthy of it; if I have not written any very good books, it is because I had not the leisure to do so; [. . .] So there remains within me a wide range of abilities, inclinations and potentialities, unused but perfectly viable, which endow me with a worthiness that could never be inferred from the mere history of my actions." But in reality and for the existentialist, there is no love apart from the deeds of love; no potentiality of love other than that which is manifested in loving; there is no genius other than that which is expressed in works of art. [. . .] Why should we attribute to Racine the capacity to write yet another tragedy when that is precisely what he did not write? In life, a man commits himself, draws his own portrait and there is nothing but that portrait. No doubt this thought may seem comfortless to one who has not made a success of his life. (Sartre 1946)[7]

Sartre captures something interesting about the possibility of having wasted one's life: the fact that you might have to *answer* for it to some other person or collective whose disapproval you fear. Imagine Fielding being invited to a reunion of his high school graduating class, where the whole context is about mutual judgment and comparison to see who has done "better" through the years. That's where one might be tempted to reach for the excuses cited by Sartre. Fielding would be all right at a reunion; he has "creditable" achievements to point to, but it would feel hollow.

The last line would seem relevant to Fielding. And yet there is an ambiguity here because Fielding, as we said before, cannot be plausibly described (by a third person) as having failed in conventional terms; and Fielding himself accepts the legitimacy of such a third person's judgment. And to be fair to Fielding, he is not seeking a Sartrean *excuse* ("Circumstances have been against me") for failing to choose a more suitable career. Maybe his "sadness" comprises his dim awareness that he has not actualized a youthful potential, but I suggest he does not explore that possibility in more detail because he understands the idleness of such thoughts.

Again, Fielding's location in his life is a central aspect of his fear of having been wasting it. What makes him reluctant to confront the fear and seek clarity is precisely the possible conclusion that "that's it"—there's nothing he can do anymore to rescue or redeem his life. With such an admission comes the thought that the future closes over one entirely, and there is nothing left to live for; one can only endure until death. Fielding is not suicidal, and indeed nowhere near suicidal, but he now has an inkling of what might drive a person to suicide. His earlier life was lived in a spirit of an open future, where one can take risks with the knowledge that one can repair things or redeem oneself if they go wrong—at the very least by drawing the benefit of learning something about oneself or about the world. But Fielding's inchoate fear of having wasted his life is conditioned by a second-order fear of discovering that it is too late to do anything about it, and this second-order fear perhaps restrains him from confronting the first-order fear.[8]

Conclusion

I have been trying to make some sense of Cyril Fielding's experience in Chapter 20 of *Passage to India*. I have called it a fear of having wasted his life, despite the fact that, by his own admission, he has spent his life relatively well as a teacher and headmaster. To his frustration, he finds that he cannot articulate the object of this fear in any greater detail, either to himself or to others, and he experiences a secondary fear that it is now too late to repair his life. I argued that this was a distinct kind of fear (a distinct kind of "internal" object), and did not amount to a fear of having been inauthentic, a fear of having been negligent, or a form of regret. I suggest that this kind of fear is not unique to Fielding but is essential to the challenge of understanding one's life as one hurtles through middle age.

Acknowledgments

I would like to thank Ami Harbin and Robert Pál-Wallin for comments on earlier drafts. I also thank Alena Dvořáková for the original idea.

Notes

1 I cite from the e-version prepared by Project Gutenberg, but without standard pagination. The passage quoted is in the final paragraph of Chapter 20.

2 The greatest external threat that most of us fear is of course death. But this raises complicated questions about metaphysics and rationality that go back at least to the Ancient Roman philosopher Lucretius, and I won't discuss them here.

3 By "flourishing" I'm using the standard translation of the Greek *eudaemonia*, but without putting too much argumentative weight or precision on it. For my purposes, I'm assuming that once a person has eudaemonia, she is aware of having it and loses her fear of having wasted her life.

4 The term "outcome luck" comes from Thomas Nagel (1979). The thought is that the ultimate meaning of a particular choice between two options will be partly determined by the (more or less predictable, more or less predicted) causal outcomes of the chosen option.

5 My imaginary Schmielding feels he "coulda been a contender," in the immortal words of Terry Molloy (played by Marlon Brando) in Elia Kazan's 1954 film *On the Waterfront*.

6 McQueen (2017) actually has two examples, Kim and Joe. McQueen argues that Kim *cannot* regret her younger self's career decision because she did what she was most interested in at the time; in contrast, Joe *can* regret his younger self's career decision since he only wanted to please his parents. I am rejecting McQueen's distinction, since I think that Joe also did what he was "most interested" in at the time—pleasing his parents.

7 Note that I am citing from an online version, without pagination. See Bibliography for details.

8 Matthew Ratcliffe (2024) explores a related phenomenon, where a person feels "unable to continue as oneself," for example in response to grief. Importantly, however, this is different from Fielding's fear because, in grieving, the griever does not fear that he has been wasting his life—the grief expresses precisely the contrary.

Bibliography

Chappell, Sophie Grace. 2018. "What have I done?" *Wittgenstein, Religion and Ethics: New Perspectives from Philosophy and Theology*, edited by M. Burley. London: Bloomsbury.

Forster, Edward Morgan. 1924/2020. *A Passage to India*. E-version from Project Gutenberg. https://gutenberg.org/cache/epub/61221/pg61221-images.html.

Friedan Betty. 1963. *The Feminine Mystique*. New York: WW Norton.

Masny, Michal. 2023. "Wasted potential: The value of a life and the significance of what could have been." *Philosophy and Public Affairs* 51(1): 6–32.
McQueen, Pddy. 2017. "When should we regret?" *International Journal of Philosophical Studies* 25, no. 5: 608–623.
Moore, Michael. 2009. *Causation and responsibility: An essay in law, morals, and metaphysics*. Oxford: Oxford University Press.
Nagel, Thomas. 1979. "Moral Luck" *Mortal Questions*. Cambridge: Cambridge University Press.
Ratcliffe, Matthew. 2024. "On feeling unable to continue as oneself." *European Journal of Philosophy*, on-line early view.
Sartre, Jean-Paul. 1946/1956. "Existentialism is a humanism." Mairet (tr.). Online version. https://www.marxists.org/reference/archive/sartre/works/exist/sartre.htm.
Smith, Angela. 2005. "Responsibility for attitudes: Activity and passivity in mental life." *Ethics* 115(2): 236–271.
Solomon, Andrew. 1998. "Anatomy of melancholy." *The New Yorker*. Online version from his personal website. https://andrewsolomon.com/articles/anatomy-of-melancholy/.

Index

About the Contributors

Lily M. Abadal is Assistant Professor of Instruction at the University of South Florida. Her research mostly focuses on moral psychology and applied virtue ethics in the Neo-Aristotelian tradition.

Saraliza Anzaldúa is Assistant Professor of Philosophy at the California Institute of Integral Studies. Ya's main areas of research are monster theory and Indigenous philosophies of Mexico. Saraliza's greatest fear is teaching a three-hour seminar without coffee.

Lok Chui Choo is Lecturer at the University of Hawaii at Manoa. She received her PhD in Philosophy from Nanyang Technological University in 2023. Her research focuses on classical Chinese philosophy (Confucianism, Daoism), ethics, and moral psychology.

Christopher Cowley is based at Charles University, Prague. He works on issues in ethics and autobiography.

Guy Crain is Professor of Philosophy and Director of the philosophy program at Rose State College in Midwest City, Oklahoma. His publications include articles on topics such as trolley problems, virtue theory, and the ethics of interpersonal violence. He is a cohost of the *Curiosity Porn* podcast.

Andrew Culbreth is Assistant Professor in the Department of Philosophy at Boston College. His work focuses on ancient Greek philosophy, especially Plato's and Aristotle's ethics and philosophical psychology. He is also an affiliated researcher with the Moral Injury Lab at the University of Virginia.

Rodrigo Díaz is *Juan de la Cierva* fellow at the Institute of Philosophy at the Spanish National Research Council (CSIC). His research focuses on the nature of emotions and their role in moral judgment and motivation. He studies these topics using an interdisciplinary approach, combining traditional philosophical methods and empirical research tools.

Kris Goffin is currently a YUFE4postdocs/Marie Sklodowska-Curie-funded postdoc at Maastricht University on the Philosophy of AI. His research focuses on aesthetics, philosophy of cognitive science (including AI), and mind, with research on implicit bias (such as implicit prejudices and stereotypes), emotions, moral psychology, aesthetic experiences, and various interactions between these topics (such as bias in art). In his current research, he focuses on bias in AI applications. Previously, he did interdisciplinary research on implicit bias and implicit racism at UAntwerp and KULeuven and received a Postdoctoral Fellowship from the Flemish Research Foundation (FWO).

Parker Haratine (PhD, University of St. Andrews) specializes in medieval philosophy and contemporary philosophical and analytic theology. He has published on historic thinkers such as Augustine and Anselm and contemporary topics such as goodness, sin, and evil.

Ami Harbin is Associate Professor of Philosophy and Women and Gender Studies at Oakland University and author of *Fearing Together: Ethics for Insecurity* (2023) and *Disorientation and Moral Life* (2016).

Timothy R. Kearl is Assistant Professor at Flagler College. He works mainly in epistemology, action theory, and metaphysics.

Charlie Kurth is Professor of Philosophy at Clemson University and Core Fellow at the Helsinki Collegium for Advanced Studies. He is the author of *The Anxious Mind* (2018), *Emotion* (2022), and numerous articles on topics in emotion theory, the philosophy of science, the philosophy of mind, and ethics.

Lawrence Lengbeyer, PhD, is Associate Professor of Philosophy in the Department of Leadership, Ethics, and Law at the United States Naval Academy. His research can be described as focused on moral psychology, though this requires overlooking the eclecticism of his intellectual interests, the result of sixteen years of diverse studies: applied mathematics (Harvard); social psychology and social/political theory (Cambridge); law and hermeneutics (Yale); and philosophy, supplemented by psychology, and linguistics (Stanford). He and his wife Audrey are passing along their loves of learning, music-making, laughing, and sleeping to their four cheerful unschooled daughters.

Robert Pál-Wallin is a doctoral candidate in the Department of Philosophy at Lund University. He is a member of the Lund Gothenburg Responsibility Project, and his main areas of research include philosophy of emotion, value theory, moral responsibility, and moral psychology.

Panu Pihkala is Researcher with the title of Docent in the Faculty of Theology at the University of Helsinki. He is an expert in interdisciplinary eco-anxiety research and hosts the podcast *Climate Change and Happiness* together with Dr. Thomas Doherty (https://climatechangeandhappiness.com). He also serves as an adviser for many projects about eco-anxiety. He has been awarded several prizes in Finland for his books about eco-emotions.

Songyao Ren is Assistant Professor of Philosophy at the University of Texas at Dallas. She specializes in ethics, moral psychology, and Chinese philosophy. Her work has appeared in *Philosophical Psychology*, *History of Philosophy Quarterly*, and *Asian Philosophy*, among others. Her current book project studies Stoicism and Zhuangism with an eye on constructing an account of emotional equanimity that can serve as an attractive ethical ideal.

Christine Tappolet is Full Professor in the Philosophy Department at the Université de Montréal. Her research interests lie mainly in metaethics, moral psychology, and emotional theory. She has edited a number of volumes, including, with Sarah Stroud, *Weakness of Will and Practical Irrationality* (2003) and, with Fabrice Teroni and Anita Konzelmann Ziv, *Shadows of the Soul: Philosophical Perspectives on Negative Emotions* (2018). In addition to close to a hundred articles and chapters, she is the author of several books, including *Emotions, Values, and Agency* (2016) and *Philosophy of Emotions: A Contemporary Introduction* (2023).

Robert H. Wallace is Assistant Professor of Philosophy at California Polytechnic State University, San Luis Obispo. He works on issues concerning agency and responsibility and related topics.

www.ingramcontent.com/pod-product-compliance
Ingram Content Group UK Ltd.
Pitfield, Milton Keynes, MK11 3LW, UK
UKHW020214290926
15470UKWH00001B/180